The Pillars of Society, John Gabriel Borkman, When We Dead Awaken

This is the fourth volume of a six-volume collection presenting all sixteen of Ibsen's major plays written in the thirty-four years from 1865 to 1899. Each volume offers a cross-section of these plays so as to illustrate the different phases of his dramatic genius.

This volume contains his first great modern prose play and his last two. *The Pillars of Society*, written between 1875 and 1877, exhibits many of the classic elements which recur in the subsequent plays—a marriage founded on a lie, women stunted by social conventions, an arrogant man destroying the happiness of those around him. *John Gabriel Borkman* (1896), according to Edvard Munch, is "the most powerful winter landscape in Scandinavian art"; and Ibsen's last play, *When We Dead Awaken* (1899), also dealing with "the coldness of heart", showed, said Bernard Shaw, "no decay of Ibsen's highest qualities. His magic is nowhere more potent."

Michael Meyer's translations have won praise for their accuracy and liveliness on both stage and page. They have been performed extensively in the theatre and on radio and television. "Where previous translators have adopted either a stiffly Victorian style, or one so modern as to destroy the illusion that we were seeing a period play, Mr Meyer has found a form of speech common both to the period in which the plays were written and to the present." (*The Times*) "Meyer's translations of Ibsen are a major fact in one's general sense of post-war drama. Their vital pace, their unforced insistence on the poetic centre of Ibsen's genius, have beaten academic versions from the field." (George Steiner, *The New Statesman*)

Michael Meyer is also Ibsen's biographer and a leading authority on his work. This edition includes Meyer's illuminating introductions to each play, as well as a chronology of Ibsen's life and writings.

The front cover shows Vinternatt i Rondane *(1914) by Harald Sohlberg, reproduced by kind permission of Einar Sohlberg and of Nasjonalgalleriet, Oslo. The portrait of Ibsen on the back cover is by Erik Werenskiold and is reproduced of Jans E. Werenskiold and by courtesy of Nasjonalgalleriet, Oslo.*

Jean Anouilh
John Arden
Peter Barnes
Brendan Behan
Aphra Behn
Bulgakov
Edward Bond (three volumes)
Bertolt Brecht (three volumes)
Howard Brenton (two volumes)
Georg Büchner
Caldéron
Anton Chekhov
Caryl Churchill (two volumes)
Noël Coward (five volumes)
Sarah Daniels
David Edgar (two volumes)
Euripides (two volumes)
Michael Frayn
Gorky
Henrik Ibsen (six volumes)
Lorca (two volumes)
Marivaux
David Mercer
Arthur Miller (three volumes)
Molière
Peter Nichols
Clifford Odets
Joe Orton
Louise Page
A. W. Pinero
Luigi Pirandello
Stephen Poliakoff
Terence Rattigan (two volumes)
Sophocles (two volumes)
Wole Soyinka
August Strindberg (three volumes)
J. M. Synge
Oscar Wilde
P. G. Wodehouse

HENRIK IBSEN

Plays : Four

The Pillars of Society
John Gabriel Borkman
When We Dead Awaken

Translated from the Norwegian and introduced by
Michael Meyer

METHUEN DRAMA

This collection was first published in Great Britain in paperback in 1980
by Eyre Methuen Ltd.
Reprinted in this corrected edition in 1991 by Methuen Drama, Michelin
House, 81 Fulham Road, London SW3 6RB.

The Pillars of Society was first published in this translation in 1963 by
Rupert Hart-Davis Ltd. Copyright © Michael Meyer 1963. Introduction
copyright © Michael Meyer 1963. Corrected for this edition, 1980, 1991.

John Gabriel Borkman was first published in this translation in 1960 by
Rupert Hart-Davis Ltd. Copyright © Michael Meyer 1960. Introduction
copyright © Michael Meyer 1960. Corrected for this edition, 1980, 1991.

When We Dead Awaken was first published in this translation in 1960 by
Rupert Hart-Davis Ltd. Copyright © Michael Meyer 1960. Introduction
copyright © Michael Meyer 1960. Corrected for this edition, 1980, 1991.

ISBN 0 413 46360 5

Printed and bound in Great Britain by
Cox and Wyman Ltd., Reading

Contents

HENRIK JOHAN IBSEN: A Chronology

1828 Born at Skien in south-east Norway on 20 March, the second child of Knud Ibsen, a merchant, and his wife Marichen, *née* Altenburg.

1834–5 Father becomes ruined. The family moves to Venstoep, a few miles outside Skien.

1844 Ibsen (aged fifteen) becomes assistant to an apothecary at Grimstad, a tiny seaport further down the coast. Stays there for six years in great poverty.

1846 Has an illegitimate son with a servant-girl, Else Sofie Jensdatter.

1849 Writes his first play, *Catiline* (in verse).

1850 Leaves Grimstad to become a student in Christiania (now Oslo). Writes second play, *The Warrior's Barrow*.

1851 Is invited to join Ole Bull's newly formed National Theatre at Bergen. Does so, and stays six years, writing, directing, designing costumes and keeping the accounts.

1852 Visits Copenhagen and Dresden to learn about the theatre. Writes *St John's Eve*, a romantic comedy in verse and prose.

1853 *St John's Eve* acted at Bergen. Failure.

1854 Writes *Lady Inger of Oestraat*, an historical tragedy in prose.

1855 *Lady Inger of Oestraat* acted at Bergen. Failure. Writes *The Feast at Solhaug*, another romantic verse-and-prose comedy.

1856 *The Feast at Solhaug* acted at Bergen. Small success. Meets Suzannah Thoresen. Writes *Olaf Liljekrans*, a third verse-and-prose comedy.

1857 *Olaf Liljekrans* acted at Bergen. Failure. Leaves Bergen to become artistic manager of the Christiania Norwegian Theatre. Writes *The Vikings at Helgeland*, an historical prose tragedy.

1858 Marries Suzannah Thoresen. *The Vikings at Helgeland* staged. Small success.

1859 His only child, Sigurd, born.

1860–1 Years of poverty and despair. Unable to write.

1862   Writes *Love's Comedy*, a modern verse satire, his first play for five years. It is rejected by his own theatre, which goes bankrupt.

1863   Ibsen gets part-time job as literary adviser to the Danish-controlled Christiania Theatre. Extremely poor. Applies unsuccessfully to Government for financial support. Resorts to moneylenders. Writes *The Pretenders*, another historical prose tragedy. Is granted a travel stipend by the Government; this is augmented by a collection raised by Bjœrnson and other friends.

1864   *The Pretenders* staged in Christiania. A success. He leaves Norway and settles in Rome. Remains resident abroad for the next twenty-seven years. Begins *Emperor and Galilean*.

1865   Writes *Brand*, in verse (as a play for reading, not acting), in Rome and Ariccia.

1866   *Brand* published. Immense success; Ibsen becomes famous throughout Scandinavia (but it is not acted for nineteen years).

1867   Writes *Peer Gynt*, in verse (also to be read, not acted), in Rome, Ischia and Sorrento. It, too, is a great success; but is not staged for seven years.

1868   Moves from Rome and settles in Dresden.

1869   Attends opening of Suez Canal as Norwegian delegate. Completes *The League of Youth*, a modern prose comedy.

1871   Revises his shorter poems and issues them in a volume. His farewell to verse; for the rest of his life he publishes exclusively in prose.

1873   Completes (after nine years) *Emperor and Galilean*, his last historical play. Begins to be known in Germany and England.

1874   Returns briefly to Norway for first time in ten years. The students hold a torchlight procession in his honour.

1875   Leaves Dresden, after seven years and settles in Munich. Begins *The Pillars of Society*, the first of his twelve great modern prose dramas.

1876   *Peer Gynt* staged for first time. *The Vikings at Helgeland* is performed in Munich, the first of his plays to be staged outside Scandinavia.

1877   Completes *The Pillars of Society*. This makes him famous in Germany, where it is widely acted.

1878   Returns to Italy for a year.

1879   Writes *A Doll's House* in Rome and Amalfi. It causes an immediate sensation, though a decade elapses before it makes Ibsen internationally famous. Returns for a year to Munich.

1880   Resettles in Italy for a further five years. First performance of an Ibsen play in England (*The Pillars of Society* for a single matinée in London).

1881   Writes *Ghosts* in Rome and Sorrento. Violently attacked; all theatres reject it, and bookshops return it to the publisher.

1882   Writes *An Enemy of the People* in Rome. Cordially received. *Ghosts* receives its first performance (in Chicago).

1884   Writes *The Wild Duck* in Rome and Gossensass. It, and all his subsequent plays, were regarded as obscure and were greeted with varying degrees of bewilderment.

1885   Revisits Norway again, for the first time since 1874. Leaves Rome and resettles in Munich.

1866   Writes *Rosmersholm* in Munich.

1888   Writes *The Lady from the Sea* in Munich.

1889   Meets and becomes infatuated with the eighteen-year-old Emilie Bardach in Gossensass. Does not see her again, but the experience shadows the remainder of his writing. Janet Achurch acts Nora in London, the first major English-speaking production of Ibsen.

1890   Writes *Hedda Gabler* in Munich.

1891   Returns to settle permanently in Norway.

1892   Writes *The Master Builder* in Christiania.

1894   Writes *Little Eyolf* in Christiania.

1896   Writes *John Gabriel Borkman* in Christiania.

1899   Writes *When We Dead Awaken* in Christiania.

1901   First stroke. Partly paralysed.

1903   Second stroke. Left largely helpless.

1906   Dies in Christiania on 23 May, aged seventy-eight.

The Pillars of Society

INTRODUCTION

Ibsen completed *The Pillars of Society* a few months after his forty-ninth birthday; he wrote it in Munich between 1875 and 1877. Enormously successful and influential at the time of its appearance, and indeed for the next quarter of a century, it has rarely been performed during the past fifty years, having rather glibly been relegated to the category of polemical dramas that have lost their topicality. It is still often thought of nowadays as an apprentice work of documentary rather than practical interest. But John Barton's successful production for the Royal Shakespeare Company at the Aldwych Theatre in 1977—the first in London since 1926—surprised the critics by showing the play to be full of theatrical life, thereby doing it the same service that Michael Elliott's 1959 production at Hammersmith did for *Brand*. *The Pillars of Society* is tightly plotted and beautifully characterized; and at this distance of time we can see that its true subject is not women's rights or the evil practices of nineteenth-century shipowners, but human emotions and relationships. The ending has been condemned as facilely happy, but the same accusation was, until recently, made against *Little Eyolf* and *The Lady from the Sea*, and has been proved false if the plays are capably handled. The chief obstacles to a professional production are the size of the cast and a tendency to verbosity on the part of Bernick and, more particularly, Dr Roerlund the schoolmaster. Trim them down, and *The Pillars of Society* stands as an absorbing example of Ibsen in his less familiar mood of humane comedy—the mood which pervades *Love's Comedy*, *The League of Youth* and much of *Peer Gynt* and *The Wild Duck*, and of which isolated characters in his more sombre plays, such as George Tesman in *Hedda Gabler*, Ballested in *The Lady from the Sea*, and Vilhelm Foldal in *John Gabriel Borkman*, are belated manifestations.

The Pillars of Society is often referred to as the first of Ibsen's social prose dramas. That honour in fact belongs to *The League of Youth*, a vigorous and delightful comedy completed eight years earlier which hardly deserves the oblivion which has enveloped it. To *The League of Youth*, too, belongs the credit of being Ibsen's first attempt to write dialogue that was genuinely modern and colloquial. His earlier prose plays, such as *St John's Eve*, *Lady Inger of Oestraat*, *The Vikings at Helgeland* and *The Pretenders*, had been written in a formalized style. But *The League of Youth*, often assumed by those who have not read it to be an earnest political tract, is a loosely constructed and light-hearted frolic almost in the manner of Restoration comedy,[1] which happens to have a pushing young politician as its chief character—"Peer Gynt as a politician," someone has described it. *The Pillars of Society* is in a much truer sense the forerunner of the eleven great plays which followed it. Apart from the tightness of its construction, it contains, as *The League of Youth* does not, the elements we commonly associate with an Ibsen play—a marriage founded on a lie, passionate women stunted and inhibited by the conventions of their time, and an arrogant man of high intellectual and practical gifts who destroys, or nearly destroys, the happiness of those nearest to him. It also exhibits, unlike his earlier plays, what Henry James admiringly described as "the operation of talent without glamour . . . the ugly interior on which his curtain inexorably rises and which, to be honest, I like for the queer associations it has taught us to respect: the hideous carpet and wallpaper (one may answer for them), the conspicuous stove, the lonely central table, the 'lamps with green shades' as in the sumptuous first act of *The Wild Duck*, the pervasive air of small interests and standards, the sign of limited local life." Above all, *The Pillars of Society* has, despite its overtones of comedy, that peculiarly Ibsenish quality of

[1] It was influenced by the eighteenth-century Norwegian dramatist Ludvig Holberg, one of the few authors Ibsen really admired.

11

austerity; what Henry James, on another occasion, described as "the hard compulsion of his strangely inscrutable art."

It is indicative of the technical problems posed by this new form of tightly plotted social realism that *The Pillars of Society* took Ibsen longer to write than any of his other plays except the triple-length *Emperor and Galilean*. No less than five separate drafts of the first act have survived, and over a period of nearly eight years his letters are scattered with excuses for its lack of progress. He began to brood on it as early as December 1869, just after finishing *The League of Youth*. On the fourteenth of that month he wrote to his publisher Frederik Hegel: "I am planning a new and serious contemporary drama in three acts, and expect to start work on it in the immediate future." The following month (25 January 1870) he informed Hegel that he hoped to have it ready by the following October, but on 11 April he wrote: "My new play has not yet got beyond the draft, and since I have to get my travel notes into order it looks like being delayed for some time." These travel notes referred to the visit he had made to Egypt in November 1869 to attend, as official Norwegian representative, the opening of the Suez Canal.

October 1870 arrived, and so far from having the play ready he could only tell Hegel that it "has sufficiently developed in my mind for me to hope that any day now I may be able to start writing it." Two sets of notes have survived from this year which contain the first germs of the play. By now he had found a more impressive excuse than the Suez Canal: the Franco-Prussian War, which had started in July of that year. In such an atmosphere (he was living in Germany) how could he concentrate on writing a social drama set in a small Norwegian seaport? He returned instead to the broader historical canvas of *Emperor and Galilean*, on which he had been working intermittently since 1864.

It was in fact another five years before he began the actual writing of *The Pillars of Society*. Apart from completing *Emperor and Galilean*, he prepared for publication a selection of his poems covering the past twenty years; it was his deliberate farewell to poetry, the form which had been his

12

earliest love. He explained this decision in a letter written to Edmund Gosse on 15 January 1874, shortly after the publication of *Emperor and Galilean*, and although his remarks were made with specific reference to that play, they apply even more strongly to the works which followed. I quote the passage in Gosse's own translation:

"The illusion I wanted to produce is that of reality. I wished to produce the impression on the reader that what he was reading was something that had really happened. If I had employed verse, I should have counteracted my own intention and prevented the accomplishment of the task I had set myself. The many ordinary and insignificant characters whom I have introduced into the play would have become indistinct, and indistinguishable from one another, if I had allowed all of them to speak in one and the same rhythmical measure. We are no longer living in the age of Shakespeare. Among sculptors, there is already talk of painting statues in the natural colours. Much can be said both for and against this. I have no desire to see the Venus de Milo painted, but I would rather see the head of a negro executed in black than in white marble.

"Speaking generally, the style must conform to the degree of ideality which pervades the representation. My new drama [*Emperor and Galilean*] is no tragedy in the ancient acceptation; what I desired to depict were human beings, and therefore I would not let them talk in 'the language of the gods.'"

In the summer of 1874 Ibsen returned to Norway for the first time since he had left it ten years earlier. There the strife between the conservatives and the liberals had reached its height and, as a result of *The League of Youth*, which was an attack on the hollowness of radical politicians, Ibsen found the conservatives hailing him as their champion. He had, however, no intention of attaching himself to any political party, and when he read in the right-wing newspaper *Morgenbladet* an editorial demand that a candidate for a professorship at the University should be rejected on the grounds that he was a freethinker, Ibsen seized the opportunity to advertise his independence. He withdrew his subscription to *Morgenbladet* and changed to the left-wing newspaper *Dagbladet*. The uneasiness of the conservatives on hearing this—Ibsen was famous enough by now for the students to arrange a torchlight procession in his honour before he left—would have been considerably increased if they had known what he was preparing for them.

After two and a half months in Norway, he returned briefly to Dresden and then, the following spring (1875), he moved to Munich, a city which he found much more to his liking and where he was to spend most of the next sixteen years. At last, in the autumn of that year, nearly six years after he had first begun to brood on it, he settled down to the actual writing of *The Pillars of Society*. At first things went well. On 23 October he wrote to Hegel: "My new play is progressing swiftly; in a few days I shall have completed the first act, which I always find the most difficult part. The title will be: *The Pillars of Society*, a Play in Five [*sic*] Acts. In a way it can be regarded as a counterblast to *The League of Youth*, and will touch on several of the more important questions of our time." On 25 November he writes: "Act 1 of my new play is finished and *fair-copied*; I am now working on Act 2." By 10 December he is "working at it daily and am now doubly anxious to get the manuscript to you as quickly as possible." On 26 January 1876 he expects to "have it ready by May."

But now things began to go less smoothly. After 26 February, when he writes to the director of the Bergen Theatre that it "will probably be printed during the summer," there is no further mention of the play in his letters until 15 September, when he explains rather lengthily to Hegel that he has been so distracted by productions or plans for productions of his earlier plays—*The Pretenders* in Meiningen, Schwerin and Berlin, *The Vikings at Helgeland* in Munich, Leipzig, Vienna and Dresden—that he has been "compelled to postpone completion of my new play; but on my return to Munich at the beginning of next month, I intend to get it polished off." But progress continued to be slow. 1877 arrived, and on 9 February he could only tell Hegel, who must by now have been growing a little impatient: "I shall have my new play ready in the summer, and will send you the manuscript as soon as possible." However, on 20 April he wrote that it "is now moving rapidly towards its conclusion," and at last, on 24 June 1877, he was able to report: "Today I take advantage of a free moment to tell you that on the 15th inst. I completed my new play and am now going ahead with the fair-copying." He posted the fair copy to Hegel in five instalments between 29 July and 20 August 1877.

The Pillars of Society was published by Hegel's firm, Gyldendal of Copenhagen, on 11 October 1877, and achieved immediate and widespread success. Throughout Scandinavia, the liberals and radicals hailed it with as much delight as that with which the conservatives had greeted *The League of Youth*. The first edition of 6,000 copies sold out in seven weeks, and a further 4,000 had to be printed. It was first performed on 18 November 1877 in Copenhagen, where it was received with great enthusiasm, and it was equally acclaimed in Christiania,[1] Stockholm and Helsinki. It also gave Ibsen his first real breakthrough in Germany. In the absence of any copyright protection, three separate German translations were published early in 1878 (one of them by a man described by Ibsen as "a frightful literary bandit"), and in February of that year it was produced at five different theatres in Berlin within a fortnight. Twenty-seven German and Austrian theatres staged it within the year. In England, William Archer, then aged twenty-two, made a "hurried translation" entitled, rather uninspiringly, *The Supports of Society*; an analysis by him of the play, with extracts from his translation, was published in the *Mirror of Literature* on 2 March 1878. Since "no publisher would look at" this version, he made another and more careful one, under the new title of *Quicksands*, and this was performed for a single matinée at the Gaiety Theatre, London, on 15 December 1880—a noteworthy occasion, for it was the first recorded performance of any Ibsen play in

[1] In Swedish at the Moellergaten Theatre. Ibsen refused to allow the Christiania Theatre to stage it because "the new director is a quite useless man," and the play was not performed in Norwegian in the capital until the following spring.

England. *The Pillars of Society* was not staged in America, at any rate in English—though it had been acted there in German—until 13 March 1891, when it was produced at the Lyceum Theatre, New York. In 1892 it was performed in Australia and South Africa, in 1893 in Rome; and in 1896 Lugné-Poe staged it at his Théâtre de l'Œuvre in Paris. By the end of the century, according to Archer, it had been performed no less than 1,200 times in Germany and Austria, a remarkable record for those days.

The Pillars of Society dealt with two problems of extreme topicality for the eighteen-seventies, and it is a measure of the play's emotional and dramatic content that it has retained its validity despite the fact that both issues have long since been settled. One was the question of women's rights; the other, that of "floating coffins," i.e. unseaworthy ships which were deliberately sacrificed with their crews so that their owners could claim insurance. Controversy over the former problem reached its height in Norway during the seventies. The Norwegian novelist Camilla Collett had fired a warning shot as early as 1853, with her novel *The Judge's Daughters*. In 1869 John Stuart Mill published *The Subjection of Women*, which Ibsen's friend Georg Brandes translated into Danish the same year. Matilda Schjoett's *Conversation of a Group of Ladies about the Subjection of Women* (published anonymously in 1871) and Camilla Collett's *Last Papers* (1872) set the issue squarely before the Norwegian public; in 1874 a Women's Reading Society was founded in Christiania, and in 1876 Asta Hanseen, a great champion of the cause, began a series of lectures on women's rights, but was so furiously assailed that in 1880 she emigrated to America. She was the original of Lona Hessel (Ibsen at first gave the character the surname of Hassel, but changed it, presumably so as to avoid too direct an identification with Hanseen). Camilla Collett exerted a direct influence on Ibsen, for he had seen a good deal of her in Dresden in 1871, and again in Munich in the spring of 1877 when he was writing the play, and when they had many arguments about marriage and other female problems. Another influence was Ibsen's wife Susannah; the subject of women's rights was one about which she had long felt strongly. Ibsen had already touched tentatively on this problem in *The League of Youth*, and he was to deal with it more minutely in his next play, *A Doll's House*. His original intention in *The Pillars of Society* was to be even more outspoken than he finally was, for in one of the preliminary drafts Dina announces her decision to go off with her lover without marrying him; but he evidently doubted whether the theatres would stage a play which suggested anything quite so daring, and legalized their relationship.

The problem of the "floating coffins" was first forced upon Ibsen's attention by an English Member of Parliament. In 1868 Samuel Plimsoll had sought in the House of Commons to have the State interfere against the cold-blooded and un-scrupulous sacrifice of human life by sending men to sea in rotten ships. In 1873 he succeeded in getting a law passed to enforce seaworthiness; but this proved too slack. On 22 July 1875 he created a tremendous commotion in Parliament by a boldly outspoken attack on the people responsible for such a policy; he called the owners of such ships murderers and the politicians who supported them scoundrels. This so roused the conscience of the nation that a temporary bill went through in a few days, and its principles were made permanent by the Merchant Shipping Act of the following year. Plimsoll's pro-test echoed throughout the world, and in a seafaring country such as Norway it rang especially loudly. A particularly scan-dalous case had occurred in Christiania during Ibsen's visit there in 1874. On 2 September of that year, at the annual general meeting of the shipping insurance company Norske Veritas, questions were asked about a ship which, after having been declared seaworthy, sprang a leak while at sea and was shown to be completely rotten. At the annual general meeting a year later two similar cases were mentioned, and a storm of indignation was aroused. The matter was reported in detail in the newspapers, and Ibsen can hardly have failed to read about it.

The Pillars of Society is full of memories of Grimstad, the little port where Ibsen had spent his years as a chemist's apprentice (just as *The League of Youth* is full of memories of his birthplace, Skien). The *Palm Tree* was the name of a Grimstad ship. Touring theatrical companies played in the hall of a sailmaker named Moeller; an actress belonging to one of them had returned there after being involved in a scandal, and had tried to keep herself by taking in washing and sewing like Dina Dorf's mother, but had been shooed out of town by the local gossips. Foreign ships came in for repairs, and foreign visitors turned the place upside-down, like the crew of the *Indian Girl*. In the autumn of 1849, six months before Ibsen left for Christiania, the Socialist Marcus Thrane had arrived in Grimstad and founded a Workers' Association, like the one Aune belonged to. And the Bernicks had their origin in a family named Smith Petersen. Morten Smith Petersen, the original of Karsten Bernick, returned to Grimstad from abroad in the eighteen-forties, and ran his aged mother's business for a while, but finally had to close it down. He then started his own shipyard and an insurance company, and eventually founded the Norske Veritas company which earned the notoriety referred to above. He had died in 1872, but his sister Margrethe Petersen survived. She was an elementary schoolteacher, and was the original of Martha Bernick.

The rich quantity of notes and draft material which has been preserved enables us to plot the development of *The Pillars of Society* in some detail. His first notes, made in 1870, begin: "The main theme must be how women sit modestly in the background while the men busily pursue their petty aims with an assurance which at once infuriates and impresses." The main characters are to be an "old white-haired lady" with two sons, one a shipowner, the other a ship's officer who has been abroad for ten years on foreign service. The shipowner's wife, "a fêted beauty before she married, is full of poetry but is bitter and unsatisfied; she makes demands of life which are, or seem, excessive." In other words, Mrs Bernick, as originally conceived, is a forerunner of the great line of Ibsen heroines—Nora Hellmer, Mrs Alving, Rebecca West, Ellida Wangel, Hedda Gabler, Rita Allmers, the Rentheim twins in *John Gabriel Borkman*, and Maja and Irene in *When We Dead Awaken*. Martha, too, appears in these early notes, jotted down five years before the play was written: "her sister, still unsure of herself; has grown up quietly admiring the man who is absent and far away." But although several of the characters of *The Pillars of Society* as we know it are here, the plot as originally conceived bears little relation to that of the final version; the naval officer falls in love with the sister (i.e., Martha), but she is already in love with a student, and the officer's mother persuades him to give up the girl and go away. "The greatest victory," she tells him, "is to conquer oneself" —a kind of echo of Brand's "The victory of victories is to lose everything." There is also reference to "the foster-daughter of sixteen, sustained by daydreams and expectations" (i.e., Dina). The play at this stage was to be "a comedy," presumably of the same genre as *The League of Youth*.

In his next notes, made five years later, we find much more of the play as we know it. A scenic synopsis includes the schoolmaster reading to the assembled wives, the husbands discussing the railway, the foster-daughter (here called Valborg) impatient and longing to get away (to her mother, who is still alive), and Lona's arrival with the steamer; Act 1 ends with her "appearing in the doorway to the garden as the curtain falls." In Act 2, "the returned wanderers [i.e., Lona and the Captain] start turning things upside-down in the town. Rumours about the Captain's great wealth and the earlier scandal concerning Valborg's mother. The schoolmaster begins to think of getting engaged to Valborg. Conflict begins between the factory-owner and the Captain." Act 3: "News about irregularities in the repairs to the ship. The engagement is announced and celebrated. The Captain decides to leave the country. Fresh information from the yards. The factory-owner hesitates; for the moment, nothing must be said." Act 4: "Secret understanding between the Captain and Valborg. The railway project secured. Great ovations. Olaf runs away with the Captain and Valborg. Exciting final catastrophe."

The list of characters has by now grown considerably.

Apart from Bennick [*sic*], his wife, his blind mother and his sister Margrete (Martha), Miss "Hassel," the schoolmaster "Roerstad," Valborg (who suddenly becomes Dina), and Captain John Tennyson (later Rawlinson), we also have Madame Dorf, young Mrs Bernick's father Mads Toennesen (a "shipowner and master builder nicknamed 'The Badger' "), his other son Emil (altered to Hilmar), and Evensen, "a supply teacher." As synopsis follows synopsis, the list of characters changes; Aune, Sandstad and "Knap" appear, Bennick becomes Bernick, and the whole of the older generation is removed—Bernick's mother, Madame Dorf, Evensen the supply teacher and, eventually, Mads Toennesen, though he was to reappear three plays later as Morten Kiil in *An Enemy of the People*.

The drafts which follow comprise four versions of Act 1 or part of it, a draft of the whole play, and Ibsen's final fair copy in the version familiar to us. The first draft of Act 1 is different from the final version in numerous respects, and makes interesting reading. Among other things it contains a rare example of Ibsen trying to write English. The clerk Knap announces in Norwegian that since "the Captain fell overboard in the North Sea and the mate has delirium tremens," the *Indian Girl* has arrived under the command of "a sailor who was on board as a passenger . . . John Rawlinson, Esqr., New Orleans." Captain Rawlinson then appears and the following lively exchange takes place in English:

BERNICK: Good morning, master Rawlinson! This way, if you please, sir! I am master Bernick!

CAPTAIN RAWLINSON (*waves his handkerchief and cries*): Very well, Karsten; but first three hurrah for the old *grævling*![1]

The draft makes very spirited reading, and it is only when we compare it with the final version that we realize how much Ibsen gained in the rewriting. Bernick has much superfluous talk trimmed down, Lona is given a far more effective entrance, Aune (the only sympathetic portrait of a working-class man Ibsen ever attempted) is introduced quickly instead

---

[1] The Norwegian word for badger.

of having to wait until Act 2, a good deal of argument as to the pros and cons of the railway is cut, and we are told far more about the characters' past, notably Lona's quarrel with Bernick and the returned brother's supposed intrigue with Madame Dorf. Hilmar (who with his hypochondria and fanciful speech anticipates Hjalmar Ekdal in *The Wild Duck*) and Lona are much more sharply characterized; and the "floating coffin" issue, absent from the first draft, is introduced. The subsequent drafts show Ibsen groping painfully towards his final conception, and together they chart his progress from the vigorous but rather artless method of *The League of Youth* towards the compactness and inevitability of *A Doll's House*.

The Pillars of Society was not the first realistic prose play. Apart from *The League of Youth*, Bjoernson's two plays *A Bankrupt* and *The Editor*, both written in 1875, were explorations in this field. But these are not plays in the truest sense; they are melodramas which indict individual figures. *The Pillars of Society* was the first play to combine the three elements of colloquial dialogue, objectivity, and tightness of plot which are the requirements and characteristics of modern prose drama. The effect of the play on the younger generation of its time has been recorded by Otto Brahm, one of the founders of the Freie Bühne in Berlin, a theatre comparable in influence to Antoine's Théâtre Libre and Stanislavsky's Moscow Arts. In 1878, when Brahm was twenty-two, he saw *The Pillars of Society* at a small theatre in Berlin. Many years later he recalled that this was "the first strong theatrical impression" that he received. "It was," he said, "my first intimation of a new world of creative art."

MICHAEL MEYER

CHARACTERS

KARSTEN BERNICK	shipowner and consul
BETTY	his wife
OLAF	their son, aged thirteen
MARTHA	Karsten's sister
JOHAN TOENNESEN	Betty's younger brother
LONA HESSEL	her elder half-sister
HILMAR TOENNESEN	Betty's cousin
DR ROERLUND	a schoolmaster
MR RUMMEL	a wholesale dealer
MR VIGELAND	a merchant
MR SANDSTAD	a merchant
DINA DORF	a young girl living with the Bernicks
KRAP	a chief clerk
AUNE	a shipyard foreman
MRS RUMMEL	
MRS HOLT	the postmaster's wife
MRS LYNGE	wife of the local doctor
MISS RUMMEL	
MISS HOLT	

Townspeople and other residents, foreign seamen, steam-ship passengers, etc.

The action takes place in KARSTEN BERNICK'S house in a small Norwegian seaport.

22

ACT ONE

A spacious garden room in KARSTEN BERNICK'S *house. Downstage left, a door leading to* BERNICK'S *room; upstage in the same
wall is a similar door. In the centre of the opposite wall is a large
entrance door. The rear wall is composed almost entirely of fine,
clear glass, with an open door giving on to a broad verandah over
which an awning is stretched. Steps lead down from the verandah
into the garden, part of which can be seen, enclosed by a fence
with a small gate. Beyond the fence is a street, the far side of
which is lined with small wooden houses painted in bright colours.
It is summer and the sun is shining warmly. Now and then
people wander along the street; they stop and speak to each other,
buy things from a little corner shop, etc.*

*In the garden room a group of ladies is seated round a table. At
the head of it sits* MRS BERNICK; *on her left,* MRS HOLT *and her
daughter; beyond them,* MRS RUMMEL *and* MISS RUMMEL. *On*
MRS BERNICK'S *right sit* MRS LYNGE, MARTHA BERNICK *and*
DINA DORF. *All the ladies are busy sewing. On the table lie large
heaps of linen cut into shapes and half-finished, and other articles
of clothing. Further upstage, at a little table on which stand two
potted plants and a glass of lemonade,* DR ROERLUND, *the schoolmaster, sits reading aloud from a book with gilt edges, though
only the odd word can be heard by the audience. Outside in the
garden,* OLAF BERNICK *is running about, shooting at a target
with a bow and arrow.*

After a few moments, AUNE, *a shipyard foreman, enters quietly
through the door on the right. The reading is interrupted briefly;*
MRS BERNICK *nods to* AUNE *and points to the door on the left.*
AUNE *walks quietly over and knocks softly on* BERNICK'S *door.
Pause. He knocks again.* KRAP, *the chief clerk, comes out of the
room with his hat in his hand and papers under his arm.*

KRAP: Oh, it's you?

AUNE: Mr Bernick sent for me.

KRAP: I know: but he can't see you himself. He's deputed me to tell you—

AUNE: You? I'd much rather speak to—

KRAP: He's deputed me to tell you this. You're to stop giving these talks to the men on Saturday evenings.

AUNE: Oh? I thought my free time was my own—

KRAP: You don't get free time in order for you to stop the men working. Last Saturday you told them their interests were threatened by the new machines and these new methods we've introduced down at the yard. Why d'you do it?

AUNE: For the good of the community.

KRAP: That's odd. Mr Bernick says this kind of thing will disintegrate the community.

AUNE: I don't mean by community what Mr Bernick does, Mr Krap. As foreman of the Workers' Association I—

KRAP: You're Mr Bernick's foreman. And the only community to which you owe allegiance is the Bernick Shipbuilding Company. That's where we all get our living. Well, now you know what Mr Bernick had to say to you.

AUNE: Mr Bernick wouldn't have said it like that, Mr Krap. But I know whom I've to thank for this. It's that damned American ship that's put in for repairs. Those people expect us to work like they do over there, and it isn't—

KRAP: Yes, well I haven't time to go into all that. Now you've heard Mr Bernick's orders, so stop this nonsense. Run back to the yard, now. I'm sure they need you there. I'll be down myself shortly. Pardon me, ladies!

He bows and goes out through the garden and down the street. AUNE exits quietly, right. DR ROERLUND, who has continued his reading during the foregoing dialogue, which has been conducted in subdued voices, finishes his book and closes it with a snap.

ROERLUND: And that, dear ladies, concludes our story.

MRS RUMMEL: Oh, what an instructive book!

MRS HOLT: And so moral!

MRS BERNICK: Yes, a book like that certainly gives one food for thought.

ROERLUND: Indeed, yes. It provides a salutary contrast to the horrors that confront us daily in the newspapers and magazines. This rouged and gilded exterior which Society flaunts before our eyes—what does it really hide? Hollowness and corruption—if I may use such words. No solid moral foundation. These so-called great modern communities are nothing but whited sepulchres.

MRS HOLT: How true!

MRS RUMMEL: We only need look at the crew of that American ship that's in port.

ROERLUND: I would rather not sully your ears by speaking of such human refuse. But even in respectable circles, what do we see? Doubt and unrest fermenting on every side; spiritual dissension and universal uncertainty. Out there, family life is everywhere undermined. An impudent spirit of subversion challenges our most sacred principles.

DINA (*without looking up*): But hasn't there been great progress too?

ROERLUND: Progress? I don't understand—

MRS HOLT (*amazed*): Dina, really!

MRS RUMMEL (*simultaneously*): Dina, how can you?

ROERLUND: I hardly think it would be healthy if this progress you speak of were to gain favour in our community. No; we in this little town should thank God that we are as we are. The occasional tare is, alas, to be found among the wheat here as elsewhere; but we strive with all the might that God has given us to root it up. We must keep our community pure, ladies. We must hold these untried theories which an impatient age would force upon us at arm's length.

MRS HOLT: Yes, there are many too many of them about.

MRS RUMMEL: Yes, last year we were only saved from having that horrible railway forced upon us by the skin of our teeth.

MRS BERNICK: Karsten put a stop to that.

ROERLUND: Providence, Mrs Bernick, Providence. You may rest assured that in refusing to countenance the scheme your husband was but the instrument of a Higher Purpose.

MRS BERNICK: But the way they attacked him in the newspapers! Oh, but dear Dr Roerlund, we've completely forgotten to thank you. It really is more than kind of you to sacrifice so much of your time for us.

ROERLUND: Oh, nonsense. My school has its holidays.

MRS BERNICK: Well, yes, but it's still a sacrifice, Dr Roerlund.

ROERLUND (*moves his chair closer*): Pray do not speak of it, dear lady. Are you not all making sacrifices for a noble cause? And do you not make them gladly and willingly? These depraved sinners whose moral condition we are striving to ameliorate are as wounded soldiers upon a battlefield; and you, dear ladies, are the Sisters of Mercy, the ministering angels who pick lint for these fallen creatures, wind your bandages gently round their wounds, tend and heal them—

MRS BERNICK: How wonderful to be able to view everything in such a charitable light.

ROERLUND: It is a gift one is born with; but much can be done to foster it. It is merely a question of having a serious vocation in life and viewing everything in the light of that vocation. What do you say, Miss Bernick? Do you not find that life has a more solid moral foundation since you decided to devote yourself to the noble task of educating the young?

MARTHA: I don't really know what to say. Sometimes as I sit there in the schoolroom I wish I were far away, on the wild sea.

ROERLUND: Temptation, my dear Miss Bernick! You must bar the door against such unruly guests. The wild sea—well, of course you don't mean that literally; you are thinking of the turbulent ocean of modern society in which so many human souls founder. Do you really envy that life you hear murmuring, nay, thundering outside? Only look down into the street. People walk there in the sunshine sweating and wrestling with their petty problems. No, we are better off who sit coolly here behind our windows with our backs turned on the direction from which unrest and disturbance might come.

MARTHA: Yes, of course. I'm sure you're right—

ROERLUND: And in a house such as this—a good, clean home,

26

where family life may be seen in its fairest form—where peace and harmony reign— (*To* MRS BERNICK) Are you listening for something, Mrs Bernick?

MRS BERNICK (*has turned towards the door downstage left*): How loudly they're talking in there!

ROERLUND: Is something important being discussed?

MRS BERNICK: I don't know. My husband seems to have someone with him.

HILMAR TOENNESEN, *with a cigar in his mouth, enters through the door on the right, but stops when he sees the ladies.*

HILMAR: Oh, I beg your pardon— (*Turns to leave*)

MRS BERNICK: No, come in, Hilmar; you're not disturbing us. Did you want something?

HILMAR: No, I was just looking in. Good morning, ladies. (*To* MRS BERNICK) Well, what's going to be the outcome?

MRS BERNICK: How do you mean?

HILMAR: Your husband's called a council of war.

MRS BERNICK: Oh? But what on earth about?

HILMAR: Oh, it's some nonsense about that confounded railway again.

MRS RUMMEL: How disgraceful!

MRS BERNICK: Poor Karsten! As if he hadn't enough worries already!

ROERLUND: But how is this possible, Mr Toennesen? Mr Bernick made it perfectly clear last year that he wouldn't have anything to with any railway.

HILMAR: Yes, that's what I thought. But I met Krap just now, and he tells me that the question's being reconsidered, and that Bernick's having a meeting with three of the other local plutocrats.

MRS RUMMEL: Yes, I thought I heard my husband's voice.

HILMAR: Oh yes, Rummel's there all right; and Sandstad who owns that big store up the hill; and Michael Vigeland—you know, the one they call Holy Mick—

ROERLUND *coughs.*

Oh, sorry, Doctor.

27

MRS BERNICK: Just when everything was so nice and peaceful here.

HILMAR: Well, personally I shouldn't be sorry if they started squabbling again. Give us a bit of fun—

ROERLUND: I think we can do without that kind of fun.

HILMAR: Depends on your temperament. Certain natures need to be harrowed by conflict occasionally. Provincial life doesn't provide many opportunities, worse luck; and not everybody has the guts to—(*Glances at* ROERLUND'S *book*) *Woman as the Servant of Society*. What's this rubbish?

MRS BERNICK: Good heavens, Hilmar, you mustn't say that! You can't have read it.

HILMAR: No, and I don't intend to.

MRS BERNICK: You don't seem in a very good temper today.

HILMAR: I'm not.

MRS BERNICK: Didn't you sleep well last night?

HILMAR: No, I slept rottenly. I took a walk yesterday evening —for my health, you know—and wandered into the Club and read a book some chap had written about the North Pole. I find it very good for my nerves to read about man's struggle with the elements.

MRS RUMMEL: It doesn't appear to have agreed with you, Mr Toennesen.

HILMAR: No, it didn't really agree with me. I tossed and turned all night. Dreamed I was being chased by a horrible walrus.

OLAF (*who has come up on to the verandah*): Have you been chased by a walrus, Uncle?

HILMAR: I dreamed it, you young jackass. Are you still playing with that silly bow? Why don't you get yourself a proper rifle?

OLAF: Oh, I'd love one! But—

HILMAR: There's some sense in having a rifle. That slow pressure on the trigger, you know—good for the nerves.

OLAF: And I could shoot bears with it, Uncle! But Father won't let me.

MRS BERNICK: You mustn't put such ideas into his head, Hilmar.

28

HILMAR: Hm! Fine lot his generation's going to be! All this talk about the importance of sport, and all they do is play silly games, when they ought to be toughening their characters by staring danger unflinchingly in the face. Don't stand there pointing that bow at me, you little fool, it might go off.

OLAF: But Uncle, there's no arrow in it.

HILMAR: You can never be sure. There might be. Point it somewhere else, I tell you. Why the devil don't you go over to America on one of your father's ships? You could hunt buffaloes there. Or fight redskins.

MRS BERNICK: Hilmar, really!

OLAF: Oh yes, Uncle, I'd love to! And I might meet Uncle Johan and Aunt Lona!

HILMAR: Hm—I shouldn't bother about that.

MRS BERNICK: You can go back into the garden now, Olaf.

OLAF: Can I go out into the street too, Mother?

MRS BERNICK: Yes, but not too far.

OLAF *runs out through the garden gate.*

ROERLUND: You ought not to stuff the child's head with such ideas, Mr Toennesen.

HILMAR: Oh, no. Of course not. He's got to spend the rest of his life sitting safe at home, like all the others.

ROERLUND: Why don't you go to America yourself?

HILMAR: I? In my state of health? But of course no one in this town bothers about that. Besides, one has certain responsibilities towards the community one lives in. There's got to be someone here to keep the flag of ideals flying. Ugh, now he's started shouting again.

LADIES: Who? Shouting? Who is shouting?

HILMAR: I don't know. They're raising their voices in there, and it's very bad for my nerves.

MRS RUMMEL: Ah, that's my husband, Mr Toennesen. He's so used to addressing public meetings.

ROERLUND: The others aren't doing too badly either, by the sound of it.

HILMAR: But of course! The moment their pockets are threatened— Oh, everyone here's so petty and materialistic. Ugh!

MRS BERNICK: Well anyway, that's better than the old days, when people thought of nothing but dissipation.

MRS LYNGE: Were things really so dreadful here before?

MRS RUMMEL: Indeed they were, Mrs Lynge. You may think yourself fortunate that you didn't live here then.

MRS HOLT: Yes, there have certainly been great changes. When I think of what things were like when I was a young girl—

MRS RUMMEL: Oh, you only need to look back fifteen years. My word, the goings on there used to be! Why, there was a dance club, *and* a musical society—

MARTHA: And a dramatic society. I remember that well.

MRS RUMMEL: Yes, it was they who put on that play of yours, Mr Toennesen.

HILMAR (*upstage*): Really? Oh, I don't—er—

ROERLUND: Mr Toennesen wrote a play?

MRS RUMMEL: Why, yes. Long before you came here, Dr Roerlund. It only ran for one night.

MRS LYNGE: Wasn't that the play you were telling me about in which you acted one of the young lovers, Mrs Rummel?

MRS RUMMEL (*shoots a glance at* ROERLUND): I? I really don't recall that, Mrs Lynge. But I do remember all the dreadful parties that used to go on.

MRS HOLT: Yes, I know houses where they used to hold big parties twice a week.

MRS LYNGE: And I hear there was a company of strolling players that used to come here.

MRS RUMMEL: Yes, they were the worst of all—

MRS HOLT *coughs uneasily.*

Er—strolling players, did you say? No, I don't remember them.

MRS LYNGE: But I hear they got up to all kinds of wicked pranks. Tell me, is there any truth in those stories?

MRS RUMMEL: None whatever, Mrs Lynge, I assure you.

MRS HOLT: Dina, my love, pass me that piece of linen, will you?

MRS BERNICK (*simultaneously*): Dina dear, run out and ask Katrine to bring us some coffee.

MARTHA: I'll come with you, Dina.

30

DINA and MARTHA *go out through the door upstage left.*

MRS BERNICK: If you'll excuse me for a moment, ladies, I think we'll take coffee outside.

She goes out on to the verandah and lays a table. DR ROERLUND *stands in the doorway talking to her.* HILMAR TOENNESEN *sits down outside and smokes.*

MRS RUMMEL (*quietly*): My goodness, Mrs Lynge, how you frightened me!

MRS LYNGE: I?

MRS HOLT: Yes, but you started it really, Mrs Rummel.

MRS RUMMEL: I? How can you say such a thing, Mrs Holt? I never let a single word pass my lips.

MRS LYNGE: But what is all this?

MRS RUMMEL: How could you bring up the subject of—! I mean, really! Didn't you see Dina was here?

MRS LYNGE: Dina? But good heavens, is there anything the matter with—?

MRS HOLT: And in this house? Don't you know it was Mrs Bernick's brother who—?

MRS LYNGE: What about him? I don't know anything—I'm a newcomer here—

MRS RUMMEL: You mean you haven't heard about—? Hm. (*To* MISS RUMMEL) Hilda dear, run down into the garden for a few minutes.

MRS HOLT: You too, Netta. And be sure you're nice to poor dear Dina when she comes back.

MISS RUMMEL *and* MISS HOLT *go into the garden.*

MRS LYNGE: Well? What was this about Mrs Bernick's brother?

MRS RUMMEL: Don't you know it was he who was involved in that dreadful scandal?

MRS LYNGE: Mr Toennesen was involved in a dreadful scandal?

MRS RUMMEL: Oh good heavens no, Mr Toennesen is her cousin, Mrs Lynge. I'm talking about her brother—

MRS HOLT: The Prodigal of the family—

MRS RUMMEL: His name was Johan. He ran away to America.

31

MRS HOLT: Had to, you understand.

MRS LYNGE: And it was he who was involved in this dreadful scandal?

MRS RUMMEL: Yes. It was a kind of a—what shall I call it?—a kind of a—with Dina's mother. Oh, I remember it as if it had happened yesterday. Johan Toennesen was working in old Mrs Bernick's office. Karsten Bernick had just come back from Paris—he hadn't got engaged yet—

MRS LYNGE: Yes, but the dreadful scandal?

MRS RUMMEL: Well, you see, that winter a theatrical troupe was here in town—

MRS HOLT: And among them was an actor named Dorf, and his wife. All the young men were quite crazy about her.

MRS RUMMEL: Yes, heaven knows what they could see in her. Well, Mr Dorf came home late one night—

MRS HOLT: Unexpectedly, you understand—

MRS RUMMEL: And what should he find but—no, I really can't bring myself to speak of it.

MRS HOLT: No, Mrs Rummel, he didn't *find* anything. The door was locked. From the inside.

MRS RUMMEL: Yes, well, that's what I'm saying—he found the door locked. And, would you believe it, he—the man who was inside—had to jump out of the window!

MRS HOLT: Right out of one of the top windows!

MRS LYNGE: And the man was Mrs Bernick's brother?

MRS RUMMEL: It was indeed.

MRS LYNGE: And that was why he ran away to America?

MRS HOLT: Yes. Well, of course he had to.

MRS RUMMEL: And then afterwards they discovered something almost equally dreadful. Would you believe it, he'd stolen some of the firm's money!

MRS HOLT: But we don't know that for sure, Mrs Rummel. It may only have been gossip.

MRS RUMMEL: Oh, but now, really! Didn't the whole town know about it? Didn't old Mrs Bernick practically go bankrupt because of it? My husband told me so himself. But Heaven forbid that *I* should say anything!

32

MRS HOLT: Well, anyway, Mrs Dorf didn't get the money because she—

MRS LYNGE: Yes, what happened between Dina's parents after that?

MRS RUMMEL: Well, Dorf went away and left his wife and child. But Madam had the cheek to stay here a whole year more. Of course, she didn't dare show her face at the theatre. She kept herself by taking in washing and sewing—

MRS HOLT: And tried to start a dancing academy.

MRS RUMMEL: Of course, nothing came of it. What parents would entrust their children to the care of a person like that? Besides, as things turned out she didn't last long. She wasn't used to hard work, not that fine lady. She picked up some chest trouble, and died.

MRS LYNGE: Well, that was a dreadful scandal indeed.

MRS RUMMEL: Yes, it's been a terrible cross for the Bernicks to bear. It's been the one skeleton in their cupboard, as my husband once phrased it. So don't ever mention the subject in this house, Mrs Lynge.

MRS HOLT: Or the half-sister, for heaven's sake!

MRS LYNGE: Mrs Bernick has a half-sister too?

MRS RUMMEL: Did have—fortunately. It's all over between them now. Oh, she was a queer one all right. Would you believe it, she cut her hair off, and when it rained she walked round in gumboots just like a man!

MRS HOLT: And when the half-brother—the Prodigal—ran away, and the whole town quite naturally raised a hue and cry against him, do you know what she did? Went over and joined him!

MRS RUMMEL: Yes, but the scandal she created before she went, Mrs Holt!

MRS HOLT: Hush, let's not talk of that.

MRS LYNGE: My goodness, was she involved in a scandal too?

MRS RUMMEL: Well, it was like this. Karsten Bernick had just got engaged to Betty Toennesen; and he was going in to announce the news to her aunt, with his newly-betrothed on his arm—

Mrs Holt: The Toennesens had lost their parents, you see—

Mrs Rummel: —when Lona Hessel got up from the chair she was sitting on and gave Karsten Bernick for all his fine airs and breeding such a box on the ears she nearly split his eardrums.

Mrs Lynge: You don't mean it!

Mrs Rummel: As heaven is my witness.

Mrs Holt: And packed her bags and went to America.

Mrs Lynge: Then she must have had her eye on him too!

Mrs Rummel: Of course she had! She'd been flouncing round here imagining that he'd marry her the moment he got back from Paris.

Mrs Holt: Yes, fancy her being able to believe that! A man of the world like Karsten Bernick—so genteel and well-bred—the perfect gentleman—every woman's dream—

Mrs Rummel: And so virtuous with it all, Mrs Holt. So moral.

Mrs Lynge: But what has this Miss Hessel been doing in America?

Mrs Rummel: Ah. Over that hangs a veil which had best not be lifted, as my husband once phrased it.

Mrs Lynge: What do you mean?

Mrs Rummel: Well, the family's no longer in contact with her, as you can imagine. But the whole town knows this much, that she's sung for money over there in—hm—places of entertainment—

Mrs Holt: And given lectures in public—

Mrs Rummel: And brought out a wicked book.

Mrs Lynge: My goodness!

Mrs Rummel: Yes, Lona Hessel is another skeleton in the Bernick family cupboard. Well, now you know the whole story, Mrs Lynge. Of course I've only told you all this so that you'll be on your guard.

Mrs Lynge: My goodness yes, you can be sure I will. But that poor Dina Dorf! I feel really sorry for her.

Mrs Rummel: Oh, it was a great stroke of luck as far as she was concerned. Just imagine if she'd been left in the hands of those parents of hers! We all lent her a helping hand, of course, and did what we could to try to guide her along the

34

right paths. Then Miss Bernick arranged for her to come and live here.

MRS HOLT: But she's always been a difficult child. Well, what can you expect, when you think of the example she's been set? A girl like that isn't like one of us. We have to take her as we find her, Mrs Lynge.

MRS RUMMEL: Hush, here she is. (*Loudly*) Yes, dear Dina's a very clever girl. Oh, hullo, Dina, are you back? We're just finishing.

MRS HOLT: Dina, my sweet, how lovely your coffee smells. There's nothing like a nice cup of morning coffee—

MRS BERNICK (*outside on the verandah*): Everything is ready, ladies!

MISS BERNICK *and* DINA *have meanwhile been helping the* MAID *to bring in the coffee things. All the* LADIES *go out on to the verandah and sit down. They talk to* DINA *with ostentatious amiability. After a few moments, she comes into the room and looks for her sewing.*

MRS BERNICK (*outside at the coffee table*): Dina, won't you join us?

DINA: No, thank you. I don't want any.

She sits down to her sewing. MRS BERNICK *and* DR ROERLUND *exchange a few words; then he comes into the room.*

ROERLUND (*pretends to need something from the table; then says softly*): Dina.

DINA: Yes.

ROERLUND: Why don't you want to sit outside with us?

DINA: When I came in with the coffee I could see from the expression on that new lady's face that they'd been talking about me.

ROERLUND: But didn't you also notice how friendly she was to you on the verandah?

DINA: That's just what I can't bear.

ROERLUND: You have a stubborn nature, Dina.

DINA: Yes.

ROERLUND: Why?

35

DINA: That's the way I am.

ROERLUND: Couldn't you try to make yourself different?

DINA: No.

ROERLUND: Why not?

DINA (*looks at him*): I'm one of the depraved sinners.

ROERLUND: Dina!

DINA: Mother was a depraved sinner too.

ROERLUND: Who has told you about these things?

DINA: No one. They never tell me anything. Why don't they? They all treat me so gently, as though I might break into pieces if— Oh, how I hate all this kindness!

ROERLUND: Dina dear, I understand so well how confined you feel here, but—

DINA: Yes, if only I could go far away. I'm sure I could manage on my own if only I didn't live among people who were so—so—

ROERLUND: So what?

DINA: So virtuous and moral.

ROERLUND: Dina, you can't mean that.

DINA: Oh, you know what I mean. Every day Hilda and Netta are brought here so that I can model myself on them. I can never be as clever as them. I don't want to be. Oh, if only I were far away! Then I might be able to become someone.

ROERLUND: You are someone, Dina.

DINA: What's the use, here?

ROERLUND: Then you mean you're seriously thinking of going away?

DINA: I wouldn't stay a day longer, if you weren't here.

ROERLUND: Tell me, Dina. Why do you like being with me?

DINA: Because you teach me so much about what's beautiful.

ROERLUND: I teach you about what is beautiful?

DINA: Yes. Or rather—you don't teach me anything; but when I hear you talk, I understand what beauty is.

ROERLUND: What do you mean by beauty?

DINA: I've never thought.

ROERLUND: Well, think now. What do you mean by beauty?

DINA: Beauty—is something that is big—and far away.

ROERLUND: Hm. Dina my dear, I'm deeply concerned about you.

DINA: Is that all?

ROERLUND: You know how very dear you are to me.

DINA: If I were Hilda or Netta you wouldn't be afraid to let people see it.

ROERLUND: Oh, Dina, you don't understand all the little things a man has to— When a man is chosen to be a moral pillar for the society he lives in—well, he can't be sufficiently careful. If only I could be sure that people would not misinterpret my motives—! Well, it can't be helped. You must and shall be rescued. Dina, is it a bargain that when I come—when circumstances permit me to come to you and say: "Here is my hand"—you will take it and be my wife? Will you promise me that, Dina?

DINA: Yes.

ROERLUND: Thank you—thank you! Because I, too—oh, Dina, you are so very dear to me. Hush, someone's coming! Dina —please—for my sake—go outside and join the others.

She goes out and joins the LADIES. *As she does so* MR RUMMEL, MR SANDSTAD *and* MR VIGELAND *enter from the room down-stage left, followed by* MR BERNICK, *with a sheaf of papers in his hand.*

BERNICK: Right, then, we're agreed.

VIGELAND: Yes, yes. May God's blessing rest upon our plans!

RUMMEL: Never you fear, Bernick. A Norseman's word is his bond. You know that.

BERNICK: There's to be no going back, now. No one's to drop out, whatever opposition we may encounter.

RUMMEL: We stand or fall together, Bernick.

HILMAR (*who has come to the door of the verandah*): Fall? What's going to fall? Railway shares?

BERNICK: On the contrary. The railway is to go ahead.

RUMMEL: Full steam, Mr Toennesen.

HILMAR (*comes closer*): Really?

ROERLUND: What?

MRS BERNICK (*at the verandah door*): But Karsten dear, surely you—?

BERNICK: Betty dear, how can these things possibly interest

37

you? (*To the* THREE GENTLEMEN) Well, we must get out a prospectus as quickly as possible. Our names will head the list, of course. The positions we occupy in the community render it our duty to support this cause to the fullest limit of our generosity.

SANDSTAD: Of course, of course.

RUMMEL: We'll see it through, Bernick. You have our word.

BERNICK: Oh yes, I'm not worried about the outcome. But we must use our authority and influence; once we can show that every section of the community is actively participating, the municipality will feel compelled to subscribe its share.

MRS BERNICK: Karsten, you must come outside and tell us all about it.

BERNICK: My dear Betty, this is not a matter for women to concern themselves with.

HILMAR: You seriously mean you're letting this railway project go through after all?

BERNICK: Yes, of course.

ROERLUND: But Mr Bernick, last year you—

BERNICK: Last year the situation was different. The plan then was for a line to run along the coast—

VIGELAND: Which would have been utterly superfluous, Dr Roerlund. After all, we have ships—

SANDSTAD: And it'd have been prohibitively expensive—

RUMMEL: Yes, and would have damaged important interests in our town.

BERNICK: The main point is that the project as then conceived would not have benefited the community as a whole. That is why I opposed it; and as a result, they have decided to run the line inland.

HILMAR: Yes, but then it won't touch any of the towns round here.

BERNICK: It will touch our town, my dear Hilmar. We have arranged for a branch line to be built.

HILMAR: Oh? That's a new idea, isn't it?

RUMMEL: Yes—magnificent idea, isn't it? What?

ROERLUND: Hm.

VIGELAND: There's no denying that Providence might almost

have designed that little valley especially so as to accommo-
date a branch line.

ROERLUND: Do you really think so, Mr Vigeland?

BERNICK: Yes, I must confess that I, too, feel it was the hand
of Providence that sent me up-country on business last
spring and directed my footsteps into this valley, which I
had never seen before. Suddenly it struck me like an
inspiration that through this valley we could lay a branch
line to our little town. I arranged for an engineer to survey
the land and I have here his provisional calculations and
estimates. Nothing now stands in our way.

MRS BERNICK (*still in the doorway, with the other* LADIES): But
Karsten dear, why have you kept all this hidden from us?

BERNICK: My dear Betty, you wouldn't have been able to
understand what it was all about. In any case I haven't
mentioned it to anyone until today. But now the decisive
moment has arrived. Now we can work openly and with all
our strength. Yes, I shall force this project through, even if
it means staking everything I possess.

RUMMEL: Us too, Bernick. You can rely on us.

ROERLUND: You really expect so much from this project then,
gentlemen?

BERNICK: Of course we do! Think what a stimulus it will give
to our whole community! Think of the great tracts of forest
it will render accessible! Think of the mines it will enable
us to work! Think of the river with its waterfalls one above
the other, and the factories we could build to utilize their
power! A whole wealth of new industries will spring into
being!

ROERLUND: But are you not afraid of the possible consequences
of more frequent contact with the depraved world outside?

BERNICK: No need to fear that, my dear Doctor. Nowadays
our industrious little community rests, thank God, on a
sound moral foundation. We have all, if I may say so,
helped to cleanse it; and we shall continue to keep it clean,
each in his own way. You, Dr Roerlund, will maintain your
splendid work at the school and in the home. We, the

practical men of affairs, will strengthen the community by spreading prosperity over as broad a circle as possible. And our womenfolk—yes, ladies, come closer, you may listen to what I have to say—our womenfolk, I say, our wives and daughters—continue, ladies, I beseech you, to labour untiringly in the cause of charity, and to be a help and a shield to your dear ones, as my beloved Betty and Martha are to me and to Olaf— (*Looks round*) Yes, where is Olaf today?

MRS BERNICK: Oh, now the holidays have begun it's hopeless to try to keep him indoors.

BERNICK: I suppose that means he's down on the waterfront again. He'll have an accident before he's finished, you mark my word.

HILMAR: Oh, rubbish. A little skirmish with the elements—

MRS RUMMEL: Oh, I think it's so wonderful the love you show your family, Mr Bernick.

BERNICK: Well, the family is the basis on which society rests. A good home, loyal and trustworthy friends, a small close-knit circle with no intrusive elements to cast their shadow—

KRAP *enters right with letters and newspapers.*

KRAP: The foreign mail, Mr Bernick. And a telegram from New York.

BERNICK (*takes it*): Ah, this'll be from the owners of the *Indian Girl.*

RUMMEL: Has the post come? Then I must ask you to excuse me—

VIGELAND: Me too.

SANDSTAD: Goodbye, Mr Bernick.

BERNICK: Goodbye, gentlemen, goodbye. And don't forget, we meet at five o'clock this afternoon.

THE THREE GENTLEMEN: Yes, yes. Of course.

They go out right.

BERNICK (*reads the telegram*): Oh no, really, this is typically American! How absolutely disgraceful!

MRS BERNICK: Oh, Karsten, what is it?

BERNICK: Look at this, Mr Krap. Here, read it.

KRAP (*reads*): "Execute minimum repairs. Despatch *Indian Girl* as soon as seaworthy. Safe season. At worst, cargo will keep her afloat." Well, bless my soul!

BERNICK: "Cargo will keep her afloat"! Those fellows know perfectly well that if anything goes wrong that cargo'll send the ship to the bottom like a stone.

ROERLUND: Well, that only goes to show what the moral climate is like in these so-called great communities.

BERNICK: You're right. They don't even respect human life, as long as they make their profit. (*To* KRAP) Can we make the *Indian Girl* seaworthy in four or five days?

KRAP: Yes, if Mr Vigeland lets us stop work on the *Palm Tree*.

BERNICK: Hm. He won't do that. Well, look through the mail. By the way, did you see Olaf down on the jetty?

KRAP: No, sir.

He goes into the room downstage left.

BERNICK (*reads the telegram again*): Eighteen human lives at stake! And those gentlemen don't turn a hair.

HILMAR: Well, it's a sailor's job to brave the elements. It must be exhilarating to have nothing but a thin plank between yourself and eternity. Good for the nerves—

BERNICK: I'd like to meet the shipowner in this town who could reconcile his conscience to giving an order like this. There isn't a man in this community, not one— (*Sees* OLAF) Ah, here he is. Thank goodness for that.

OLAF, *with a fishing-line in his hand, has run up the street and in through the garden gate.*

OLAF (*still in the garden*): Uncle Hilmar, I've been down looking at the steamer!

BERNICK: Have you been on that jetty again?

OLAF: No, I only went out in a boat. Just fancy, Uncle Hilmar, a whole circus has come ashore, with horses and animals! And there were lots of tourists too!

MRS RUMMEL: I say, are we going to see a circus?

ROERLUND: We? I hardly think so.

MRS RUMMEL: No, no—of course, I didn't mean *us*—I only—

DINA: I should like to see a circus.

OLAF: Yes, so would I!

HILMAR: You little fool, what's worth seeing there? *Dressage*, and all that nonsense. Now, to see a gaucho galloping across the pampas on his snorting mustang—that'd be different! Oh dear, these provincial backwaters—

OLAF (*tugs* MARTHA'S *sleeve*): Look, Aunt Martha, look! There they are!

MRS HOLT: Oh, my goodness!

MRS LYNGE: Dear me, what horrible people.

A crowd of TOURISTS *and* TOWNSPEOPLE *appears in the street.*

MRS RUMMEL: My word, they're proper vagabonds. Look at that woman in the grey dress, Mrs Holt. She's carrying a knapsack on her back!

MRS HOLT: Yes. Fancy, she's got it tied to her parasol! I expect she's the ringmaster's—er—wife.

MRS RUMMEL: There's the ringmaster! The one with the beard. I say, he looks just like a pirate! Don't look at him, Hilda.

MRS HOLT: Nor you, Netta.

OLAF: Mother, he's waving to us!

BERNICK: What!

MRS BERNICK: Olaf, what on earth do you mean?

MRS RUMMEL: My goodness, yes! The woman's waving too!

BERNICK: This really is intolerable.

MARTHA (*gives an involuntary cry*): Oh!

MRS BERNICK: What is it, Martha?

MARTHA: Oh, nothing. I thought for a moment it—

OLAF (*cries excitedly*): Look, look! Here come the horses and animals! And there are the Americans, too! All the sailors from the *Indian Girl!*

"Yankee Doodle" is heard, accompanied by a clarinet and drum.

HILMAR (*puts his hands over his ears*): Ugh, ugh, ugh!

ROERLUND: I think we should isolate ourselves for a while, ladies. This is not for us. Let us return to our work.

MRS BERNICK: Ought we perhaps to draw the curtains?
ROERLUND: That is exactly what I had in mind.

The LADIES *take their places again at the table.* DR ROERLUND *closes the verandah door and draws the curtains across it and the windows. The room is plunged into semi-darkness.*

OLAF (*peering out*): Mother, now the ringmaster's lady's washing her face at the pump.
MRS BERNICK: What! In the middle of the market-place?
HILMAR: Well, if I was crossing a desert and happened on a well, I don't suppose I'd bother to look round to see if— ugh, that dreadful clarinet!
ROERLUND: This is becoming a matter for the police.
BERNICK: Ah well, they're foreigners; one mustn't judge them too severely. These people are not born with the sense of decorum which makes us instinctively obey the laws of propriety. Let them go their way. What are they to us? This ribald behaviour, offensive to every standard of decency, fortunately has no place in our community. What the—!

The STRANGE LADY *strides in through the door, right.*

THE LADIES (*in terrified whispers*): The circus woman! The ringmaster's—er—!
MRS BERNICK: Good heavens! What is the meaning of this?
MARTHA (*jumps to her feet*): Oh!
THE LADY: Morning, Betty dear. Morning, Martha. Morning, brother-in-law.
MRS BERNICK (*with a scream*): Lona!
BERNICK (*takes a step backwards*): Good God!
MRS HOLT: Oh, dear heaven!
MRS RUMMEL: It can't be possible!
HILMAR: Well! Ugh!
MRS BERNICK: Lona! Is it really you!
MISS HESSEL: Really me? Sure it's me. Come on, kiss me and prove it!
HILMAR: Ugh! Ugh!
MRS BERNICK: You mean you've come here to—?
BERNICK: To perform?

43

MISS HESSEL: Perform? What do you mean, perform?

BERNICK: In the—er—circus.

MISS HESSEL (*roars with laughter*): Karsten, have you gone nuts? You think I've joined the circus? No—I've learned a few tricks, and acted the clown in more ways than one— (MRS RUMMEL *coughs*)—but I haven't started jumping through hoops yet.

BERNICK: Then you're not—!

MRS BERNICK: Thank heaven for that!

MISS HESSEL: No, we came respectably, with the other tourists. Steerage—but we're used to that.

MRS BERNICK: Did you say *we*?

BERNICK (*takes a step towards her*): Whom do you mean by *we*?

MISS HESSEL: Me and the kid, of course.

THE LADIES (*shriek*): Kid?

HILMAR: What!

ROERLUND: Well, really!

MRS BERNICK: But Lona, what do you mean?

MISS HESSEL: Who do you think I mean? John, of course; he's the only kid I have, to my knowledge. Johan, you used to call him.

MRS BERNICK: Johan!

MRS RUMMEL (sotto voce *to* MRS LYNGE): The Prodigal!

BERNICK (*unwillingly*): Is Johan with you?

MISS HESSEL: Yes, of course. Never go anywhere without him. Say, you *are* all looking down in the mouth. Why are you sitting in the dark? What's that white stuff you're all sewing? Is someone dead?

ROERLUND: Madam, you find yourself at a meeting of the Society for the Redemption of Fallen Women.

MISS HESSEL (*lowers her voice*): What! You mean all these respectable-looking ladies are—?

MRS RUMMEL: Now, really!

MISS HESSEL: Oh, I get it, I get it. Well, if it isn't Mrs Rummel! And Mrs Holt! Say, we three haven't grown any shorter in the tooth since we last met! Now, listen, all of you. Let the Fallen Women wait for twenty-four hours; they won't fall any further. This is an occasion for celebration!

ROERLUND: A homecoming is not always an occasion for celebration.

MISS HESSEL: Is that so? How do you interpret your Bible, Reverend—

ROERLUND: I am not a Reverend.

MISS HESSEL: Never mind, you'll become one. Say, this charity stuff stinks awful. Just like a shroud. Of course, I'm used to the prairies. Air's fresher there.

BERNICK (*mops his brow*): Yes, it is rather close in here.

MISS HESSEL: Take it easy, Karsten. You'll surface. (*Pulls aside the curtains*) Let's have some daylight in here for when the kid comes. Wait till you see him! He's scrubbed himself as clean as a—

HILMAR: Ugh!

MISS HESSEL (*opens the door and windows*): That's to say, he *will* have, once he gets a chance up at the hotel. On that ship he got as filthy as a pig.

HILMAR: Ugh! Ugh!

MISS HESSEL: Ugh? Well, bless me if it isn't—! (*Points at HILMAR and asks the others*) Does he still sit around here saying "Ugh!"?

HILMAR: I *don't* sit around. I only stay here because my health doesn't permit me to work.

ROERLUND (*coughs*): Ladies, I hardly think—

MISS HESSEL (*catches sight of OLAF*): Is this yours, Betty? Give us your paw, kid. Are you afraid of your ugly old aunt?

ROERLUND (*puts his book under his arm*): Ladies, I hardly think the atmosphere here is conducive to further work today. We meet again as usual tomorrow?

MISS HESSEL (*as the other LADIES rise to leave*): Sure, why not? You can count me in.

ROERLUND: You? Forgive my asking, madam, but what can you possibly contribute to our Society?

MISS HESSEL: Fresh air—Reverend!

ACT TWO

The garden room in BERNICK'S *house.* MRS BERNICK *is seated alone at the work-table with her sewing. After a few moments,* BERNICK *enters right with his hat on, carrying gloves and a stick.*

MRS BERNICK: Home already, Karsten?

BERNICK: Yes. I have an appointment here.

MRS BERNICK (*sighs*): Oh, dear. Johan again, I suppose.

BERNICK: No, no, it's with one of the men. (*Takes off his hat*) Where are all the ladies today?

MRS BERNICK: Mrs Rummel and Hilda hadn't time.

BERNICK: Oh? They sent their excuses?

MRS BERNICK: Yes; they had so much to do at home.

BERNICK: But of course. And the others won't be coming either, I suppose?

MRS BERNICK: No, they're busy too.

BERNICK: I could have told you that yesterday. Where's Olaf?

MRS BERNICK: I sent him out for a walk with Dina.

BERNICK: Hm. Dina. Flighty young hussy. Striking up like that with Johan the very first day he arrived—

MRS BERNICK: But Karsten dear, Dina knows nothing about—

BERNICK: Well, he ought to have had the tact not to pay her so much attention. I saw the look Vigeland gave them.

MRS BERNICK (*puts her sewing in her lap*): Karsten, why do you think they've come?

BERNICK: Well, I dare say that farm of his isn't doing too well —she said yesterday they'd had to travel steerage—

MRS BERNICK: Yes, I'm afraid you must be right. But fancy *her* coming with him! After the dreadful way she insulted you!

BERNICK: Oh, that was a long time ago. Forget about it.

MRS BERNICK: How can I forget about it? After all, he is my

46

brother—but it's not so much him I'm thinking of as all the unpleasantness it's causing you. Oh, Karsten, I'm so dreadfully frightened—

BERNICK: Frightened? Of what?

MRS BERNICK: Mightn't they arrest him for stealing that money from your mother?

BERNICK: Don't be so silly. No one can prove anything was taken.

MRS BERNICK: Oh, but the whole town knows. And you've said yourself that—

BERNICK: I have said nothing. The town knows nothing. All they heard was just vague gossip.

MRS BERNICK: You are so magnanimous, Karsten.

BERNICK: Try to forget these old memories, Betty. You don't know how it distresses me to be reminded about all this. (*Walks up and down; then he throws down his stick*) Why on earth must they come home just at this moment, when I don't want any trouble in the town; or in the press? It'll get into every local paper for miles around. Whether I welcome them or whether I turn my back on them, people will talk about it and read something into it. They'll dig the whole story up again, just the way you're doing. And in a community like ours— (*Throws down his gloves on the table*) And I haven't a single person I can talk to or look to for support.

MRS BERNICK: Have you no one, Karsten?

BERNICK: No, who could there be? Oh, why in God's name must they come *now*? They're sure to create a scandal of some kind or another. Especially she. It really is intolerable having people like that in one's own family.

MRS BERNICK: Well, I can't help it if—

BERNICK: You can't help what? That they're your relations? No, you can't help that.

MRS BERNICK: I didn't ask them to come.

BERNICK: Oh, here we go again. "I didn't ask them to come. I didn't write and beg them. I didn't drag them here by the hair." I know it all by heart!

MRS BERNICK (*begins to cry*): Oh, why must you be so unkind?

47

BERNICK: That's right. Start crying, and give the town something else to talk about. Stop this foolishness, Betty. Go and sit outside, someone might come. Do you want people to see you've been crying? A fine thing it'd be if people got to hear that— hush, someone's coming.

There is a knock on the door.

Come in!

MRS BERNICK *goes out on to the verandah with her sewing.* AUNE *enters, right.*

AUNE: Good morning, Mr Bernick.

BERNICK: Good morning. Well, I suppose you can guess why I've sent for you?

AUNE: Mr Krap said something yesterday about your not being satisfied with—

BERNICK: I'm dissatisfied with the way things are going down at the yard, Aune. You're not getting on with those repairs. The *Palm Tree* ought to have been under sail days ago. Mr Vigeland comes here to complain every day. He's a difficult man to have as a partner.

AUNE: The *Palm Tree* can sail the day after tomorrow.

BERNICK: At last! But that American ship, the *Indian Girl*, has been lying here for five weeks—

AUNE: The American? I understood we were to put all our men on to your ship till she was ready.

BERNICK: I gave no such orders. My instructions were that you should go full steam ahead with the American too. You haven't.

AUNE: But her bottom's rotten, Mr Bernick. The more we patch her the worse she gets.

BERNICK: That's not the real reason. Mr Krap's told me the whole story. You don't understand how to use these new machines I've bought—or rather, you won't use them.

AUNE: Mr Bernick, I'm nearly sixty and ever since I was a boy I've been accustomed to the old methods—

BERNICK: We can't use those nowadays. Look, Aune, you mustn't think I'm doing this for money. Luckily I don't

48

need any more of that. I've got to think of the community of which I'm a member, and of the business of which I am the head. Progress has got to come from me or it won't come at all.

AUNE: I want progress too, Mr Bernick.

BERNICK: Yes, for your own narrow circle, the working class. Oh, I know you agitators. You make speeches and get the people worked up, but the moment anyone takes any practical steps towards improving matters, as with these machines, you refuse to co-operate, and get frightened.

AUNE: I am frightened, Mr Bernick. I'm frightened for all the mouths from which these machines will take the bread. You keep on saying we've got to think of the community, but I reckon the community owes us a duty too. What's the use of society employing knowledge and capital to introduce all these new inventions before it's educated a generation that knows how to use them?

BERNICK: You read and think too much, Aune. And what good do you get from it? It just makes you discontented with your position in society.

AUNE: It isn't that, Mr Bernick. I can't bear to see one good man after another getting sacked and their families going hungry to make way for these machines.

BERNICK: When printing was invented, many scribes went hungry.

AUNE: Would you have welcomed it if you'd been a scribe?

BERNICK: I didn't send for you to argue with you. The *Indian Girl*'s got to be ready to sail the day after tomorrow.

AUNE: But, Mr Bernick—

BERNICK: The day after tomorrow, do you hear? At the same time as our own ship; not an hour later. I've good reasons for wanting to get the job done quickly. Have you read the news-paper this morning? Then you know that the Americans have been causing trouble again. Those ruffians are turning the whole town upside down; not a night goes by without them starting a brawl in the streets or in a drinking-house. To say nothing of other things I'd rather not mention.

AUNE: Yes, they seem a bad lot.

49

BERNICK: And who gets the blame for all this? I do! It all comes back on to my head. These newspaper fellows grumble and try to insinuate that we've put all our labour strength on to the *Palm Tree*. And I, who am supposed to influence my fellow citizens by setting them a good example, have all this dirt thrown at me. Well, I'm not standing for it. I'm not used to having my name dragged in the mud like this.

AUNE: Oh, you don't need to bother about that kind of thing, Mr Bernick.

BERNICK: Just now I do. I need all the respect and goodwill I can muster from my fellow citizens. I've big plans afoot, as I daresay you've heard, and if malicious-minded people succeed in shaking the community's trust in me, it could cause me very great difficulties. So I want at all costs to avoid giving these damned scribblers any food for gossip, and that's why I say the job's got to be done by the day after tomorrow.

AUNE: Mr Bernick, you might as well tell me it's got to be done by this afternoon.

BERNICK: You mean I'm demanding the impossible?

AUNE: With our present labour strength, yes.

BERNICK: Very well. Then I'll have to start looking elsewhere.

AUNE: You don't mean you're going to dismiss still more of the older men?

BERNICK: No, that's not what I was thinking.

AUNE: It'd create bad feeling in the town if you did that. And in the newspapers.

BERNICK: Probably it might, so I won't. But if the *Indian Girl* isn't ready to sail by the day after tomorrow, there'll be a notice of dismissal served on you.

AUNE: On me! (*Laughs*) You're joking, sir.

BERNICK: I shouldn't take that for granted if I were you.

AUNE: Dismiss me? But my father and his father worked all their lives in this yard. And so have I.

BERNICK: Who's making me do this?

AUNE: You're asking the impossible, Mr Bernick.

BERNICK: A good worker doesn't know the meaning of the

50

word impossible. Yes or no? Give me a straight answer, or you'll get your notice now.

AUNE (*takes a step towards him*): Mr Bernick, have you ever seriously thought what it means to give an old worker the sack? You think he can look round for something else? Oh, yes; he can do that; but that isn't the whole story. You ought to be present some time in a workman's house on the evening when he comes home and throws down his bag of tools behind the door.

BERNICK: Do you think I'm finding it easy to do this? Haven't I always been a good master to you?

AUNE: So much the worse for me, sir. It means no one at home will put the blame on you. They won't say anything to my face—they wouldn't dare—but they'll shoot a glance at me when they think I'm not looking and say to themselves: "Oh well, he must have deserved it." Don't you see, sir, that's the one thing I can't bear! Poor as I am, I've always been used to being regarded as lord and master in my own house. My humble home is a little community just as yours is, Mr Bernick, and I've been able to sustain it and keep it going because my wife has believed in me and my children have believed in me. And now it's all going to fall to the ground.

BERNICK: Well, if there's no alternative the lesser must make way for the greater. The individual must be sacrificed for the common cause. That's the only answer I can give you; it's the way of the world. You're a stubborn man, Aune. You oppose me, not because you must but because you won't accept the fact that machines can work better than flesh and blood.

AUNE: And you're so dead set on this, Mr Bernick, because you know that if you sack me at least you'll have shown the press you're anxious to do as they say you should.

BERNICK: Well, suppose I am? I've told you how much this means to me; either I have every newspaper in the district putting me in the pillory, or else I get them on my side just at the moment when I'm working to get a big project under way for the good of the community. Well then, how else can I act? My choice is either to keep your home going or to suppress the building of hundreds of new homes— hundreds of homes that will never be built, never have a fire in their hearth, unless I succeed in achieving what I'm now working for. Well, I leave the choice to you.

AUNE: I see. In that case I've no more to say.

BERNICK: Hm. My dear Aune, it really grieves me deeply that we have to part.

AUNE: We're not parting, Mr Bernick.

BERNICK: What do you mean?

AUNE: Working men have a sense of honour too.

BERNICK: Of course they have. Then you think you can promise—?

AUNE: The *Indian Girl* will be ready to sail the day after tomorrow.

Touches his forehead and goes out right.

BERNICK: Well, I've made that obstinate old fool see sense. That's a good omen, anyway.

HILMAR TOENNESEN *enters through the garden gate, smoking a cigar.*

HILMAR (*on the verandah*): Morning, Betty. Morning, Bernick.

MRS BERNICK: Good morning.

HILMAR: You've been crying. You know, then?

MRS BERNICK: Know what?

HILMAR: That the scandal's started. Ugh!

BERNICK: What do you mean?

HILMAR (*comes into the room*): Those two Americans are walking round the town in broad daylight with our little Dina Dorf.

MRS BERNICK (*follows him*): Hilmar, you're joking!

HILMAR: I'm afraid it's the truth. Lona was actually so tactless as to shout at me. Of course I pretended not to hear her.

BERNICK: And I suppose this hasn't exactly passed unnoticed.

HILMAR: You bet your life it hasn't. People stood still and stared at them. The news spread through the town like wildfire; like a prairie blaze. In every house people stood at their windows and waited for the procession to pass; they were packed behind their curtains like sardines—ugh! You must forgive me, Betty; I can't help saying "Ugh!," this makes me so nervous. If it goes on, I shall have to think about taking a holiday. Rather a long one.

MRS BERNICK: But you ought to have spoken to him and made it clear that—

HILMAR: What, in public? No, I'm sorry! But fancy him daring to show his face in this town at all! Well, we'll see if the newspapers can't put a spoke in his wheel. I'm sorry, Betty, but—

BERNICK: The newspapers, did you say? Have you heard anything to suggest that they may take action?

HILMAR: Oh yes, there's no doubt about that. When I left you yesterday afternoon, I took a walk up to the Club, for my health. It was quite evident from the silence that fell when I entered that they'd been talking about our American friends. Well, then that tactless editor fellow—you know, Hammer—came in and congratulated me out loud on my rich cousin's return home.

BERNICK: Rich—?

HILMAR: Yes, that's what he said. Of course I gave him a pretty piercing look and made it quite clear that I knew nothing about any riches as far as Johan Toennesen was concerned. "Oh, really?" he said. "That's strange. People usually do all right in America provided they have some capital, and your cousin didn't go empty-handed, did he?"

BERNICK: Hm. Look, do me the goodness to—

MRS BERNICK (*worried*): There you are, Karsten—

HILMAR: Yes, well anyway, he's given me a sleepless night. And he has the cheek to stroll round this town looking as innocent as an angel. Why didn't that illness he had knock him off? It's really monstrous how indestructible some people are.

MRS BERNICK: Hilmar, what are you saying?

HILMAR: Oh, I'm not saying anything. But look at him, he's survived railway accidents and attacks by grizzlies and

Blackfoot Indians without a scratch to show for it all. Didn't even get scalped. Ugh, here they are!

BERNICK (*glances up the street*): Olaf's with them!

HILMAR: But of course! They want to remind everyone that they belong to the best family in town. Look at all those people coming out of the chemist's to stare at them and make remarks. My nerves won't stand this. How a man can be expected to keep the flag of ideals flying under circumstances like these I really don't know—

BERNICK: They're coming here. Now listen, Betty, it's my express wish that you treat them with every courtesy.

MRS BERNICK: May I, Karsten?

BERNICK: Yes, yes; and you too, Hilmar. With luck they won't stay long, and while we're alone together I don't want there to be any insinuations. We must on no account embarrass them.

MRS BERNICK: Oh, Karsten, how magnanimous you are!

BERNICK: Yes, well; never mind that.

MRS BERNICK: No, you must let me thank you. And forgive me for becoming so emotional just now. Oh, you were quite justified in—

BERNICK: Never mind, I say, never *mind*.

HILMAR: Ugh!

JOHAN TOENNESEN *and* DINA *enter through the garden, followed by* MISS HESSEL *and* OLAF.

MISS HESSEL: Morning, everyone.

JOHAN: We've been giving the old place the once-over, Karsten.

BERNICK: Yes, so I hear. Plenty of changes, eh?

MISS HESSEL: Everywhere there's evidence of Karsten Bernick's great and good works. We've been around the gardens you presented to the town—

BERNICK: Oh, you've been there?

MISS HESSEL: "The Gift of Karsten Bernick," it says over the entrance. Yes, you seem to be the king-pin here all right.

JOHAN: Fine ships you've got too. I ran into the captain of the *Palm Tree*—he's an old school friend of mine—

MISS HESSEL: And you've built a new school; and I hear we can thank you for the waterworks and the gas tank.

BERNICK: Well, one must do something for the community one lives in.

MISS HESSEL: The sentiment does you credit, brother-in-law. It made me proud to see what a high opinion everyone has of you. I don't reckon myself vain, but I couldn't resist reminding one or two people we spoke to that Johan and I belong to the family.

HILMAR: Ugh!

MISS HESSEL: What's "Ugh!" about that?

HILMAR: All I said was "Hm!"

MISS HESSEL: Did you? Oh, that's all right. Well, you don't seem to have any visitors today.

MRS BERNICK: No, we're alone.

MISS HESSEL: We met a couple of your Salvationists in the market-place. They seemed to be in a great hurry. But we haven't had a real chance to talk yet, have we? Yesterday you had those three Railway Kings and the Reverend—

HILMAR: Schoolmaster.

MISS HESSEL: Well, I call him Reverend. But tell me, what do you think of what I've been doing for the past fifteen years? Hasn't he grown into a fine boy? Who'd ever think he was the same as that young good-for-nothing who ran away from home?

HILMAR: Hm.

JOHAN: Oh Lona, stop boasting.

MISS HESSEL: O.K., so I'm proud of it! Hell, it's the only thing I've ever achieved in the world; but it makes me feel I've done something to justify my existence. Yes, Johan, when I think how you and I started out there, with just our four bare paws—

HILMAR: Hands—

MISS HESSEL: I said paws. They were black.

HILMAR: Ugh!

MISS HESSEL: Yes, and empty.

HILMAR: Empty? Well, I must say—

MISS HESSEL: What must you say?

HILMAR: I must say—ugh! (*Goes out on to the verandah*)

MISS HESSEL: What's the matter with him?

BERNICK: Oh, never mind him; he's been rather nervous these last few days. Er—wouldn't you like to have a look round the garden? You haven't seen it properly yet, and I happen to have an hour free just now.

MISS HESSEL: That's a fine idea. I'd love to.

MRS BERNICK: There've been some big changes there too, as you'll see.

BERNICK, MRS BERNICK *and* MISS HESSEL *descend into the garden. We see them occasionally during the following scene.*

OLAF (*in the doorway to the verandah*): Uncle Hilmar, do you know what Uncle Johan asked me? He asked if I'd like to go with him to America.

HILMAR: You, you jackass? Why, you spend your whole time clinging to your mother's petticoats.

OLAF: I don't want to do that any longer. You wait—once I'm big, I'll—!

HILMAR: Oh, stuff! You've no stomach for danger.

They go together into the garden.

JOHAN (*to* DINA, *who has taken off her hat and is standing in the doorway on the right, shaking the dust from her dress*): I'm afraid that walk must have made you very hot.

DINA: No, I enjoyed it. I've never enjoyed a walk so much before.

JOHAN: You don't often go for walks in the morning, perhaps?

DINA: Oh, yes. But only with Olaf.

JOHAN: I see. Er—perhaps you'd rather go into the garden than stay inside here?

DINA: No, I'd rather stay here.

JOHAN: So would I. Good, that's agreed then, we'll take a walk like this every morning.

DINA: No, Mr Toennesen. You mustn't.

JOHAN: Mustn't? But you promised—

DINA: Yes, but now I think about it— you ought not to be seen with me.

JOHAN: But why not?

DINA: Oh, you're a stranger here. You don't understand. I'm not—

JOHAN: Yes?

DINA: No, I'd rather not talk about it.

JOHAN: Come on. You can tell me.

DINA: Well, if you want to know—I'm not like other girls. There's something—well, something. So you mustn't.

JOHAN: Look, I don't understand this at all. You haven't done anything wrong, have you?

DINA: No—*I* haven't—but—no, I don't want to talk any more about it. You'll hear all about it from the others, I expect.

JOHAN: Hm.

DINA: But there was something else I wanted to ask you.

JOHAN: What?

DINA: Is it as easy as they say to become—someone—over there in America?

JOHAN: No, it isn't always easy. You often have to work your fingers to the bone at first, and live pretty rough.

DINA: I wouldn't mind that.

JOHAN: You?

DINA: I can work. I'm healthy and strong, and Aunt Martha's taught me a lot.

JOHAN: Well, for heaven's sake then, come back with us.

DINA: Oh, you're only joking. You said that to Olaf. But tell me one thing. Are people as—as moral over there as they are here?

JOHAN: Moral?

DINA: Yes. I mean—are they as good and virtuous as they are here?

JOHAN: Well, they haven't all got horns, the way people here seem to imagine. You needn't be afraid of that.

DINA: You don't understand. I want to go somewhere where people aren't good and virtuous.

JOHAN: Where they *aren't*? What do you want them to be, then?

57

DINA: I want them to be natural.

JOHAN: They're that all right.

DINA: Then I think it'd be good for me if I could go and live there.

JOHAN: I'm sure it would. You must come back with us.

DINA: No, I don't want to go with you. I must go alone. Oh, I'd manage. I'd make something of myself—

BERNICK (*below the verandah with the two* LADIES): No, no, stay here, Betty dear. I'll fetch it. You might easily catch cold.

He enters the room and starts looking for MRS BERNICK's *shawl.*

MRS BERNICK (*in the garden*): You must come with us, Johan. We're going down to the grotto.

BERNICK: No, I'm sure Johan would rather stay here. Dina, take my wife's shawl down to her, will you, and go along with them? Johan'll stay here with me, Betty dear. I want to hear about what life is like on the other side.

MRS BERNICK: All right, but come soon. You know where we'll be.

MRS BERNICK, MISS HESSEL *and* DINA *go out left through the garden.*

BERNICK (*watches them go for a moment, then walks across to the door upstage left and closes it. Then he goes over to* JOHAN, *clasps both his hands, shakes and presses them*): Johan! Now we're alone—thank you! Thank you!

JOHAN: Oh, nonsense.

BERNICK: My house and home, the happiness of my family, my position in the community—I owe it all to you.

JOHAN: Well, I'm glad to hear it, my dear Karsten. Some good came out of that silly business after all, then.

BERNICK (*shakes his hands again*): Thank you, thank you! There isn't one man in ten thousand who'd have done as you did.

JOHAN: Forget it! We were both young and wild, weren't we? One of us had to take the rap.

BERNICK: But who deserved to, if not the guilty one?

JOHAN: Now wait a minute! On this occasion it was the innocent one who deserved the rap. I had no worries or responsibilities; and no parents. I was glad of a chance to get away from that drudgery at the office. You had your old mother still alive; besides, you'd just got secretly engaged to Betty, and she was deeply in love with you. What would have happened to her if she'd found out that you—?

BERNICK: I know, I know; all the same—

JOHAN: And wasn't it just for Betty's sake that you broke off that business with Mrs Dorf? You'd only gone along that evening to put an end to it all—

BERNICK: Yes; why did that drunken ruffian have to come home just that evening? Yes, Johan, it was for Betty's sake; even so—that you could be so unselfish as to take the blame on yourself, and go away—

JOHAN: Forget it, my dear Karsten. After all, we agreed that this was the best solution; we had to get you out of it somehow, and you were my friend. Yes, how proud I was of that friendship! I was a poor country lad working in an office, you were rich and of good family, just back from Paris and London—and yet you chose me as your friend, though I was four years younger than you. Oh, I realize now it was because you were in love with Betty, but how proud I was! And who wouldn't have been? Who wouldn't gladly have sacrificed himself for you, especially when all it meant was giving the town something to gossip about for a month and having an excuse to get away from it all into the great wide world outside?

BERNICK: Hm. My dear Johan, to be frank I must tell you that the matter hasn't quite been forgotten yet.

JOHAN: Hasn't it? Well, what's that to me? Once I'm back on my ranch—

BERNICK: You're going back, then?

JOHAN: Of course.

BERNICK: But not too soon, I hope?

JOHAN: As soon as I can. I only came here to please Lona.

BERNICK: Oh? How do you mean?

JOHAN: Well, you see, Lona isn't young any longer, and these last few months she's been pining her heart out to get back

here; but she wouldn't ever admit it. (*Smiles*) She didn't
dare leave an irresponsible young fellow like me on my own,
when by the age of nineteen I'd already gone and—

BERNICK: Yes, well?

JOHAN: Karsten, I've got a confession to make to you which
I'm a little ashamed about.

BERNICK: You didn't tell her?

JOHAN: Yes, I did. It was wrong of me, but I had to. You've
no idea what Lona has been to me. I know you could never
get along with her, but to me she's been like a mother.
Those first years over there, when we were so poor—you've
no idea how she worked! And when I had that long illness
and couldn't earn anything, she went off and sang in cafés—
I tried to stop her but I couldn't—and gave lectures which
people laughed at, and wrote a book which she's since
laughed over herself—yes, and cried over—all just to keep
me alive. I couldn't sit there last winter and watch her
pining her heart out after the way she'd slaved and toiled
for me. Karsten, I couldn't! So I said to her: "Go, Lona.
You needn't worry about me. I'm not as irresponsible as
you think." And then—well, I told her.

BERNICK: And how did she take it?

JOHAN: Well, she quite rightly decided that since I'd proved
myself innocent there was no reason why I shouldn't come
back with her. But you don't need to worry. Lona won't
talk, and I can keep my mouth shut. Like I did before.

BERNICK: Oh, yes, yes. I trust you.

JOHAN: Here's my hand on it. Well now, we'll say no more
about that business; luckily it's the only crazy thing either
of us has ever done. I intend to enjoy the few days I'm
going to be here. You can't imagine what a lovely walk we
had this morning. Who'd ever have imagined that that
little girl who used to run around here and act cherubs at
the theatre would ever—by the way, Karsten, what happened to her parents—afterwards?

BERNICK: My dear chap, I don't know any more than what I
wrote to you just after you sailed. You got my two letters all
right?

60

JOHAN: Yes, yes, I have both of them. That drunken scoundrel left her, then?

BERNICK: Yes, and got himself killed in a brawl.

JOHAN: She died not long afterwards, didn't she? But you did all you could for her, I presume? Secretly, I mean?

BERNICK: She was proud. She revealed nothing, and refused to accept a penny.

JOHAN: You did the right thing in bringing Dina to live with you.

BERNICK: Of course, of course. Actually, it was Martha who arranged that.

JOHAN: Was it Martha? Yes, by the way, where is Martha today?

BERNICK: Where is she? Oh, when she isn't at the school she's busy with her invalids.

JOHAN: So it was Martha who took care of her?

BERNICK: Yes, Martha's always had rather a weakness for looking after children. That was why she took this job at the council school. Damn stupid idea.

JOHAN: Yes, she looked pretty worn-out yesterday. I'm afraid you're right, she isn't really strong enough for that kind of work.

BERNICK: Oh, she's strong enough for it. But it's so unpleasant for me. It makes it look as though I wasn't prepared to maintain my own sister.

JOHAN: Maintain her? I thought she had money of her own—

BERNICK: Not a penny. You remember what a difficult situation mother was in when you left? Well, she managed to keep going for a while, with my help, but I wasn't really happy with that as a long-term policy. I thought I'd go in with her, but even that wasn't enough. In the end, I had to take over the whole business, and when we finally drew up the accounts there was scarcely anything left of mother's share. Soon afterwards she died and of course Martha was left practically penniless.

JOHAN: Poor Martha!

BERNICK: Poor? What do you mean? You don't imagine I let her want for anything? Oh no, I think I may say I'm a good brother to her. She lives with us, naturally, and eats at our table; her teacher's salary is sufficient for her clothing needs, and—well, she's a single woman, what more does she want?

JOHAN: Hm; we don't reason like that in America.

BERNICK: No, I dare say not, in an unstable society like theirs. But here in our little community, which immorality hasn't yet, thank God, begun to corrupt, the women are content to occupy a modest and unassuming position. Anyway, it's Martha's own fault; she could have been provided for long ago, if she'd been so minded.

JOHAN: Could have married, you mean?

BERNICK: Yes, and very advantageously. She's had several good offers; strangely enough, considering she's a woman with no money and no longer young, and really rather ordinary.

JOHAN: Ordinary?

BERNICK: Oh, don't think I hold it against her. Indeed, I wouldn't have it otherwise. You know how it is, in a big house like ours it's always useful to have a—well—placid-natured person around whom one can ask to do anything.

JOHAN: Yes, but what about her?

BERNICK: What do you mean, what about her? Oh, I see. Well, she's got plenty to interest herself; she's got me and Betty and Olaf and—me. It isn't good for people to be always thinking of themselves first, least of all women. After all, each of us has a community of one kind or another to work for, be it great or small. I do so, anyway. (*Indicates* KRAP, *as the latter enters right*) Here's an example for you. This business I have to deal with now, do you suppose it's to do with my own company? Not a bit of it. (*Quickly, to* KRAP) Well?

KRAP (*shows him a sheaf of papers and whispers*): All the documents for the transaction are in order.

BERNICK: Good! Splendid! Well, brother-in-law, I'm afraid you'll have to excuse me for a while. (*Lowers his voice as he presses his hand*) Thank you, Johan, thank you! You may rest assured that anything I can ever do for you—well, you understand. (*To* KRAP) Come with me.

They go into BERNICK'S *office.*

JOHAN (*looks after him for a moment*): Hm.

He turns to go down into the garden. As he does so, MARTHA
enters right with a small basket on her arm.

JOHAN: Why, Martha!

MARTHA: Oh—Johan—is it you?

JOHAN: You've been out early too.

MARTHA: Yes. Wait here a minute, I'm sure the others will be
along soon.

Turns to go out, left.

JOHAN: Look, Martha, are you always in such a hurry?

MARTHA: Am I—?

JOHAN: Yesterday you seemed to be avoiding me—I didn't
manage to get a word with you—and today—

MARTHA: Yes, but—

JOHAN: We always used to be inseparable. Ever since we
were children.

MARTHA: Oh, Johan. That's many, many years ago.

JOHAN: For heaven's sake! It's only fifteen years. You think
I've changed?

MARTHA: You? Oh yes—you have too—although—

JOHAN: What do you mean?

MARTHA: Oh, nothing.

JOHAN: You don't sound very glad to see me again.

MARTHA: I've waited so long, Johan. Too long.

JOHAN: Waited? For me to come back?

MARTHA: Yes.

JOHAN: Why did you think I'd want to come back?

MARTHA: To repair the wrong you did.

JOHAN: I?

MARTHA: Have you forgotten that a woman died in destitu-
tion and disgrace because of you? Have you forgotten that
because of you the best years of a young child's life were
embittered?

JOHAN: You don't mean that you—? Martha, did your brother
never—?

63

MARTHA: Do what?

JOHAN: Did he never—I mean—did he never say anything in mitigation of what I did?

MARTHA: Oh, Johan, you know how strict Karsten's principles are.

JOHAN: Hm. Yes, yes, I know how strict my old friend Karsten's principles are. But this is—! Oh, well. I spoke to him just now. I think he's changed somewhat.

MARTHA: How can you say that? Karsten has always been a fine man.

JOHAN: Yes, I didn't mean it like that; but never mind. Hm! Well, now I understand how you've been thinking about me. You've been awaiting the return of the prodigal.

MARTHA: Listen, Johan. I'll tell you how I've been thinking about you. (*Points down into the garden*) You see that girl playing down there on the grass with Olaf? That is Dina. You remember that strange letter you wrote to me when you ran away? You wrote that I must believe in you. I have believed in you, Johan. Those wicked things people talked about afterwards—you did them in a fit of madness, you didn't know what you were doing—

JOHAN: What do you mean?

MARTHA: Oh, you know what I mean; don't let's talk about it any more. Anyway, you had to go away and start—a new life. Listen, Johan. You remember how we two used to play games together when we were children? Well, I have acted as your proxy here. The duties that you forgot to fulfil here, or couldn't fulfil, I have fulfilled for you. I tell you this so that you shan't have that to reproach yourself with too. I have been a mother to that wronged child; I've brought her up, as well as I could—

JOHAN: And wasted your whole life for her sake.

MARTHA: It hasn't been wasted. But you took so long in coming, Johan.

JOHAN: Martha—if only I could tell you the—! Well, anyway let me thank you for being such a loyal friend to me.

MARTHA (*smiles sadly*): Hm. Well, now we've had our talk, Johan. Hush, someone's coming. Goodbye. I can't wait now.

64

She goes out through the door upstage left. MISS HESSEL enters from the garden, followed by MRS BERNICK.

MRS BERNICK (*still in the garden*): For heaven's sake, Lona, what are you thinking of?

MISS HESSEL: Let me go! I tell you I must speak with him.

MRS BERNICK: But it'd create the most dreadful scandal. Oh, Johan, are you still here?

MISS HESSEL: Get along now, son. Don't stand hanging round indoors; go down into the garden and talk to Dina.

JOHAN: Yes, I was just thinking of doing that.

MRS BERNICK: But—

MISS HESSEL: Johan, have you bothered to take a close look at Dina?

JOHAN: Why, yes, I think so.

MISS HESSEL: So you damn well should. Now there *is* something for you.

MRS BERNICK: But Lona—!

JOHAN: Something for me?

MISS HESSEL: Yes, well, something to look at, anyway. O.K., then, get going!

JOHAN: Yes, yes, I'm going. I'm going!

He goes down into the garden.

MRS BERNICK: Lona, I'm speechless! Surely you can't be serious about this?

MISS HESSEL: Of course I'm serious! She's a healthy, honest girl, and in her right mind, isn't she? She'd make just the wife for Johan. That's the kind of girl he needs over there, not an old half-sister.

MRS BERNICK: Dina! Dina Dorf! But Lona, think—

MISS HESSEL: All I'm thinking about is the boy's happiness. He needs me to give him a push, he's a bit timid where these things are concerned; never really had an eye for girls.

MRS BERNICK: What, Johan? I should have thought we had sufficient evidence to the contrary—unfortunately—

MISS HESSEL: Oh, to hell with that, that's ancient history! Where's Karsten? I want to talk to him.

MRS BERNICK: Lona, you mustn't do this, I tell you.

MISS HESSEL: I'm going to do it. If the boy likes her, and she likes him, let them have one another. Karsten's a clever guy, he'll manage to find a way—

MRS BERNICK: Do you really imagine that these American improprieties will be permitted here?

MISS HESSEL: Betty, don't talk nonsense.

MRS BERNICK: And that a man with such strict moral principles as Karsten—

MISS HESSEL: Oh, nonsense, they're not that strict.

MRS BERNICK: How dare you!

MISS HESSEL: All I'm saying is that Karsten isn't any more moral than most other men.

MRS BERNICK: You still hate him, don't you? But what do you want here, if you can't forget—? I don't understand how you dare to look him in the face after the disgraceful way you behaved towards him.

MISS HESSEL: Yes, Betty, I did overstep the mark a bit that time.

MRS BERNICK: And he's forgiven you so generously, though he never did you any wrong. It wasn't his fault that you set your cap at him. But ever since that moment you've hated me too. (*Bursts into tears*) You've always begrudged me my happiness. And now you come here to shame me, by showing the town what kind of a family I've made Karsten marry into! I'm the person everyone will blame, and that's what you want. Oh, it's hateful of you! (*She goes out weeping through the door upstage left*)

MISS HESSEL (*watches her go*): Poor Betty!

BERNICK *enters from his office.*

BERNICK (*still in the doorway*): Yes, yes, Krap. Good. Excellent. Send four hundred crowns to provide food for the poor. (*Turns*) Lona! (*Comes closer*) Are you alone? Isn't Betty with you?

MISS HESSEL: No. Shall I go and fetch her?

BERNICK: No, no, it doesn't matter. Oh, Lona, you can't

imagine how I've been longing for a chance to talk frankly with you. To ask your forgiveness.

MISS HESSEL: Look, Karsten, don't let's get sentimental. It doesn't suit us.

BERNICK: You must listen to me, Lona. I know appearances seem to be against me now that you know about Dina's mother. But I swear to you it was only a temporary infatuation. I did love you once, honestly and truly.

MISS HESSEL: Why do you think I've come back?

BERNICK: Whatever you have in mind, I beseech you not to do anything before you have given me the chance to vindicate myself. I can, Lona; at any rate I can explain to you why I acted as I did.

MISS HESSEL: Now you're afraid. You once loved me, you say. Yes, you told me so often enough in your letters—and perhaps it was true in a way, as long as you were living out there in a world which was big and free and gave you the courage to think bigly and freely yourself. You probably thought I had a bit more character and will and independence than most of the others here. Besides, it was a secret between the two of us; no one could make funny remarks about your vulgar taste.

BERNICK: Lona, how can you think that—?

MISS HESSEL: But when you came back here and heard how people were laughing at me, and making fun of what they called my peculiarities—

BERNICK: Well, you were rather headstrong in those days.

MISS HESSEL: Only because I wanted to shock the prudes this town was full of—the ones in trousers as well as the ones in petticoats. Well, then you met that charming young actress—

BERNICK: It was a momentary infatuation, nothing more. I swear to you that not a tenth part of all the rumours and slander that went round about me was true.

MISS HESSEL: Possibly. But then Betty came home, pretty and rich, and everyone's darling; and the news got around that she was to inherit all her aunt's money and I was to get nothing—

BERNICK: Yes, that was the crux of it, Lona. I shan't beat

about the bush. I didn't love Betty; I didn't break with you because my affections had changed. It was only for the money. I needed it; I *had* to make sure I got it.

MISS HESSEL: And you can tell me that to my face!

BERNICK: Yes, I do. Please listen to me, Lona—

MISS HESSEL: But you wrote to me that you'd fallen passionately in love with Betty, asked me to be magnanimous, begged me for Betty's sake to say nothing about the fact that there had been anything between us—

BERNICK: I had to, I tell you.

MISS HESSEL: Then, by God, I don't regret what I did.

BERNICK: Let me explain to you calmly and objectively how things stood. My mother, you recall, was head of the family business; but she had no business sense whatever. I was urgently summoned home from Paris; things had become critical; I had to get the firm back on its feet again. What did I find? I found a business tottering on the verge of bankruptcy. We had to keep it absolutely secret, of course, but this ancient and respected house which had flourished for three generations was facing ruin. I was her son, her only son. I had to look round for some means of saving it.

MISS HESSEL: So you saved the House of Bernick at the expense of a woman.

BERNICK: You know quite well that Betty loved me.

MISS HESSEL: What about me?

BERNICK: Believe me, Lona, you would never have been happy with me.

MISS HESSEL: Was it out of consideration for my happiness that you jilted me?

BERNICK: You think I acted from selfish motives? If it had only been my interests that had been at stake, I would gladly and fearlessly have started again from nothing. But you don't understand how a man of business identifies himself with the business he inherits and with the vast responsibilities it brings with it. Do you realize that the happiness or misery of hundreds, even thousands of people depends on him? Has it ever occurred to you that the whole of our

68

community, which both you and I call our home, would have been shattered if the House of Bernick had failed?

MISS HESSEL: Is it also for the sake of the community that for the past fifteen years your life has been based upon a lie?

BERNICK: A lie?

MISS HESSEL: How much does Betty know about the circumstances that lay behind her marriage with you?

BERNICK: Do you really believe I'd hurt her by revealing such things? What dividends would that pay?

MISS HESSEL: What dividends, did you say? Ah, well, you're a business man—I suppose you know best about dividends. Now listen to me, Karsten. I'm going to talk calmly and objectively to you. Tell me; are you really happy?

BERNICK: In my family life, you mean?

MISS HESSEL: Of course.

BERNICK: Yes, Lona, I am. The sacrifice you made for me wasn't in vain. I think I can say I've grown happier year by year. Betty's so good and acquiescent. During the years we've lived together she has learned to mould her character to mine—

MISS HESSEL: Hm.

BERNICK: She used to have a lot of over-romantic ideas about love; she couldn't accept that as the years pass it must shrink into the calm candle-flame of friendship.

MISS HESSEL: But she accepts that now?

BERNICK: Completely. As you can imagine, her daily association with me hasn't been without a maturing influence on her. People have to learn to reduce their demands on each other if they are to fulfil their functions in the community in which it has pleased God to place them. Betty has gradually learned to realize this, with the result that our house is now an example to our fellow citizens.

MISS HESSEL: But these fellow citizens know nothing about this lie?

BERNICK: Lie?

MISS HESSEL: Yes, the lie on which your life has been resting for the past fifteen years.

BERNICK: You call that a—?

MISS HESSEL: I call it a lie. A triple lie. You lied to me, you lied to Betty and you lied to Johan.

BERNICK: Betty has never asked to be told the truth.

MISS HESSEL: Because she doesn't know.

BERNICK: And you won't ask it. For her sake you won't.

MISS HESSEL: Oh, no. I can put up with ridicule; I've a broad back.

BERNICK: Johan won't, either. He's told me so.

MISS HESSEL: But what about you, Karsten? Isn't there something in you that cries out to be freed from this lie?

BERNICK: Do you expect me voluntarily to sacrifice the happiness of my family and my position in society?

MISS HESSEL: What right have you to that position?

BERNICK: Every day for the past fifteen years I have purchased a grain of that right—by my conduct, and my work, and my achievements.

MISS HESSEL: Yes, you've achieved plenty all right—for yourself and for others. You're the richest and most powerful man in town; no one dares oppose you, because you're supposed to be a man without fault or dishonour; your home is regarded as a pattern for other homes; your career as an example for other men to follow. But all this honour, and you too, rest on a quicksand. A moment may come, a word may be spoken, and you and all your honour will sink to the bottom, if you don't save yourself in time.

BERNICK: Why have you come, Lona?

MISS HESSEL: I want to help you to get firm ground under your feet, Karsten.

BERNICK: Revenge! You want revenge? Yes, that's it, of course. But you won't succeed! There's only one person who knows the truth, and he'll hold his tongue.

MISS HESSEL: Johan?

BERNICK: Yes, Johan. If anyone else accuses me, I shall deny everything. If anyone tries to destroy me, I shall fight for my life! You'll never succeed, I tell you! The only person who could destroy me is silent. And he's going away.

RUMMEL *and* VIGELAND *enter right.*

70

RUMMEL: Good morning, good morning, my dear Bernick. You must come along with us to the Chamber of Commerce. You know, to discuss the railway.

BERNICK: I can't. Not just now.

VIGELAND: But Mr Bernick, you must—!

RUMMEL: You must, Bernick. There are people working against us. That damned newspaper editor, Hammer, and the others who wanted the coast line, are saying there are private interests behind this new proposal.

BERNICK: Well, tell them—

VIGELAND: It won't help what *we* tell them, Mr Bernick.

RUMMEL: No, no, you must come yourself. No one will dare to suspect you of anything like that.

MISS HESSEL: Why, the very idea!

BERNICK: I can't, I tell you. I'm not well. That is—well, anyway, wait a minute and give me time to collect myself.

ROERLUND *enters right.*

ROERLUND: Excuse me, Mr Bernick. I've just seen something that has deeply disturbed me.

BERNICK: Yes, yes, what is it?

ROERLUND: I must ask you a question. Is it with your consent that the young girl who has found asylum beneath your roof is walking the public streets in the company of a person who—

MISS HESSEL: What person, Reverend?

ROERLUND: Of the person from whom, of all people, she should be kept at the greatest possible distance.

MISS HESSEL *laughs loudly.*

ROERLUND: Is it with your consent, Mr Bernick?

BERNICK (*looks for his hat and gloves*): I know nothing about it. Excuse me, I'm in a hurry—I have to attend a meeting of the Chamber of Commerce.

HILMAR (*enters from the garden and goes over to the door upstage left*): Betty, Betty!

MRS BERNICK (*in the doorway*): What is it?

HILMAR: You really must go down into the garden and put a

stop to the way a certain person is flirting with Dina Dorf. It made me quite nervous to listen to them.

MISS HESSEL: Oh? What did this person say?

HILMAR: Only that he wants her to go with him to America! Ugh!

ROERLUND: Can this be possible!

MRS BERNICK: What are you saying!

MISS HESSEL: But it'd be a wonderful thing!

BERNICK: Impossible. You must have misheard.

HILMAR: Ask him yourself, then. Here come the happy pair. Keep me out of it, though.

BERNICK (to RUMMEL and VIGELAND): Go ahead, I'll join you in a moment.

RUMMEL and VIGELAND go out right. JOHAN and DINA enter from the garden.

JOHAN: Lona, Lona, she's coming with us!

MRS BERNICK: Johan, you must be mad!

ROERLUND: I refuse to believe my ears! This is the most disgraceful scandal! By what arts of seduction have you—?

JOHAN: Now, take it easy—!

ROERLUND: Answer me, Dina. Do you seriously intend to do this? Have you made this decision freely and voluntarily?

DINA: I must get away from here.

ROERLUND: But with him! With him!

DINA: Name me any other man here who would have the courage to take me away with him.

ROERLUND: Right, then you'll have to be told who he is.

JOHAN: Be quiet!

BERNICK: Don't say another word!

ROERLUND: If I remained silent I should be betraying the community whose moral and manners I have been chosen to protect; and I should be failing my duty towards this young girl in whose upbringing I have had no small share, and who is to me—

JOHAN: Be careful what you say!

ROERLUND: She shall know the truth! Dina, it was this man who was responsible for your mother's misery and shame.

72

BERNICK: Dr Roerlund!

DINA: He! (*To* JOHAN) Is this true?

JOHAN: Karsten, you answer her.

BERNICK: Silence, all of you! The subject is closed.

DINA: It is true, then.

ROERLUND: Of course it is true. And that's not all. This person in whom you have placed your trust did not leave home empty-handed. Old Mrs Bernick's money—her son can testify.

MISS HESSEL: Liar!

BERNICK: Ah!

MRS BERNICK: Oh, my God, my God!

JOHAN (*raises his arm*): You dare to—

MISS HESSEL: Don't hit him, Johan.

ROERLUND: Yes, go on, hit me! The truth shall out—and it is the truth—Mr Bernick has said so himself, and the whole town knows it. Well, Dina, now you know the kind of man he is.

Short silence.

JOHAN (*quietly, grips* BERNICK'S *arm*): Karsten, Karsten, what have you done?

MRS BERNICK (*in tears, softly*): Oh, Karsten, that I should have involved you in such a scandal!

SANDSTAD (*hurries in right and shouts, with his hand still on the door-handle*): Mr Bernick, you must come at once! The railway is hanging by a thread!

BERNICK (*abstractedly*): What? What must I do?

MISS HESSEL (*earnestly, meaningly*): You must do your duty to the community, brother-in-law.

SANDSTAD: Yes, hurry! We need all your moral authority behind us.

JOHAN (*close to* BERNICK): Bernick, you and I will talk about this tomorrow.

He goes out through the garden. BERNICK *helplessly and blindly walks out right with* SANDSTAD.

ACT THREE

The same. BERNICK *enters angrily through the door upstage left with a cane in his hand, leaving the door ajar behind him.*

BERNICK: There, now! He's been asking for that. I fancy he won't forget that hiding in a hurry. (*Speaks to someone through the open door*) What? Oh, Betty, you mother the boy too much. You make excuses for him and take his side whatever he does. Irresponsible little brat! Not irresponsible? What would you call it, then? Sneaking out of the house at night, stealing one of the fishermen's boats, stays away half the day and frightens the life out of me—! As if I hadn't enough on my mind already! And then the young puppy has the nerve to threaten me that he'll run away! Well, just let him try! You? No, I'm sure you don't; you don't care what happens to him. I really believe if he went and killed himself, you'd— Oh, don't you? Possibly, but when I die I shall leave something behind me that I want carried on; I don't fancy the idea of being left childless. Don't argue, Betty, I've given my orders; he's not to leave the house. (*Listens*) Be quiet now, I don't want anyone to notice anything.

KRAP *enters right.*

KRAP: Can you spare me a moment, Mr Bernick?
BERNICK (*throws down the cane*): Yes, yes, by all means. Have you come from the yard?
KRAP: Yes, I've just left there. Hm.
BERNICK: Well? Everything's going ahead all right with the *Palm Tree*, isn't it?
KRAP: Oh, the *Palm Tree* will be able to sail tomorrow, but—

74

BERNICK: Is it the *Indian Girl*? Don't tell me that stubborn old fool—

KRAP: The *Indian Girl* will be able to sail tomorrow too—but she won't get very far.

BERNICK: What do you mean?

KRAP: Excuse me, Mr Bernick, but that door's open and I think there's someone in there.

BERNICK (*closes the door*): Well, what have you got to tell me that mustn't be overheard?

KRAP: It's this. Your foreman seems determined to send the *Indian Girl* to the bottom with all hands.

BERNICK: Aune? Good God, what on earth makes you think that?

KRAP: Can't think of any other explanation, Mr Bernick.

BERNICK: Well, tell me. But be brief.

KRAP: Yes, Mr Bernick. Well, you know how slowly the work's been going since we got those new machines and took on those untrained workmen.

BERNICK: Yes, yes.

KRAP: But when I went down there this morning I noticed they'd made the most extraordinary progress on the American ship. That big patch on her hull—you know, where she's gone rotten—

BERNICK: Yes, yes, what about it?

KRAP: Completely repaired! Apparently. They've sheathed it. Looks as good as new. Aune himself had been working on her all night with a lantern.

BERNICK: Well?

KRAP: I thought about it. Didn't like it. The men were having lunch, so I went and took a good look at her, outside and in. No one saw me. I had difficulty in getting down into the hold, because they've reloaded the cargo, but I saw enough to confirm my suspicions. There's something funny going on, Mr Bernick.

BERNICK: You must be mistaken, Mr Krap. I can't believe Aune would do a thing like that.

KRAP: I don't like saying it, but it's the truth. Something funny going on, I said to myself. He hadn't put in any new

75

timbers, as far as I could see; just plugged and caulked her, and covered it up with plates and tarpaulins and so on. Real shoddy workmanship! The *Indian Girl* will never reach New York. She'll go to the bottom like a cracked kettle.

BERNICK: This is dreadful! But what motive do you suppose he can have?

KRAP: Probably wants to bring the machines into discredit. Revenge; wants to force you to take the old workmen back.

BERNICK: And for that he's willing to sacrifice all those human lives.

KRAP: He said the other day: "There aren't any human beings in the *Indian Girl*. Only beasts."

BERNICK: Possibly; but what about all the capital investment that will be lost? Hasn't he thought of that?

KRAP: Aune doesn't hold with capital investment, Mr Bernick.

BERNICK: True enough. He's a trouble-maker, a demagogue. All the same—to be so devoid of conscience—! Look here, Krap, we must check on this. Not a word about it to anyone. It'll be bad for the yard if this leaks out.

KRAP: Of course, but—

BERNICK: You must try to get down there again during the dinner break. I must have the truth about this.

KRAP: I'll get it for you, Mr Bernick. But may I ask—what will you do if—?

BERNICK: Report the matter, of course. We can't let ourselves be accessories to a criminal action. I can't afford to have that on my conscience. Besides, it will make a good impression on both the press and the community if they see that I am putting personal considerations aside so that justice may take its course.

KRAP: Very true, Mr Bernick.

BERNICK: But first we must have the truth. Meanwhile, not a word to anyone.

KRAP: You can trust me, Mr Bernick. I'll get the truth for you.

He goes out through the garden and down the street.

BERNICK (*to himself*): Terrible! But—no, it's impossible! It couldn't happen.

He turns to enter his office. HILMAR TOENNESEN *enters right.*

HILMAR: Morning, Bernick. Well, congratulations on your triumph at the Chamber of Commerce yesterday.

BERNICK: Oh, thank you.

HILMAR: Brilliant victory, they tell me. Public-spirited visionary routs chauvinistic self-interest. Like a colonial power disciplining the savages. Remarkable achievement after that unpleasant little scene you'd—

BERNICK: Yes, yes, never mind that.

HILMAR: I gather the final *coup de grâce* hasn't been delivered yet, though.

BERNICK: You mean the railway?

HILMAR: Yes. You know what our beloved editor Mr Hammer is cooking up, I presume?

BERNICK (*tensely*): No. What?

HILMAR: He's cottoned on to that rumour that's floating around. Says he's going to make it front-page news.

BERNICK: What rumour?

HILMAR: Why, all that buying up of property along the route of the branch line.

BERNICK: What? Is there a rumour to that effect?

HILMAR: Yes, it's all over town. I heard about it at the Club. It seems one of our lawyers has been secretly buying up all the forests and mines and waterfalls on behalf of an anonymous client.

BERNICK: Do they say who this client is?

HILMAR: The members thought he must be acting for a syndicate in some other town that had heard about your plans and thought they'd get in quickly before property values began to soar. Disgusting, isn't it, what? Ugh!

BERNICK: Disgusting?

HILMAR: Yes, absolute strangers trespassing on our property like that. And fancy one of our own lawyers lending himself to such a scheme! Now it'll be these damned outsiders who'll reap all the profit.

77

BERNICK: But it's only an unconfirmed rumour.

HILMAR: Yes, but everyone believes it, and tomorrow or the day after Hammer will publish it as a fact. Everyone at the Club's feeling very bitter about it already. I heard several people say that if the rumour's confirmed they'll withdraw their support.

BERNICK: But that's impossible!

HILMAR: Oh? Why do you suppose those hucksters were so keen to go in with you? Do you think they hadn't already started licking their lips at the—?

BERNICK: Impossible, I tell you! We have *some* public spirit in this little community—!

HILMAR: Here? Look, you're an optimist and you judge other people by yourself. But I know our town pretty well, and I tell you there isn't one person here—apart from ourselves, of course—not one, I tell you, who attempts to keep the flag of ideals flying. (*Upstage*) Ugh, here they are!

BERNICK: Who?

HILMAR: The two Americans. (*Looks out, right*) Who's that with them? Oh dear, isn't that the captain of the *Indian Girl*? Ugh!

BERNICK: What on earth can they want with him?

HILMAR: Birds of a feather, I suppose. He's probably been a pirate, or a slave-trader; and heaven knows what they haven't got up to in the past fifteen years.

BERNICK: No, you've no right to think of them like that.

HILMAR: You *are* an optimist. Well, if they're descending on us again, I'll be off.

He goes towards the door, left. MISS HESSEL *enters right.*

MISS HESSEL: Hullo, Hilmar. Am I chasing you away?

HILMAR: Not at all. I just happen to be in a hurry. I've something I have to say to Betty.

Enters the room upstage left.

BERNICK (*after a short silence*): Well, Lona?

MISS HESSEL: Well?

BERNICK: How do you feel about me today?

78

MISS HESSEL: The same as yesterday. One lie more or less—

BERNICK: I must make you understand. Where is Johan?

MISS HESSEL: He's coming. He had something he wanted to ask someone.

BERNICK: After what you heard yesterday, surely you must understand that everything I have built up here will be destroyed if the truth gets out.

MISS HESSEL: I understand that.

BERNICK: I need hardly tell you that I was not guilty of this theft which was rumoured to have been committed.

MISS HESSEL: Oh, naturally. But who was the thief, then?

BERNICK: There was no thief. No money was stolen. Not a penny was missing.

MISS HESSEL: What?

BERNICK: I repeat; not a penny.

MISS HESSEL: Then how did that monstrous rumour get round that Johan—?

BERNICK: Lona, I can talk to you as I wouldn't to anyone else. I shan't hide anything from you. I was partly responsible for spreading that rumour.

MISS HESSEL: You? You could do a thing like that to him, when to save your skin he'd—?

BERNICK: You mustn't judge me without remembering how things stood at the time. I explained it to you yesterday. I came home and found my mother involved in a whole string of stupid enterprises. One misfortune followed after another; every disaster that could happen to us happened; our house stood on the verge of ruin. I felt desperate and reckless. Oh, Lona, I think it was mainly in the hope of trying to forget it all that I got myself involved in that—business which ended in Johan going away.

MISS HESSEL: Hm.

BERNICK: You can imagine how all sorts of rumours spread about after you and he had left. It wasn't the first thing of that kind he'd done, they said; Dorf had been well paid to go away and keep his mouth shut; others said she'd been given the money. Just then it was beginning to get whispered that our house was having difficulty in fulfilling its

79

obligations. What more natural than that the scandal-mongers should put two and two together? When she stayed on here in obvious poverty, people said he'd taken the money with him to America; the gossip increased and the sum multiplied like a snowball.

MISS HESSEL: And you, Karsten—?

BERNICK: I seized on this rumour as a drowning man clutches at a raft.

MISS HESSEL: You encouraged it?

BERNICK: I didn't contradict it. Our creditors were beginning to get restive; I had to find some way of calming them; it was essential that no one should doubt our solidarity. We'd had a temporary setback; they mustn't foreclose on us; we only needed a little time, and everyone would get their money.

MISS HESSEL: And everyone got their money?

BERNICK: Yes, Lona. This rumour saved our house, and made me the man I am now.

MISS HESSEL: In other words, a lie made you the man you are now.

BERNICK: Who suffered by it—then? Johan had sworn he'd never come back.

MISS HESSEL: You ask who suffered by it. Look at yourself, Karsten, and tell me honestly; don't you think you've suffered?

BERNICK: Look at any man you choose to name; you'll find every one of them has at least one skeleton hidden in his cupboard.

MISS HESSEL: And you call yourselves pillars of society?

BERNICK: Society has none better.

MISS HESSEL: If that's what your society is like, what does it matter whether it survives or is destroyed? What do people here set store by? Lies and pretences—that's all. You, the chief citizen of the town, sit here in honour and happiness, power and glory, simply because you once branded an innocent man as a criminal.

BERNICK: Do you think I don't know how deeply I wronged him? And do you think I'm not ready to right that wrong?

MISS HESSEL: How? By talking?

BERNICK: I can't do that, Lona.

MISS HESSEL: How else can such a wrong be righted?

BERNICK: I am rich, Lona. Johan can ask anything he wants—

MISS HESSEL: Yes, offer him money, and see what he replies.

BERNICK: Do you know what he intends to do?

MISS HESSEL: No. Since yesterday he's said nothing. It's as though all this has suddenly made him into a man.

BERNICK: I must talk to him.

MISS HESSEL: Here he is.

JOHAN *enters right.*

BERNICK (*goes towards him*): Johan—!

JOHAN (*waves him aside*): First you listen to me. Yesterday morning I gave you my word to keep my mouth shut.

BERNICK: You did.

JOHAN: I didn't know then that—

BERNICK: Johan, just let me briefly explain the circumstances—

JOHAN: There's no need; I know all about the circumstances. The firm was in difficulties; I'd left the country; you had a name and a reputation at stake. Oh, I don't blame you so much for that; we were young and reckless in those days. But now the truth will have to be revealed. I need it.

BERNICK: I can't reveal the truth just now. I need all the moral credit I can muster.

JOHAN: I don't mind about the lies you've been spreading about me. It's this business with Dina's mother. You've got to admit it was you. Dina's going to become my wife, and I want to live with her here, and build a new life with her here, in this town.

MISS HESSEL: You want to do that?

BERNICK: With Dina? As your wife? Here?

JOHAN: Yes, here. I want to stay here to silence all these liars and scandalmongers. But she won't marry me unless you clear my name.

BERNICK: Don't you realize that if I admit to the one I'm automatically confessing to the other? You think I only

81

need to show the firm's books to prove nothing was stolen? But I can't do that—our books weren't kept very carefully in those days. And even if I could, what good would it do? I'd stand revealed as a man who'd saved his skin by telling a lie, and had allowed this lie with all its consequences to be believed for fifteen years without raising a finger to contradict it. You don't know this community as well as you used to, or you'd realize that to do this would ruin me completely.

JOHAN: All I can say is that I intend to make Mrs Dorf's daughter my wife and live with her here in this town.

BERNICK (*wipes the sweat from his forehead*): Listen, Johan— and you too, Lona. I'm in a very particular position just now. If you do this to me you'll destroy me, and not only me but a future of great prosperity and happiness for the community which nurtured you.

JOHAN: And if I don't I shall destroy my own chances of happiness for ever.

MISS HESSEL: Go on, Karsten.

BERNICK: Now listen. It's to do with this question of the railway, and that isn't such a simple matter as you may think. I suppose you've heard there was talk last year about building a coast line? A good many influential voices were raised in support of it, both here and elsewhere in the neighbourhood, especially in the press; but I managed to stop it, because it would have damaged our steamship trade along the coast.

MISS HESSEL: Have you an interest in this steamship trade?

BERNICK: Yes. But no one dared to suspect me of acting from that motive. My name and my reputation forbade that. In any case, I could have carried the loss; but the town couldn't have. So they decided to run the line inland. Once this had been decided I secretly took steps to assure myself that it would be practicable for a branch line to be extended here.

MISS HESSEL: Why secretly, Karsten?

BERNICK: Have you heard about the big purchases that have been made of forests and mines and waterfalls—?

MISS HESSEL: Yes, by a syndicate from one of the other towns.

BERNICK: Under present conditions these properties are virtually worthless to their various owners, so they went comparatively cheaply. If one had waited till the project of the branch line had been made public, the prices of these properties would have rocketed exorbitantly.

MISS HESSEL: Yes, well; what of it?

BERNICK: Now we come to something that could bear two different interpretations—something that a member of our community could only admit to if his name and reputation were such as to set him above suspicion.

MISS HESSEL: Yes?

BERNICK: It was I who bought all those properties.

MISS HESSEL: You?

JOHAN: On your own?

BERNICK: On my own. If the branch line gets built, I am a millionaire. If it doesn't get built, I am ruined.

MISS HESSEL: That was a big risk, Karsten.

BERNICK: I have risked all the money I possess.

MISS HESSEL: I'm not thinking of your money. When it gets known that—

BERNICK: Yes, that's the point. With the reputation I have now I can accept the responsibility for this act, carry it through to its conclusion and say to my fellow citizens: "Look! I have taken this risk for the sake of the community."

MISS HESSEL: Of the community?

BERNICK: Yes. And no one will question my motive.

MISS HESSEL: But there are others here who've acted more openly than you, and with no ulterior motive.

BERNICK: Who?

MISS HESSEL: Rummel, Sandstad and Vigeland, of course.

BERNICK: In order to win their support I was compelled to take them into my confidence.

MISS HESSEL: Oh?

BERNICK: They demanded a fifth of the profits, to be shared amongst them.

MISS HESSEL: Oh, these pillars of society!

BERNICK: Doesn't society itself force us to use these back-

83

stairs methods? What would have happened if I hadn't acted secretly? Everyone would have charged in, they'd have divided and dispersed the properties and bungled and wrecked the whole enterprise. There isn't one man in this town apart from me who understands how to organize a project of this magnitude. Up here, it's only the families who have migrated from the cities who have any talent for big business. That's why my conscience tells me I have acted correctly in this matter. Only in my hands can these properties be of any permanent value to the thousands of people whom I intend that they shall benefit.

MISS HESSEL: I think you're right there, Karsten.

JOHAN: But I don't know these thousands of people, and my life and my happiness are at stake.

BERNICK: The prosperity of your birthplace is also at stake. If anything comes to light which casts a shadow on my early career, all my enemies will unite to destroy me. A youthful indiscretion won't be forgiven in this community. People will examine my whole life under a microscope, dig up a hundred trivial incidents and reinterpret them in the light of this revelation. They will destroy me with their rumours and innuendoes. I shall have to withdraw from the railway project; and if I do that, it will fail, and I shall be ruined and ostracized.

MISS HESSEL: Johan, after what you've just heard you must go away and keep your mouth shut.

BERNICK: Yes, yes, Johan, you must!

JOHAN: All right. I'll go. And I'll keep my mouth shut. But I shall come back, and when I do I shall speak.

BERNICK: Stay over there, Johan. Keep quiet about this, and I'll gladly give you a share of—

JOHAN: Keep your money. Give me back my name and my honour.

BERNICK: And sacrifice my own?

JOHAN: You and your community must work that out between you. I want to marry Dina; I must and shall marry her. So I'm leaving tomorrow. In the *Indian Girl*—

BERNICK: The *Indian Girl*?

84

JOHAN: Yes. The captain's promised to take me with him. I'm going back to America, to sell my ranch and put my affairs in order. In two months I shall be here again.

BERNICK: And then you'll talk?

JOHAN: Then the guilty will have to pay for his crime.

BERNICK: Are you forgetting that I shall also have to pay for a crime of which I am not guilty?

JOHAN: Who was it who profited by the false rumour of fifteen years ago?

BERNICK: You're making me desperate. If you speak, I shall deny everything. I shall say there's a conspiracy against me; a plot for revenge. I shall say you have come here to blackmail me.

MISS HESSEL: Karsten!

BERNICK: I'm desperate, I tell you; and I'm fighting for my life. I shall deny everything, everything!

JOHAN: I have your two letters. I found them in my trunk with my other papers. I read them again this morning. They're plain enough.

BERNICK: And you intend to publish them?

JOHAN: If you force me to.

BERNICK: And in two months you say you will be back?

JOHAN: I hope so. The winds are favourable. In three weeks I shall be in New York—if the *Indian Girl* doesn't sink—

BERNICK (*starts*): Sink? Why should the *Indian Girl* sink?

JOHAN: No, why should she?

BERNICK (*scarcely audibly*): Sink?

JOHAN: Well, Bernick, now you know how things are. You'd better start thinking. Goodbye. You can give my love to Betty, though she's hardly received me in a very sisterly manner. But I want to see Martha. She must tell Dina—she must promise me—

He goes out through the door upstage left.

BERNICK (*to himself*): The *Indian Girl*? (*Quickly*) Lona, you must stop him!

MISS HESSEL: You can see for yourself, Karsten. I haven't any power over him any longer.

85

She follows JOHAN *into the room left.*

BERNICK (*ponders uneasily*): Sink?

AUNE *enters right.*

AUNE: Excuse me, Mr Bernick. Can you spare me a moment?

BERNICK (*turns angrily*): What do you want?

AUNE: I'd like permission to ask you a question.

BERNICK: All right, but be quick. What is it?

AUNE: I wanted to ask if you're still resolved to dismiss me if the *Indian Girl* doesn't sail tomorrow?

BERNICK: Why ask me that? She'll be ready now, won't she?

AUNE: She'll be ready. But if she wasn't, it'd mean my dismissal?

BERNICK: Why are you asking me these foolish questions?

AUNE: I'd like to know, Mr Bernick. Answer me; would it mean my dismissal?

BERNICK: Do I usually stand by my word?

AUNE: Then tomorrow I'd lose my position in my home, and among the people I belong to. I'd lose my influence among the workmen; lose my chance to do anything for the poor and humble of this community.

BERNICK: Aune, we've discussed all that.

AUNE: Right, then the *Indian Girl* can sail.

Short silence.

BERNICK: Look, I can't have eyes everywhere; I can't be personally responsible for everything. You give me your promise, don't you, that the repairs have been executed satisfactorily?

AUNE: You didn't give me much time, Mr Bernick.

BERNICK: But the work has been done properly?

AUNE: The weather's good, and it's midsummer.

Another silence.

BERNICK: Have you anything else to say to me?

AUNE: I don't know of anything else, Mr Bernick.

BERNICK: Then—the *Indian Girl* will sail—

86

AUNE: Tomorrow?

BERNICK: Yes.

AUNE: Very good.

Touches his forehead and goes. BERNICK *stands for a moment, torn by doubt; then he strides quickly over to the door as though to call* AUNE *back, but stops uneasily with his hand on the door-handle. As he does so, the door is opened from the outside and* KRAP *enters.*

KRAP (*quietly*): Oh, so he's been here. Has he confessed?

BERNICK: Hm—did you discover anything?

KRAP: What's the need? Couldn't you see from his eyes that he had a bad conscience?

BERNICK: Oh, nonsense, one can't *see* things like that. I asked you if you discovered anything.

KRAP: Couldn't get to her. Too late; they'd already started hauling her out of the dock. But the very fact that they were in such a hurry proves—

BERNICK: It proves nothing. They've completed the inspection, then?

KRAP: Of course, but—

BERNICK: There, you see! And they've found nothing to complain of.

KRAP: Mr Bernick, you know what these inspections are, especially in a yard with a reputation like ours.

BERNICK: Nevertheless, it means that no blame can be attached to us.

KRAP: But, Mr Bernick, surely you could see from the way Aune—

BERNICK: Aune has convinced me that there is nothing to fear.

KRAP: And I tell you I'm morally convinced that—

BERNICK: Look here, Krap, what the devil are you getting at? I know you've a grudge against this man, but if you want to pick a quarrel with him you'll have to find other grounds than this. You know how vitally important it is for me—for the company—that the *Indian Girl* sails tomorrow.

KRAP: All right. Let her sail. But how far she'll go—hm!

VIGELAND: Good morning, Mr Bernick, good morning! Can you spare me a moment?

BERNICK: Yes, of course, Mr Vigeland.

VIGELAND: I just wanted to ask if you agree that the *Palm Tree* shall sail tomorrow.

BERNICK: Why, yes. It's all settled.

VIGELAND: Only that the captain came just now to tell me there's a gale warning.

KRAP: The barometer's fallen heavily since this morning.

BERNICK: Oh? Do they expect a storm?

VIGELAND: Well, a stiff breeze. But no head wind; on the contrary—

BERNICK: Hm. Well, what do you say?

VIGELAND: I say, as I said to the captain: "The *Palm Tree* rests in the hand of Providence." Besides, she's only got the North Sea to cross on her first leg; and freight charges are pretty high in England just now, so—

BERNICK: Yes, it'd certainly be expensive to delay her.

VIGELAND: She's solidly built; and anyway, she's fully insured. She's a good risk; not like that *Indian Girl*—

BERNICK: What do you mean?

VIGELAND: She's sailing tomorrow, too.

BERNICK: Yes, we've worked overtime on her; besides—

VIGELAND: Well, if that old coffin can sail—especially with the crew she's got—it'd be a poor thing if we were afraid to—

BERNICK: Quite, quite. You have the ship's papers with you?

VIGELAND: Yes, here.

BERNICK: Good. Mr Krap, will you see to them?

KRAP: This way, Mr Vigeland. We'll soon get this settled.

VIGELAND: Thank you. And the outcome, Mr Bernick, we leave in the hands of the Almighty.

He goes with KRAP *into the room downstage left.* ROERLUND *enters through the garden.*

ROERLUND: Why, fancy seeing you here at this time of day, Mr Bernick.

BERNICK (*abstractedly*): Mm?

ROERLUND: I really came to speak to your wife. I thought she might need a few words of consolation.

BERNICK: I'm sure she does. But I'd like to have a word with you too.

ROERLUND: With pleasure, Mr Bernick. Is something the matter? You look quite pale and upset.

BERNICK: Oh? Do I? Well, what can you expect with everything piling up on me the way it has these last few days? I've got my own business to look after without this railway— Listen, Dr Roerlund: tell me something. Let me ask you a question.

ROERLUND: By all means, Mr Bernick.

BERNICK: It's just a thought that occurred to me. When a man stands on the threshold of a great and ambitious enterprise which has as its object the creation of prosperity for thousands of people—suppose this enterprise should claim one, just one victim—?

ROERLUND: How do you mean?

BERNICK: Well, say a man is thinking of building a great factory. He knows for certain, because all his experience has taught him, that sooner or later in this factory human life will be lost.

ROERLUND: Yes, I fear that is only too likely.

BERNICK: Or a man is planning to open a mine. He employs men with children, and young men with all their lives before them. It's certain, is it not, that some of these men will lose their lives in his service?

ROERLUND: Alas, yes.

BERNICK: Well. A man in such a position knows before he starts that the project he is launching will at some stage of its development cost human life. But this project is for the general good. For every life it takes it will, equally beyond doubt, provide the means of happiness for many hundreds of people.

ROERLUND: Ah, you're thinking of the railway—all that dangerous quarrying and dynamiting and so on—

BERNICK: Yes, yes, exactly. I'm thinking of the railway. And

89

the railway will mean mines and factories— Remembering all this, do you still feel—?

ROERLUND: My dear Mr Bernick, your conscience is too tender. I believe that as long as one entrusts one's work to the hands of Providence—

BERNICK: Yes; yes, of course; Providence—

ROERLUND: —one is absolved from guilt. Build your railway, and have no fear.

BERNICK: Yes, but now I want to give you a particular example. Suppose a mountainside has to be blasted at a dangerous spot; and if this isn't done, the railway cannot be completed. I know, and the engineer knows, that it will cost the life of the man who lights the fuse; but it must be lit, and it is the engineer's duty to send a man to do it.

ROERLUND: Hm—

BERNICK: I know what you're going to say. The engineer ought to take the match and go himself to light the fuse. But such things aren't done. He must sacrifice one of his men.

ROERLUND: No engineer in this country would do it.

BERNICK: No engineer in a big country would think twice about doing it.

ROERLUND: Yes, I can quite believe that. In those depraved and unscrupulous societies—

BERNICK: Oh, there's some merit in those societies—

ROERLUND: How can you say that? Why, you yourself—

BERNICK: In big countries men at least have elbow-room to plan ambitiously for the general good. They have courage to make sacrifices for the sake of a cause; but here one's hands are tied by all kinds of petty scruples and considerations.

ROERLUND: Is a human life a petty consideration?

BERNICK: When it's weighed against the general good, yes.

ROERLUND: But the examples you suggest are quite unrealistic, Mr Bernick. I really can't make you out today. These great communities you speak of—what is a human life worth there? They think of human life simply as capital. Our ethical standpoint is completely different. Look at our great shipyards! Name one shipowner in this town who would think of sacrificing a human life for mercenary motives! And then think of those scoundrels in your great communities who, to increase their profits, send out one unseaworthy ship after another—

BERNICK: I'm not talking about unseaworthy ships!

ROERLUND: But I am talking about them, Mr Bernick.

BERNICK: Why bring that up? That's got nothing to do with it. Oh, this wretched narrowness and timidity! If a general in this country sent his men into battle and saw them shot down, he'd have sleepless nights. It isn't so in big countries. You should hear that fellow in there talking about—

ROERLUND: What fellow? The American?

BERNICK: Yes. You should hear him describe how people in America—

ROERLUND: Is he in there? Why didn't you tell me? I'll soon see to him—

BERNICK: Oh, it's no use. You won't get anywhere with him.

ROERLUND: We'll see about that. Ah, here he is.

JOHAN TOENNESEN *enters from the room on the left.*

JOHAN (*talks back through the open door*): All right, Dina, as you wish. But I'm not giving you up. I'm coming back, and when I do everything's going to be all right.

ROERLUND: May I ask what you mean by those words? What exactly do you want?

JOHAN: That young girl, before whom you slandered me yesterday, is going to be my wife.

ROERLUND: *Your*—? Do you really imagine that—?

JOHAN: I want her as my wife.

ROERLUND: Very well. I suppose you'll have to be told. (*Goes across to the door, which is still ajar*) Mrs Bernick, will you please come and witness this? You too, Miss Martha. And let Dina come too. (*Sees* MISS HESSEL) Oh. Are you here?

MISS HESSEL (*in the doorway*): Can I come too?

ROERLUND: By all means. The more the better.

BERNICK: What are you going to do?

Mrs Bernick: Oh, Dr Roerlund, I tried to stop him, but—

Roerlund: I shall stop him, Mrs Bernick. Dina, you are a
rash and thoughtless girl. But I do not reproach you. For
too long you have lacked the moral support which you so
grievously need. I reproach myself for not having provided
you with that support earlier.

Dina: You mustn't tell them now!

Mrs Bernick: What is all this?

Roerlund: I must tell them now, Dina, although your conduct yesterday and today has made it ten times more
difficult for me. But you must be saved, and all other considerations must yield to that. You remember the promise I
made you, and the answer you promised to give me when I
should decide that the time had come. Now I dare delay no
longer; therefore— (*To* Johan) This young girl after whom
you lust is betrothed to me.

Mrs Bernick: What!

Bernick: Dina!

Johan: She? To you?

Martha: No, Dina, no!

Miss Hessel: It's a lie!

Johan: Dina. Is that man speaking the truth?

Dina (*after a brief pause*): Yes.

Roerlund: Let us pray that by this the arts of the seducer
will be rendered powerless. This decision, which I have
resolved to take in order to secure Dina's happiness, may be
revealed to the rest of our community; I raise no objection.
I sincerely trust it will not be misinterpreted. Meanwhile,
Mrs Bernick, I think it would be wisest to remove her to
her room and to try to restore her calm and equilibrium.

Mrs Bernick: Yes, come with me. Oh, Dina, what a lucky
girl you are!

She leads Dina *out, left.* Dr Roerlund *goes with them.*

Martha: Goodbye, Johan.

She goes.

HILMAR (*in the verandah doorway*): Hm. Well, really! I must say—!

MISS HESSEL (*who has watched* DINA *go out; to* JOHAN): Don't lose heart, son. I'll stay here to keep an eye on the Reverend.

She goes out right.

BERNICK: Well, Johan, this means you won't be sailing in the *Indian Girl*.

JOHAN: It means I shall.

BERNICK: But you won't be coming back?

JOHAN: I'll come back.

BERNICK: After this? But what can you want here now?

JOHAN: To take my revenge on you all. To break as many of you as I can.

He goes out right. VIGELAND *and* KRAP *enter from* BERNICK'S *office.*

VIGELAND: Well, all the papers are in order now, Mr Bernick.

BERNICK: Good, good.

KRAP (*whispers*): You still want the *Indian Girl* to sail to-morrow, then?

BERNICK: Yes.

He goes into his office. VIGELAND *and* KRAP *go out right.* HIL-MAR *is about to follow them when* OLAF *pokes his head cautiously out of the doorway to the room left.*

OLAF: Uncle! Uncle Hilmar!

HILMAR: Ugh, is it you? Why aren't you upstairs? You're under house arrest.

OLAF (*takes a step towards him*): Ssh! Uncle Hilmar, have you heard the news?

HILMAR: Yes, I hear you've had a hiding today.

OLAF (*scowls towards his father's office*): He won't hit me again. But have you heard that Uncle Johan's sailing to America tomorrow?

HILMAR: What's that to do with you? Now you run upstairs again.

OLAF: I'll fight those redskins yet.

HILMAR: Oh, stuff! A little coward like you?

OLAF: Just you wait till tomorrow. You'll see.

HILMAR: Jackass!

He goes out through the garden. OLAF runs back into the room and shuts the door as he sees KRAP enter right.

KRAP (*goes over to* BERNICK'S *door and half-opens it*): Excuse me disturbing you again, Mr Bernick, but there's a dreadful storm blowing up. (*Waits for a moment; there is no reply*) Shall the *Indian Girl* sail?

Short pause.

BERNICK (*from his room*): The *Indian Girl* shall sail.

KRAP closes the door and goes out right.

ACT FOUR

The same. The work-table has been moved out. It is a stormy afternoon, already twilight; during the scene it grows gradually darker. A FOOTMAN *lights the chandelier. Two* MAIDS *bring in pots of flowers, lamps and candles, and place them on the tables and in brackets on the walls.* RUMMEL, *in tails, with gloves and a white cravat, is standing in the room giving orders.*

RUMMEL (*to the* FOOTMAN): Only every second candle, Jacob. We mustn't look too festive; it's meant to be a surprise. Oh, and all these flowers—? Ah, well, let them stay. People will think they're always here—

BERNICK *enters from his office.*

BERNICK (*in the doorway*): What's the meaning of all this?
RUMMEL: Oh dear, you weren't meant to see. (*To the* SERVANTS) All right, you can go now.

The FOOTMAN *and* MAIDS *go out through the door upstage left.*

BERNICK (*comes closer*): Rummel, what on earth does all this mean?
RUMMEL: It means that your proudest moment has come. The whole town is marching here in procession this evening to pay homage to its foremost citizen.
BERNICK: What!
RUMMEL: With banners and a brass band. We were going to have torches, but the weather was so doubtful we didn't dare risk it. Still, there's to be an illumination. That'll look well in the newspapers.
BERNICK: Look, Rummel, I'd rather we didn't have this.
RUMMEL: Well, it's too late now. They'll be here in half an hour.

BERNICK: But why didn't you tell me about it before?

RUMMEL: I was afraid you might object to the idea. I had a word with your wife, and she gave me permission to make a few arrangements. She's looking after the refreshments herself.

BERNICK (*listens*): What's that? Are they coming already? I think I hear singing.

RUMMEL (*at the verandah door*): Singing? Oh, that's only the Americans. The *Indian Girl* is being hauled out to the buoy.

BERNICK: Is she hauling out? Yes. No, I can't this evening, Rummel. I'm not feeling well.

RUMMEL: Yes, you look off-colour. But you must pull yourself together. Damn it, man, you must! I and Sandstad and Vigeland attach the utmost importance to this ceremony. So spectacular a display of public feeling will completely crush our opponents. Rumours are spreading in the town; the news of the property deals is bound to come out soon. You must let them know this evening, against a background of songs and speeches, and the merry clink of glasses—in short, in an atmosphere of holiday and carnival—how much you have staked for the welfare of the community. In such an atmosphere of holiday and carnival, as I have just phrased it, we can get the hell of a lot done. But we've got to have that atmosphere, or it'll be no good.

BERNICK: Yes, yes, yes—

RUMMEL: Especially when the issue is such a delicate and ticklish one. Thank heaven you've the name and reputation you have, Bernick. But listen, now. I must tell you about the arrangements. Hilmar Toennesen has written a song in your honour. It's very beautiful; it begins: "Wave high the banner of ideals!" And Dr Roerlund is to make the speech. You'll have to reply, of course.

BERNICK: I can't do that this evening, Rummel. Couldn't you—?

RUMMEL: Impossible! Much as I'd like to. The speech will naturally be addressed mainly to you. Possibly just a word or two about us too. I've been discussing it with Vigeland

96

and Sandstad. We thought you might reply with a toast to the prosperity of the community. Sandstad will say something about the harmony that exists between the various strata of our society; Vigeland will want to stress how important it is that this new enterprise should not disturb the moral foundations on which our life is so firmly based; and I'm thinking of paying a brief tribute to the ladies, whose contribution to the welfare of our community, while humble and unassuming, must not be overlooked. But you're not listening.

BERNICK: Yes, yes, I am. But tell me—is the sea very rough this evening?

RUMMEL: Are you worrying about the *Palm Tree*? She's well insured.

BERNICK: Insured, yes. But—

RUMMEL: And in good trim. That's the main thing.

BERNICK: Hm. If anything should happen to a ship, it doesn't necessarily follow that human lives will be lost. The ship and her cargo, perhaps—chests and papers—

RUMMEL: Damn, it man, chests and papers aren't that important.

BERNICK: Of course not. No, no—I only meant— Quiet! They're singing again.

RUMMEL: That'll be the crew of the *Palm Tree*.

VIGELAND *enters right.*

VIGELAND: Well, the *Palm Tree*'s hauling out now. Good evening, Mr Bernick.

BERNICK: You're a seaman. Do you still feel confident that—?

VIGELAND: Providence will decide, Mr Bernick; of that I am confident. Besides, I've been on board myself and distributed a few little tracts which I trust will ensure God's blessing on her.

SANDSTAD *and* KRAP *enter right.*

SANDSTAD (*still in the doorway*): Well, if that ship survives, I'll believe in miracles. Oh—good evening, good evening!

BERNICK: Anything wrong, Mr Krap?

97

KRAP: I said nothing, Mr Bernick.

SANDSTAD: The whole crew of the *Indian Girl* is drunk. If those brutes get that ship safely across the Atlantic, I'm a Dutchman.

MISS HESSEL *enters right.*

MISS HESSEL (*to* BERNICK): He asked me to say goodbye to you.

BERNICK: Is he aboard already?

MISS HESSEL: He will be any moment. I left him outside the hotel.

BERNICK: And he's still determined——?

MISS HESSEL: Absolutely determined.

RUMMEL (*over by the windows*): Confound these new-fangled contraptions. I can't get these curtains down.

MISS HESSEL: You want them down? I thought they were to stay up.

RUMMEL: Down to begin with, madam. I suppose you know what's going to happen?

MISS HESSEL: Yes, I know. Let me help you. (*Takes the cords*) Yes, I'll lower the curtain on my brother-in-law; though I'd sooner lift it.

RUMMEL: You can do that later. When the garden is filled with the surging throng, the curtains will be raised to reveal an amazed and happy family circle. A citizen's home should be as a house of glass, open to the gaze of all.

BERNICK *seems about to speak, but turns quickly and goes into his room.*

RUMMEL: Well, let's just run through the arrangements. Come along, Mr Krap. We need your help on a few details.

All the GENTLEMEN *go into* BERNICK'S *room.* MISS HESSEL *has drawn the curtains over the windows and is just about to do the same across the open glass door when* OLAF *jumps down on to the verandah from above. He has a plaid over his shoulder and a bundle in his hand.*

MISS HESSEL: Oh, my goodness, Olaf, how you frightened me!

98

OLAF (*hiding his bundle*): Ssh!

MISS HESSEL: Did you jump out of that window? Where are you going?

OLAF: Ssh! Don't tell anyone! I'm going to Uncle Johan. Only down to the jetty, of course—just to say goodbye to him. Good night, Aunt Lona!

He runs out through the garden.

MISS HESSEL: No, wait! Olaf, Olaf!

JOHAN TOENNESEN, *in travelling clothes, with a bag over his shoulder, enters cautiously right.*

JOHAN: Lona!

MISS HESSEL (*turns*): What! Are you here again?

JOHAN: I've still got a few minutes. I must see her just once more. We can't part like this.

MARTHA *and* DINA, *both wearing overcoats, and the latter with a small travelling-bag in her hand, enter through the door upstage left.*

DINA: I must see him, I must see him!

MARTHA: Yes, Dina. You'll see him.

DINA: There he is!

JOHAN: Dina!

DINA: Take me with you.

JOHAN: What?

MISS HESSEL: You want to go with him?

DINA: Yes! Take me with you! That man says he's going to make a public announcement this evening in front of the whole town about—

JOHAN: Dina! You don't love him?

DINA: I have never loved him. I'd die rather than be engaged to him. Oh, how he humiliated me yesterday with his fine phrases! He made me feel he was raising something contemptible up to his own level. I'm not going to be humiliated like that any more. I'm going away. Can I come with you?

JOHAN: Yes! Yes!

99

DINA: I shan't trouble you for long. Just help me to get over there; help me to find my feet—

JOHAN: Yippee! Don't you worry about that, Dina!

MISS HESSEL (*points towards* BERNICK'S *door*): Ssh! Quiet, quiet!

JOHAN: I'll take care of you, Dina!

DINA: No. I won't let you do that. I'm going to look after myself. I'll manage to do that over there. If only I can get away from here! Oh, these women—you've no idea! They've written to me today begging me to realize how lucky I am, and reminding me how noble and magnanimous he's been. Tomorrow and the next day and every day they'll be squinting at me to see whether I'm proving myself worthy of him. Oh, all this respectability frightens me so much!

JOHAN: Tell me, Dina. Is that the only reason you're leaving? Am I nothing to you?

DINA: Oh, no, Johan. You mean more to me than anyone else in the world.

JOHAN: Oh, Dina!

DINA: Everyone here tells me I ought to hate you and detest you. They say it's my duty. But I don't understand all this about duty. I never shall.

MISS HESSEL: That's right, child! Don't you!

MARTHA: Yes, Dina. Go with him. As his wife.

JOHAN: Yes! Yes!

MISS HESSEL: What? I'll have to kiss you for that, Martha. I hadn't expected that from you.

MARTHA: No, I suppose not. I hadn't expected it myself. But I've got to speak out some time. Oh, how we suffer here under this tyranny of duty and convention! Rebel against it, Dina! Marry him. Do something to defy all their stupid ideals!

JOHAN: What do you say, Dina?

DINA: Yes. I will be your wife.

JOHAN: Dina!

DINA: But first I want to work and become someone. The way you have. I don't just want to be something someone takes.

MISS HESSEL: Sensible girl! That's the way!

JOHAN: Right! I'll wait, and hope—

MISS HESSEL: You'll win her, son. But now it's time for you both to go aboard.

JOHAN: Yes—aboard! Oh, Lona, my dear sister! Here, I want a word with you—

He leads her upstage and whispers quickly to her.

MARTHA: Dina, my dear, let me look at you. Let me kiss you once again. For the last time.

DINA: Not for the last time. No, dear, dear Aunt Martha! We'll meet again!

MARTHA: No; we never shall. Promise me, Dina—don't ever come back. (*Clasps both* DINA'S *hands and looks at her*) Go, my dear child—go to your happiness across the sea. Oh, down in that schoolroom I've so often longed to be over there! It must be beautiful there. The sky is larger and the clouds fly higher than they do here. The air that blows on the faces of the people is freer—

DINA: Oh, Aunt Martha, you must come and join us. Some day.

MARTHA: I? Never; never. My little task lies here. Now I think I can resign myself to being what I must be.

DINA: I can't imagine being without you.

MARTHA: Oh, one can learn to manage without almost anything, Dina. (*Kisses her*) But you'll never have to test the truth of that, my dear. Promise me you'll make him happy.

DINA: I won't promise anything. I hate promises. What will be will be.

MARTHA: Yes, yes, my dear. Always be as you are now. Be true to yourself. And believe in yourself.

DINA: I will, Aunt Martha.

MISS HESSEL (*puts some papers which* JOHAN *has given her into her pocket*): Good boy, Johan. All right, I'll do that. But now be off with you!

JOHAN: Yes, we've no time to waste. Goodbye, Lona—thanks for everything you've done for me. Goodbye, Martha. Thank you too. You've been a wonderful friend.

MARTHA: Goodbye, Johan! Goodbye, Dina! God bless you and make you happy—always!

MARTHA *and* MISS HESSEL *hurry them to the verandah door.*
JOHAN *and* DINA *run out through the garden.* MISS HESSEL
closes the door and draws the curtain over it.

MISS HESSEL: Now we're alone, Martha. You've lost her, and I've lost him.

MARTHA: *You*'ve lost him?

MISS HESSEL: Oh, I'd half-lost him already over there. The boy wanted to stand on his own feet, so I pretended I was pining to come back here.

MARTHA: Was that why? Now I see why you came. But he wants you to go back and join them.

MISS HESSEL: An old half-sister? What good can she be to him now? Men destroy a lot of things to find happiness.

MARTHA: It happens sometimes.

MISS HESSEL: But we'll stick together, Martha.

MARTHA: Can I be of any use to you?

MISS HESSEL: Who better? We two foster-mothers—haven't we both lost our children? Now we're alone.

MARTHA: Yes; alone. You might as well know now. I loved him more than anything else in the world.

MISS HESSEL: Martha! (*Grips her arm*) Is this true?

MARTHA: That's been my life. I loved him, and waited for him. Every summer I waited for him to come through that door. At last he came; but he didn't see me.

MISS HESSEL: You loved him! But it was you yourself who put happiness into his hands.

MARTHA: What else should I have done, if I loved him? Yes, I loved him. I've only lived for him, ever since he went away. What ground did I have for hope, you're wondering? Oh, I thought I had a little. But then, when he came back, it was just as though everything had been wiped clean from his memory. He didn't see me.

MISS HESSEL: Because of Dina, Martha. You stood in her shadow.

MARTHA: I'm glad. When he left, we were the same age; but

when I saw him again—oh, that dreadful moment!—I suddenly realized that now I was ten years older than him. He'd been walking over there in the bright, quivering sunlight, drawing in youth and strength with every breath, while I'd been sitting in here, spinning and spinning—

MISS HESSEL: The thread of his happiness, Martha.

MARTHA: Yes, it was gold I was spinning. I mustn't be bitter. It's true, isn't it, Lona—we two have been good sisters to him?

MISS HESSEL (*throws her arms round her*): Martha!

BERNICK *enters from his room.*

BERNICK (*to the* GENTLEMEN *inside his room*): Yes, yes, yes, make what arrangements you please. I'll manage when the time comes— (*Closes the door*) Oh, are you here? Look, Martha, you'd better go and dress up a bit. And tell Betty to do the same. Nothing grand, of course. Just something neat and simple. You must be quick, though.

MISS HESSEL: And you must look happy and excited, Martha. This is a joyful occasion for us all.

BERNICK: Olaf must come down too. I want to have him by my side.

MISS HESSEL: Hm. Olaf—

MARTHA: I'll go and tell Betty.

She goes out through the door upstage left.

MISS HESSEL: Well. Now the great moment's arrived.

BERNICK (*paces uneasily up and down*): Yes, so it has.

MISS HESSEL: I imagine a man must feel very proud and happy at such a moment.

BERNICK (*looks at her*): Hm.

MISS HESSEL: The whole town's to be illuminated, I hear.

BERNICK: Yes, they've planned something of the kind.

MISS HESSEL: All the guilds are to march here with their banners. Your name is to shine in letters of fire. Tonight the news will be telegraphed to every corner of the land: "Surrounded by his happy family, Karsten Bernick was acclaimed by his fellow citizens as a pillar of society."

BERNICK: Yes, that's right. And they're going to give three cheers for me outside there, and the crowd will demand that I show myself in the doorway here, and I shall be forced to bow and make a speech of thanks.

MISS HESSEL: Forced?

BERNICK: Do you think I feel happy at this moment?

MISS HESSEL: No, I don't imagine you can feel all that happy.

BERNICK: You despise me, don't you, Lona?

MISS HESSEL: Not yet.

BERNICK: You've no right to do that. To despise me. Oh, Lona, you can't imagine how dreadfully alone I am in this narrow, stunted society—how, year by year, I've had to renounce my hopes of really fulfilling myself and becoming what I might and could have become. What have I accomplished? It seems a lot, but really it's nothing—a patchwork of trivialities. But they wouldn't tolerate anything else here, or anything bigger. If I tried to move a step outside their conception of right and wrong, my power would vanish. Do you know what we are, we whom they call the pillars of society? We are the instruments of society. Nothing more.

MISS HESSEL: Why have you only begun to realize this now?

BERNICK: Because I've been thinking a great deal lately— since you came back. Especially this evening. Oh, Lona, why didn't I appreciate you then for what you were?

MISS HESSEL: And if you had?

BERNICK: I'd never have let you go. And if I'd had you beside me, I wouldn't stand where I do today.

MISS HESSEL: What about Betty? Haven't you ever thought what she might have been to you?

BERNICK: I only know she hasn't been the wife I needed.

MISS HESSEL: Because you've never let her share your work with you, or tried to establish a free and truthful relationship with her. Because you've allowed her to spend her life reproaching herself for the disgrace to her family for which you yourself are responsible.

BERNICK: Yes, yes, yes. Lying and cheating—that's the cause of it all.

MISS HESSEL: Then why don't you start telling the truth?

BERNICK: Now? It's too late now, Lona.

MISS HESSEL: Tell me, Karsten. What satisfaction does all this lying and cheating bring you?

BERNICK: None. I shall be destroyed, like the whole of this rotten society. But a generation will grow up after us. It's my son I'm working for; it's for him that I'm doing all this. A time will come when society will be founded on honesty and truth, and then he will be able to live a happier life than his father has.

MISS HESSEL: With a lie as the cornerstone of his existence? Think what an inheritance you're leaving your son.

BERNICK (*in subdued despair*): I am leaving him an inheritance a thousand times worse than you know. But some time the curse must end. And yet—in spite of everything— (*Violently*) How could you do all this to me? Well, now it's happened. Now I must go on. I won't let you destroy me!

HILMAR TOENNESEN, *an open letter in his hand, hastens in right, confused.*

HILMAR: But this is utterly—! Betty, Betty!

BERNICK: What is it now? Have they come already?

HILMAR: No, no. I must speak to someone—

He goes out through the door upstage left.

MISS HESSEL: Karsten, you say we came here to destroy you. Then let me tell you the metal he's made of, this prodigal whom your virtuous community treated like a leper. He can manage without you now. He's gone.

BERNICK: But he's coming back.

MISS HESSEL: Johan will never come back. He's gone for ever, and Dina has gone with him.

BERNICK: Never come back? And Dina—gone with him?

MISS HESSEL: Yes, to become his wife. There's a slap in the face for your virtuous community! Reminds me of the day I gave you a— ah well!

BERNICK: Gone? She too? In the *Indian Girl*?

MISS HESSEL: No. He didn't dare to risk so precious a cargo

with that gang of ruffians. Johan and Dina have sailed in the *Palm Tree*.

BERNICK: Ah! Then it was all for nothing—! (*Goes quickly to the door of his room, flings it open and shouts*) Krap, stop the *Indian Girl*! She mustn't sail tonight!

KRAP (*from the other room*): The *Indian Girl* is already standing out to sea, Mr Bernick.

BERNICK (*closes the door and says dully*): Too late! And for nothing—!

MISS HESSEL: What do you mean?

BERNICK: Nothing, nothing. Get away from me—!

MISS HESSEL: Hm. Look here, Karsten. Johan told me to tell you that he's entrusted to me the keeping of his good name, which he once entrusted to you and which you robbed him of while he was away. Johan will keep his mouth shut. And I can do as I choose. Look. I have your two letters here in my hand.

BERNICK: You have them! And now—now you're going to—this evening—when the procession arrives—?

MISS HESSEL: I didn't come here to unmask you. I came to shake you from your sleep, so that you'd stand up and tell the truth. I have failed. Very well, then. Go on living your lie. Look. I'm tearing your two letters up. Take the pieces. Now you have them. There's no evidence against you now, Karsten. You've nothing left to fear. Be happy—if you can.

BERNICK (*a shiver runs through his whole body*): Lona, why didn't you do this before? Now it's too late. Now my whole life is ruined. After today, I can't go on living.

MISS HESSEL: What has happened?

BERNICK: Don't ask me. And yet—I must live! I shall live! For Olaf's sake! He'll make everything right—he'll atone for everything—!

MISS HESSEL: Karsten!

HILMAR TOENNESEN *hurries back.*

HILMAR: I can't find him. He's gone. Betty too.

BERNICK: What's the matter with you?

HILMAR: I daren't tell you.

BERNICK: What is it? You must tell me!

HILMAR: Very well. Olaf has run away. He's gone—in the *Indian Girl*.

BERNICK (*recoils*): Olaf! In the *Indian Girl*! No! No!

MISS HESSEL: Yes, it's true. Now I understand. I saw him jump out of the window.

BERNICK (*in the doorway to his room, cries desperately*): Krap, stop the *Indian Girl*! Stop her at all costs!

KRAP (*comes out*): Impossible, Mr Bernick. How can we?

BERNICK: We must stop her. Olaf is on board.

KRAP: What!

RUMMEL (*enters from* BERNICK'S *room*): Olaf run away? Impossible!

SANDSTAD (*enters*): They'll send him back with the pilot, Mr Bernick.

HILMAR: No, no. He's left me a letter. (*Shows it*) He says he'll hide among the cargo until they've reached the open sea.

BERNICK: I shall never see him again.

RUMMEL: Oh, rubbish. She's a good, strong ship, newly repaired—

VIGELAND (*who has also come out*): In your own yard, Mr Bernick.

BERNICK: I shall never see him again, I tell you. I've lost him, Lona. No—I realize it now. He never belonged to me. (*Listens*) What's that?

RUMMEL: Music. The procession's arriving.

BERNICK: I can't receive anyone. I won't!

RUMMEL: What on earth do you mean? You must!

SANDSTAD: You must, Mr Bernick. Remember what you have at stake.

BERNICK: What does that matter now? Whom have I to work for now?

RUMMEL: What a question to ask! You have us. And the community.

VIGELAND: Of course!

SANDSTAD: And you surely haven't forgotten that we too—

MARTHA *enters through the door upstage left. The music can be faintly heard from far down the street.*

MARTHA: The procession's arriving. I can't find Betty anywhere. I can't think where she—

BERNICK: Can't find her! You see, Lona! In sorrow as in joy, I stand alone.

RUMMEL: Up with those curtains! Come and help me, Mr Krap. You too, Mr Sandstad. Most regrettable that the whole family isn't here. That's not at all according to programme.

The curtains are raised from the windows and the door. The whole street is illuminated. On the house opposite is a big transparency, bearing the inscription : "Long live Karsten Bernick, The Pillar of our Society!"

BERNICK (*recoils*): Take that away! I don't want to see it! Put it out, put it out!

RUMMEL: My dear fellow, have you taken leave of your senses?

MARTHA: What's the matter with him, Lona?

MISS HESSEL: Ssh!

Whispers to her.

BERNICK: Take away this nonsense, I tell you! Can't you see that all these lights are a mockery!

RUMMEL: Well, really!

BERNICK: Oh, how could you understand? But I—I—! These are torches to light the dead to their graves!

KRAP: Hm!

RUMMEL: Now look! You're making too much of this.

SANDSTAD: The boy'll just take a trip across the Atlantic, and then you'll have him back home again.

VIGELAND: Put your trust in the hand of the Almighty, Mr Bernick.

RUMMEL: That ship's not ready to sink yet.

KRAP: Hm.

RUMMEL: It's not as though she was one of these floating coffins they send out in foreign countries—

MRS BERNICK, *a big shawl over her head, enters from the verandah.*

MRS BERNICK: Karsten, Karsten, have you heard?

BERNICK: Yes, I've heard. But you—you see nothing! You're his mother, why didn't you look after him?

MRS BERNICK: Karsten, listen—

BERNICK: Why didn't you keep a watch on him? I've lost him! Give him back to me, if you can.

MRS BERNICK: Yes, I can. I have him safe.

BERNICK: You have him?

THE OTHERS: Ah!

HILMAR: Yes, I thought as much.

MARTHA: You've got him back, Karsten!

MISS HESSEL: Yes. Now you must win him too.

BERNICK: You have him safe! Do you really mean it? Where is he?

MRS BERNICK: I shan't tell you until you've forgiven him.

BERNICK: Forgiven—! But how did you find out—?

MRS BERNICK: Do you think a mother hasn't eyes? I was terrified you might find out. Those few words he let fall yesterday—then I found his room was empty and his clothes and rucksack missing—

BERNICK: Yes, yes.

MRS BERNICK: So I ran down and got hold of Aune. We went out in his boat. The American ship was just getting ready to sail. Thank heaven, we got there in time—went aboard—had the ship searched—found him. Oh, Karsten, you mustn't punish him!

BERNICK: Betty!

MRS BERNICK: Or Aune either!

BERNICK: Aune? What do you know about him? Is the *Indian Girl* under sail again?

MRS BERNICK: No, that's just it—

BERNICK: Speak, speak!

MRS BERNICK: Aune was as frightened as I was. It took a long time to search the ship—darkness was falling, the pilot

began to complain—so Aune took his courage in his hands
and told them in your name—

BERNICK: Yes?

MRS BERNICK: To hold the ship until morning.

KRAP: Hm.

BERNICK: Oh, what luck! What incredible luck!

MRS BERNICK: You aren't angry?

BERNICK: Oh, Betty, thank God, thank God!

RUMMEL: Come, man, you're being over-sensitive.

HILMAR: Yes, as soon as anyone's bold enough to risk a little
skirmish with the elements—ugh!

KRAP (*by the windows*): The procession's just coming through
the garden gate!

BERNICK: Let them come.

RUMMEL: The whole garden's filling with people.

SANDSTAD: The street's crammed too.

RUMMEL: The entire town's here, Bernick. This is really an
inspiring moment.

VIGELAND: Let us accept it in a humble spirit, Mr Bernick.

RUMMEL: All the flags are out. What a procession! There's
the festival committee, with Dr Roerlund at its head.

BERNICK: Let them come, I say!

RUMMEL: Look; you're in a rather disturbed state of mind
just now—

BERNICK: So?

RUMMEL: Well, if you don't feel up to it, I wouldn't mind
saying a few words on your behalf.

BERNICK: No, thank you. This evening I shall speak for
myself.

RUMMEL: But do you know what you have to say?

BERNICK: Yes, Rummel. Don't worry. I know what I have to say.

*The music has ceased. The verandah door is thrown open. DR
ROERLUND enters at the head of the festival committee, accompanied by two FOOTMEN carrying a covered basket. After them
come CITIZENS of all classes, as many as the room will hold. A
huge crowd, with banners and flags, can be glimpsed outside in
the garden and the street.*

ROERLUND: Most honoured sir! I see by the amazement on your face that our intrusion into this happy family circle, where you sit gathered at your peaceful fireside surrounded by active and honourable fellow citizens, takes you completely by surprise. But our hearts commanded that we should come and pay you homage. It is not the first time we have done this, but it is the first time we have done so on such a comprehensive scale. We have often expressed to you our thanks for the solid moral foundation on which you have, as one might say, grounded our community. But tonight we hail you as the far-sighted, indefatigable and selfless—nay, self-sacrificing—fellow citizen who has seized the initiative in launching an enterprise which, so expert opinion assures us, will give a powerful impetus to the material welfare and prosperity of our community.

VOICES FROM THE CROWD: Bravo, bravo!

ROERLUND: Mr Bernick, you have for many years been a shining example to our town. I am speaking now not of your model family life, nor of your untarnished moral record. These are matters for private admiration rather than public acclaim. I speak rather of your work as a citizen, which is apparent for all to see. Stately ships sail forth from your shipyards and show our country's flag upon the furthest corners of the globe. A numerous and contented family of workers reveres you as a father. By calling into existence new branches of industry you have given prosperity to hundreds of homes. You are, in a word, the cornerstone of our community.

VOICES: Hear, hear! Bravo!

ROERLUND: But what we especially bless in you is the shining altruism which irradiates your every action—a rare quality indeed in this modern age. You are now in the process of procuring for the community a—I do not flinch from the plain, prosaic word—a railway.

MANY VOICES: Bravo, bravo!

ROERLUND: But this enterprise is threatened by obstacles deliberately placed in its path by narrow and selfish interests.

VOICES: Hear, hear!

ROERLUND: It is not unknown that certain individuals who do not belong to our community have stolen a march on our own industrious citizens, and have secured certain advantages which rightly belonged to this town.

VOICES: Yes, yes. Hear, hear!

ROERLUND: This regrettable information has, sir, doubtless come to your knowledge. None the less you are pursuing your project inflexibly, knowing that a true patriot's vision cannot be confined by the needs of his own parish.

VARIOUS VOICES: Hm. No, no! Yes, yes!

ROERLUND: It is therefore to the patriot and, in the largest sense, the model citizen, that we are gathered here tonight to pay homage. May God grant that your enterprise may result in true and lasting prosperity for this community! The railway is a road which may expose us to corrupting influences from without, but it will also be a road by which we shall swiftly be able to rid ourselves of them. We can, alas, no longer hope to isolate ourselves completely from the evil of the outside world. But the fact that on this evening of rejoicing we have, so it is rumoured, been rid with unexpected speed of one such influence—

VOICES: Ssh! Ssh!

ROERLUND: —I take as a happy omen for this enterprise. I only mention this as evidence that we stand here in a house in which ethical considerations carry greater weight than the ties of blood.

VOICES: Hear, hear! Bravo!

BERNICK (*simultaneously*): Allow me to—

ROERLUND: One word more, sir. What you have done for this parish you have, of course, done with no ulterior motive or thought of material advantage. But we trust you will not refuse to accept a small token of appreciation from your fellow citizens, least of all at this significant moment when, so men of practical experience assure us, we stand on the threshold of a new era.

MANY VOICES: Bravo! Hear, hear!

He nods to the FOOTMEN, *who bring the basket closer. During the following, members of the Committee take out and present the objects described.*

ROERLUND: We therefore have the honour, Mr Bernick, to present you with this silver coffee-service. May it adorn your table when, in the days to come, as so often in days gone by, we shall enjoy the pleasure of gathering at your hospitable board. And you too, gentlemen, who have so steadfastly supported our foremost citizen, we beg to accept these small tokens of our affection. To you, Mr Rummel, this silver cup. You have often, in well-winged words, amid the clinking of cups, championed the civic interests of this community. May you often find worthy opportunities for raising and emptying this cup. To you, Mr Sandstad, I present this album containing photographs of your fellow citizens. Your famed and acknowledged generosity places you in the agreeable position of numbering friends in every stratum of the community, regardless of political differences. And to you, Mr Vigeland, to adorn your bedside, I offer this book of sermons, printed on vellum, and luxuriously bound. Under the ripening influence of the years you have arrived at a mature wisdom; your interest in temporal matters has been purified and sublimated by reflection upon loftier and less worldly things. (*Turns to the* CROWD) And now, my friends, three cheers for Mr Bernick and his fellows in the fight! Three cheers for the pillars of our society!

WHOLE CROWD: Long live Mr Bernick! Long live the pillars of our society! Hurrah! Hurrah! Hurrah!

MISS HESSEL: Good luck, brother-in-law.

An expectant silence.

BERNICK (*begins slowly and earnestly*): Fellow citizens! Your Chairman has said that we stand this evening on the threshold of a new era; and I hope this will prove to be the case. But for this to happen, we must face the truth, which until this evening has been an outcast from this community.

(General amazement) I must therefore begin by rejecting the words of praise with which you, Dr Roerlund, as is the custom on such occasions, addressed me. I am unworthy of them, for until today I have not acted selflessly. If I have not always acted from pecuniary motives, I none the less now realize that a desire for power, for influence and for reputation, has been the driving force behind most of my actions.

RUMMEL *(aside)*: What's this?

BERNICK: However, I do not therefore reproach myself before my fellow citizens. For I still believe that I can be reckoned among the most useful of us who stand here tonight.

MANY VOICES: Hear, hear! Yes, yes!

BERNICK: I condemn myself most for having so often been weak enough to use backstairs methods, because I knew and feared our community's fondness for scenting impure motives behind everything a man does here. And that brings me to a case in point.

RUMMEL *(uneasily)*: Hm-hm!

BERNICK: Rumours have been spreading about the big purchases of land that have been made in the neighbourhood. All these purchases have been made by me, and by me alone.

VOICES *(whisper)*: What did he say? Him? Mr Bernick?

BERNICK: All that land belongs, at this moment, to me. I have of course confided this information to my partners in this enterprise, Messrs Rummel, Vigeland and Sandstad, and we have agreed that—

RUMMEL: It isn't true! Where's the proof? Show us the proof!

VIGELAND: We agreed nothing!

SANDSTAD: Well, I must say!

BERNICK: That is quite correct; we have not yet agreed on what I was about to propose. But I am confident that these three gentlemen will agree with me now when I say that I have this evening convinced myself that these properties should be turned into a public company, so that any citizen who wishes may buy a share in them.

MANY VOICES: Hurrah! Long live Mr Bernick!

RUMMEL (*quietly to* BERNICK): You damned traitor!

SANDSTAD (*also quietly*): You've cheated us!

VIGELAND: May the devil—oh, good heavens, what am I saying?

CROWD (*outside*): Hurrah, hurrah, hurrah!

BERNICK: Quiet, gentlemen! I am unworthy of this applause, for the decision I have now reached is not what I originally intended. I intended to keep all the land for myself, and I still believe that these properties can be best exploited if they come under the control of a single hand. But that is for you to decide. If it is the general wish, I am willing to administer them to the best of my ability.

VOICES: Yes! Yes! Yes!

BERNICK: But first my fellow citizens must know me as I really am. Let each man look into his own heart, and let us resolve that from tonight we shall in fact enter upon a new era. Let the old life, with its painted façade, its hypocrisy and its hollowness, its sham propriety and its miserable prejudices, survive only as a museum. And to this museum we shall give—shall we not, gentlemen?—our coffee-service, our silver cup, our photograph album and our book of sermons printed on vellum and luxuriously bound.

RUMMEL: Yes, of course.

VIGELAND (*mutters*): You've taken all the rest from us, so why not this?

SANDSTAD: Yes, yes.

BERNICK: And now to the chief issue that remains between me and my community. You have heard it asserted that evil influences have left us this evening. To that piece of news I can add another. The man in question did not leave alone. A girl went with him, to become his wife—

MISS HESSEL (*loudly*): Dina Dorf!

ROERLUND: What?

MRS BERNICK: Lona!

Great excitement.

ROERLUND: Fled? Run away—with him? Impossible!

BERNICK: To become his wife, Dr Roerlund. And I will tell you something else. (*Quietly*) Prepare yourself, Betty, for what I am about to say. (*Loudly*) I say: "Hats off to that man, for he had the courage to shoulder the blame for another man's crime." Oh, fellow citizens, I am weary of lies. They have poisoned every fibre of my being. You shall know everything. It was I who was guilty fifteen years ago.

MRS BERNICK (*quietly, emotionally*): Karsten!

MARTHA (*similarly*): Oh—Johan—!

MISS HESSEL: At last!

Dumb astonishment among the onlookers.

BERNICK: Yes, fellow citizens! I was the guilty one, and he was the one who fled. The false and evil rumours which were afterwards spread about him it is now too late to refute. But who am I to complain of this? Fifteen years ago I raised myself on these rumours. Whether they are now to bring me down is a question that each one of you must argue with his own conscience.

ROERLUND: What a thunderbolt! The town's foremost citizen! (*Softly, to* MRS BERNICK) Oh, Mrs Bernick, I feel most deeply sorry for you.

HILMAR: What an admission! Well, I must say—!

BERNICK: But you must not decide tonight. I beg each of you to return home to collect your thoughts and to look into your hearts. When you are calm again you will decide whether by speaking thus openly I have lost or won. Goodbye. I still have much to atone for; but that is between myself and my own conscience. Good night. Take away these trappings. This is not the time nor the place for them.

ROERLUND: I should think not indeed! (*Softly, to* MRS BERNICK) Run away! She was quite unworthy of me after all. (*Half-aloud to the Committee*) Well, gentlemen, after this I think we had better depart as quietly as we can.

HILMAR: How anyone is to wave the banner of ideals high after this I really—ugh!

The news meanwhile has been whispered from mouth to mouth.

The CROWD *drifts away.* RUMMEL, SANDSTAD *and* VIGELAND *also go, arguing in subdued but vehement tones.* HILMAR *wanders out right. Silence.*

BERNICK, MRS BERNICK, MARTHA, MISS HESSEL *and* KRAP *are left in the room.*

BERNICK: Betty, can you forgive me?

MRS BERNICK (*smiles*): Do you know, Karsten, this has been the happiest moment I have had for years?

BERNICK: What do you mean?

MRS BERNICK: For years now I have believed that you were once mine, but I had lost you. Now I know you were never mine; but I shall win you.

BERNICK (*throws his arms round her*): Oh, Betty, you have won me! Lona has taught me to understand for the first time what kind of woman you really are. But Olaf—Olaf!

MRS BERNICK: Yes, now you can see him. Mr Krap—

She talks quietly to KRAP *upstage. He goes out through the verandah door. During the following, all the transparencies, and the lights in the houses outside, are gradually extinguished.*

BERNICK (*quietly*): Thank you, Lona. You have saved what was best in me—and for me.

MISS HESSEL: What else do you think I wanted?

BERNICK: Yes—was it this you came back for—or was it something else? I don't understand you, Lona.

MISS HESSEL: Hm—

BERNICK: It wasn't hatred, then? And it wasn't revenge? Then why did you come back here?

MISS HESSEL: Old friendship doesn't rust, Karsten.

BERNICK: Lona!

MISS HESSEL: When Johan told me about that lie, I vowed to myself: "The hero of my youth shall stand free and true."

BERNICK: Lona, Lona! How little I have deserved this from you!

MISS HESSEL: Ah, Karsten! If we women demanded our deserts—!

117

AUNE enters from the garden with OLAF.

BERNICK (*runs towards him*): Olaf!

OLAF: Father, I promise you I won't ever again—

BERNICK: Run away?

OLAF: Yes, yes, I promise, Father.

BERNICK: And I promise you, you shall never have cause to. From now on you shall be allowed to grow up, not as the heir to my life's work, but as one who has his own life's work awaiting him.

OLAF: And may I become anything I like?

BERNICK: Yes, you may.

OLAF: Thank you. Then I don't want to become a pillar of society.

BERNICK: Oh? Why not?

OLAF: I think it must be so dull.

BERNICK: You shall be yourself, Olaf. That is all that matters. As for you, Aune—

AUNE: I know, Mr Bernick. I'm dismissed.

BERNICK: We'll stay together, Aune. And please forgive me.

AUNE: What! But the ship didn't sail this evening—

BERNICK: She shall not sail tomorrow, either. I gave you too little time. The work must be attended to more thoroughly.

AUNE: It will, Mr Bernick. And with the new machines!

BERNICK: Good. But it must be done thoroughly and honestly. There is much in us which needs to be repaired thoroughly and honestly. Well, good night, Aune.

AUNE: Good night, Mr Bernick—and thank you. Thank you!

He goes out right.

MRS BERNICK: They have all gone now.

BERNICK: And we are alone. My name does not shine in letters of fire any longer. All the lights in the windows are out.

MISS HESSEL: Would you like them lit again?

BERNICK: Not for all the money in the world. Where have I been? You will be appalled when you know. I feel as though I had just returned to health and sanity after being poisoned.

But I feel it—I *can* become young and strong again. Oh, come closer, come closer around me! Come, Betty! Come, Olaf, my son! And you, Martha. Oh, Martha! It's as though I had never seen you all these years.

MISS HESSEL: I can well believe that. Your society is a society of bachelors. You don't notice the women.

BERNICK: True, true. And because of that—now I don't want any arguing, Lona—you must not leave Betty and me.

MRS BERNICK: No, Lona, you mustn't!

MISS HESSEL: How could I run away and abandon all you youngsters just when you're beginning to start a new life? Being a foster-mother is my job, isn't it? You and I, Martha—we two old maids—! What are you looking at?

MARTHA: How light the sky has grown! It's bright and calm over the sea. The *Palm Tree* has good luck in her sails.

MISS HESSEL: And good luck on board.

BERNICK: And we—we have a long, hard day ahead of us. I most of all. But let it come. Oh, gather close around me, you loyal and true women. That is something else I've learned in these past few days. It is you women who are the pillars of society.

MISS HESSEL: Then it's a poor wisdom you've learned, brother-in-law. (*Puts her hand firmly on his shoulder*) No, Karsten. The spirit of truth and the spirit of freedom—they are the pillars of society.

John Gabriel Borkman

INTRODUCTION

John Gabriel Borkman was Ibsen's last play but one; he wrote it in 1896, at the age of sixty-eight. Its theme, like that of the strange, abbreviated experiment which followed, *When We Dead Awaken*, is, in Ibsen's own phrase, "the coldness of the heart". Edvard Munch described *John Gabriel Borkman* as "the most powerful winter landscape in Scandinavian art."

The plot of *John Gabriel Borkman* is based on a story which Ibsen had heard long ago in his student days in Christiania. In 1851 a high-ranking army officer was charged with embezzlement. At first he denied the charge, but then, like Old Ekdal before the beginning of *The Wild Duck*, he unsuccessfully tried to shoot himself. He was sentenced to four years penal servitude and, when he was released, shortly before Ibsen returned to Christiania as theatrical director, he shut himself up in his house and spent the rest of his life brooding in solitude, unable even to speak to his wife. Later, in the eighteen-eighties, a great scandal occurred at Arendal; a bank director speculated and embezzled his clients' money, and was sent to prison. Bankruptcy was a subject that held a painful interest for Ibsen, for when he had been seven this fate had befallen his father.

In the year in which the officer was charged, Ibsen, aged twenty-three, had written a poem in no way connected with that incident, but which anticipated many of the sentiments which, nearly half a century later, he was to put into Borkman's mouth. It is called *The Miner* and it tells of the fascination the poet felt for the darkness of the subterranean pit, and of his conviction that the answer to the secrets of life lay there:

Groan and thunder, mountain wall,
Before my heavy hammer blow.
Downwards I must carve my way
Till I hear the iron ore ring.

Deep in the mountain's desolate night
The rich treasure beckons me.
Diamonds and precious stones
Among the red branches of the gold.

And in the darkness there is peace.
Peace and rest for eternity.
Heavy hammer, break me the way
To the heart-chamber of what lies hidden there . . .

When I first entered here
I thought in my innocence:
'The spirits of the dark will solve for me
Life's endless riddles'.

No spirit has yet taught me that strange answer.
No ray has shone from the depths.

Was I wrong? Does this path
Not lead to the light?
But the light blinds my eyes
If I seek it in the mountains.

No, I must go down into the dark.
Eternal peace lies there.
Heavy hammer, break me the way
To the heart-chamber of what lies hidden there.

Hammer blow on hammer blow
Till the last day of life.
No ray of morning shines.
No sun of hope rises.

It is interesting that, when Ibsen recalled the trial which had so impressed him in his youth, he should have taken up the theme of the poem which he had written independently in the same year.

Another memory from fifty years before found its way into the play. As a young man, Ibsen had a friend named Vilhelm Foss, an old copying clerk who had once published a collection of verses and still cherished the hope that he might some day achieve poetic fame. Ibsen had remembered Foss when planning *The Lady from the Sea* eight years previously, for we find a reference to him in the first rough notes for that play. In the event, Ibsen found no place for him in *The Lady from the. Sea*, but he often retained a discarded character for use in a subsequent play, so that Vilhelm Foss finally achieved immortality as Vilhelm Foldal in *John Gabriel Borkman*.

A more recent and painful memory left its mark on the play. Shortly before Ibsen wrote *Borkman*, his only son, Sigurd, to whom he was deeply attached, had left home to get married. The household must have seemed empty without him, and one imagines this was in Ibsen's mind when he wrote the scene in which Erhart leaves his parents to elope with Mrs Wilton. The theme of young people rebelling against the domination of their parents had long been a favourite with Ibsen; we find it, for example, in *The Wild Duck* (Gregers Werle) and in *Ghosts*.

The danger of a loveless marriage was another theme to which Ibsen constantly returned (*Love's Comedy, The Pillars of Society, A Doll's House, The Lady from the Sea, Hedda Gabler*); so was that of the man who sacrifices the happiness of his wife or the woman he loves for the sake of a cause or a personal ambition (*Brand, An Enemy of the People, The Master Builder, When We Dead Awaken*). Ibsen's own marriage, though not unhappy, seems to have been more or less loveless; and he was obsessed by the feeling that, in choosing the life of an author, he had sacrificed his chances of happiness and, to some extent, those of his wife.

Formally the last act of *John Gabriel Borkman* marks a return towards the kind of epic-poetic-symbolic drama which Ibsen had perfected to a high degree in *Brand* and *Peer Gynt* thirty years before. After completing *Peer Gynt* in 1867 he had deliberately abandoned poetry as a dramatic medium; in a letter to Edmund Gosse, dated 15 January 1874, explaining why he had chosen to write *Emperor and Galilean* in prose, he said: "I wished to produce on the reader the impression that what he was reading was something that had actually happened. . . . We are no longer living in the age of Shakespeare. . . . What I desired to depict was human beings, and therefore I would not let them talk in 'the language of the gods'." He had done his best to remain faithful to this resolve and, although there are moments in every play he wrote in which we sense the buried river beneath the surface, it is not, I think, until the final act of *John Gabriel Borkman* that we again find the recorder of realistic dialogue being edged aside by the symbolist and the poet. In *When We Dead Awaken* this process was carried a stage further.

Ibsen's early drafts show that he originally gave Borkman the single Christian name of Jens, and then altered it successively to Jens Jørgen, Jens Adolf, Jens Gabriel, John, and finally, John Gabriel. He told his doctor, Edvard Bull, that he decided on this last combination because the English name John would suggest big business, while that of Gabriel, the archangel, would signify power and glory.

In the first draft of the play the second act opens with Borkman playing the final bars of "a piece by Beethoven" on the violin, and Frida accompanying him on the piano. But Ibsen took away Borkman's violin, so as to allow him to pace up and down the room, and altered the music from Beethoven to Saint-Saëns' *Danse Macabre*, which was especially popular in Norway during the summer of 1896, and which the young pianist, Hildur Andersen, with whom Ibsen was on terms of close friendship, often played to him.

It is not the purpose of these introductions to interpret the plays; that is something that should be left to individual directors, and few things are more irritating than a translator who tries to saddle a play with a rigid interpretation. Ibsen's plays, like Shakespeare's, are capable of many interpretations; for example, before the 1914 war Borkman was commonly presented in Scandinavian productions as a Nietzsche figure, in 1916 as a wartime speculator, in the thirties he was likened to Ivar Kreuger, the match-king, and in the forties to Hitler. Ibsen did, however, express a strong view as to how the character of Mrs Borkman should be played—one of the few occasions on which he committed himself on paper about any of his characters. In a letter to a correspondent of the newspaper *Kjøbenhavns Aftenblad*, complaining that Mrs Borkman's character had been misinterpreted in performance, Ibsen wrote:

"The main point is that Mrs Borkman loves her husband. She is not at heart a hard or evil woman; she was, to begin with, a loving wife, and has only become hard and evil because she has been deceived. Her husband has deceived her doubly —firstly, in love, and secondly, because she had believed in his genius. It is above all important that the actress should make this clear. If Mrs Borkman did not love her husband, she would long ago have forgiven him. Despite having been doubly deceived, she still waits for the sick wolf whose tread she hears every day. As he waits for 'the world' to come to him, so she waits for him to come to her. This is made clear in the dialogue, and it is above all else important that the actress who plays Mrs Borkman should bring out this side of her character."

In the absence of any hard-and-fast international copyright agreement, Ibsen earned little from foreign productions of his plays, and relied much on royalties from their sale in book-form in Scandinavia. Ever since *The Pillars of Society* he had, with formidable regularity, completed a play every second autumn, so as to have it in the bookshops in time for the Christmas sales. (The only exception during this period was *An Enemy of the People*, which he wrote the year after *Ghosts*.) His routine was to relax for a year after finishing a

127

play, and then to spend the winter considering plots and ideas, one of which he would work out during the summer. The summer was always his favourite season for writing, at any rate after he left Norway for Italy in 1864.

True to this routine, he had completed *The Master Builder* in October 1892, and *Little Eyolf* in October 1894. William Archer cannot, therefore, have been surprised when, the following June, Ibsen wrote to him: "I hope I may get down to writing a new play next year. But I don't know for sure—there's so much else I have to attend to which takes up my time." However, his fears, if he really entertained them, proved unjustified, for six months later, on 24 April 1896, he wrote to Georg Brandes that he could not travel to England, as Brandes had suggested, firstly because he did not know enough English, and secondly because he was "busy preparing a new work, and I don't want to put off writing it for longer than necessary". On 11 July he began the actual writing of his first draft. On 27 July he wrote to his publisher: "My play progresses with surprising speed and ease. Thanks to the more than southerly heat this summer, I am able to work uninterruptedly." By 26 August he had completed his first draft, and the next day he began to revise it. This took seven and a half weeks. By 18 October the final version was ready to go to press, and on 15 December *John Gabriel Borkman* was published by Gyldendal in Copenhagen in a first printing of 15,000 copies—an enormous edition for the Scandinavia of those days. (Since *The Pillars of Society*, nineteen years before, 10,000 had been the normal first printing for Ibsen's plays.)

On the day before publication (14 December 1896) *John Gabriel Borkman* was read in public in London (in Norwegian) to secure the English copyright. It was first performed on 10 January 1897, when the Finnish and Swedish theatres in Helsinki staged it simultaneously.[1] On 16 January it was produced at Frankfurt-on-Main. The German censor had demanded the excision of two passages, Ella's remark in

---

[1] Finland being a bilingual country, a Swedish theatre has long existed in Helsinki for the benefit of the Swedish-speaking minority.

Act II about "the sin for which there is no forgiveness", and Mrs Wilton's in Act IV about the importance of Erhart having another girl to fall back on if he should tire of her, or she of him. Despite the censor the performance was a success. Three days later the play received its Norwegian première, under strange circumstances. The Swedish actor, August Lindberg, had secured the rights to perform *John Gabriel Borkman* in the Norwegian provinces, and managed to stage his première at the little town of Drammen, about thirty miles from Christiania, on 19 January, six days before the Christiania Theatre were ready with theirs. To annoy the Christiania Theatre, with the management of which he was on bad terms, Lindberg ran special trains from the capital to Drammen, and so drew off a large proportion of the Christiania Theatre's public. Before the end of the month the play had also been staged in Stockholm, Berlin (where Hermann Nissen played Borkman with a make-up suggesting both Bjœrnson and Ibsen, and the play was coolly received) and Copenhagen.

In London that winter Ellen Terry tried to interest Henry Irving in the role of Borkman. He was ill and "she took advantage of his enforced immobility by reading to him the first two acts of *John Gabriel Borkman*; he read the third to her. 'What a play!' he commented, with an inflection that left no doubt as to his opinion of it."[1] We are not told which of them, if either, read the fourth act. In the event, Londoners had to wait until 3 May before they could see the play. On that afternoon it was performed at the Strand Theatre by the association known as the New Century Theatre. Borkman was played by W. H. Vernon, Mrs Borkman by Geneviève Ward, Ella by Elizabeth Robins, Erhart by Martin Harvey, Mrs Wilton by Mrs Beerbohm Tree, Foldal by James Welch, and Frida by Dora Barton. It seems to have been a very bad performance; even Bernard Shaw, anxious to encourage people to go and see it, could find little to praise. After denouncing the poverty of the sets ("I beg the New Century Theatre, when the next Ibsen play is ready for mounting, to

[1] *Henry Irving*, by Laurence Irving (1951), p. 601.

apply to me for assistance. If I have a ten-pound note, they shall have it; if not, I can at least lend them a couple of decent chairs") he continued:

"I regret to say that the shortcomings of the scenery were not mitigated by imaginative and ingenious stage management. Mr Vernon's stage management is very actor-like; that is to say, it is directed, not to secure the maximum of illusion for the play, but the maximum of fairness in distributing good places on the stage to the members of the cast. . . . The traditional stage management of tragedy ignores realism . . . it lends itself to people talking at each other rhetorically from opposite sides of the stage, taking long sweeping walks up to their "points," striking attitudes in the focus of the public vision with an artificiality, which instead of being concealed, is not only disclosed but insisted on, and being affected in all their joints by emotions which a fine comedian conveys by the faintest possible inflexion of tone or eyebrow. . . . Mr Vernon's Borkman was not ill acted; only, as it was not Ibsen's Borkman, but the very reverse and negation of him, the better Mr Vernon acted, the worse it was for the play. . . . Mr Vernon was as earthly and sane as a man need be until he went for his walk in the snow, and a Borkman who is that is necessarily a trifle dull." Shaw thought Elizabeth Robins "too young and too ferociously individualistic" for the part of Ella; and of Geneviève Ward as Mrs Borkman, he wrote: "The truth is, her tragic style, derived from Ristori, was not made for Ibsen." James Welch, "though his scene in the second act was a triumph, made a fundamental mistake in the third. . . . He played the heartbroken old man pretending to laugh—a descendant of the clown who jokes in the arena while his child is dying at home—and so wrecked what would otherwise have been the best piece of character work of the afternoon." Martin Harvey, as Erhart, "shewed, as we all knew he would shew, considerable stage talent and more than ordinary dramatic intelligence; but in the first act he was not the embarrassed young gentleman of Ibsen, but rather the 'soaring human boy' imagined by Mr Chadband". The best performances, in Shaw's view, came from Mrs Beerbohm Tree as Mrs Wilton and Dora Barton as Frida—"but then these two parts are comparatively easy". Other critics were, as can be imagined, even less favourable.

John Gabriel Borkman was first performed in America on 18 November 1897, when it was produced by the Criterion Independent Theatre in New York. Borkman was played by E. J. Henley, Mrs Borkman by Maude Banks, Ella by Ann Warrington, Erhart by John Blair, Mrs Wilton by Carrie Keeler, Foldal by Albert Brunning, and Frida by Dorothy Usner. This appears to have been a better production than the one in London; the *New York Dramatic Mirror* called Henley's performance "a memorable achievement". In the same month, Lugné-Poe, a great Ibsen enthusiast, staged the play at his Théâtre de L'Oeuvre in Paris. Prague, Vienna and Bologna soon followed suit, and by 1909 *John Gabriel Borkman* had reached even Tokyo. Ella Rentheim was one of the many Ibsen roles in which Eleonora Duse excelled; Max Reinhardt, as a young actor in Berlin, scored one of his greatest successes as Vilhelm Foldal; and Erhart Borkman was one of John Gielgud's first professional parts.

John Gabriel Borkman has since been performed eight times in London, most memorably by Frederick Valk in 1950. The 1975 Royal National Theatre production by Peter Hall proved a hollowly operatic disappointment, despite the presence of Ralph Richardson, Peggy Ashcroft and Wendy Hiller. Laurence Olivier, on television in 1958, after playing his first two acts magnificently, unaccountably shrank from the final act, but the twin sisters can seldom have been portrayed more movingly than they were by Pamela Brown and Irene Worth in this production by Casper Wrede.

MICHAEL MEYER

CHARACTERS

JOHN GABRIEL BORKMAN,	sometime banker.
MRS GUNHILD BORKMAN,	his wife.
ERHART BORKMAN,	their son, a student.
MISS ELLA RENTHEIM,	Mrs Borkman's twin sister.
MRS FANNY WILTON	–
VILHELM FOLDAL,	supernumerary clerk in a Government Office.
FRIDA FOLDAL,	his daughter.
MRS BORKMAN'S MAID.	

The action takes place during a winter evening in the Rentheim family mansion outside the Norwegian capital.

ACT I:	Mrs Borkman's sitting-room.
ACT II:	The drawing-room upstairs.
ACT III:	Mrs Borkman's sitting-room.
ACT IV:	The courtyard outside the house; and a part of the forest.

This translation was first performed on 19 November 1958, in an H. M. Tennent Globe Production for Associated Television, with the following cast:

JOHN GABRIEL BORKMAN	Laurence Olivier
MRS BORKMAN	Irene Worth
ERHART BORKMAN	Anthony Valentine
ELLA RENTHEIM	Pamela Brown
MRS WILTON	Maxine Audley
VILHELM FOLDAL	George Relph
FRIDA FOLDAL	Anne Castaldini
MAID	Carmel McSharry

Directed by Casper Wrede

ACT ONE

MRS BORKMAN'S *sitting-room, furnished with old-fashioned and faded splendour. At the back, an open sliding door leads to a garden room, with windows and a glass door. Through these can be seen the garden, with snow driving in the evening dusk. In the side wall on the right is a door leading from the hall. Further downstage is a large, old-fashioned iron stove, in which a fire is burning. On the left, some way back, a smaller, single door. Downstage on the same side is a window, hidden by thick curtains. Between the window and the door is a sofa with a horse-hair cover; in front of it stands a table with a cloth on it. On the table is a lighted lamp, with a shade. By the stove stands a high-backed armchair.*

MRS GUNHILD BORKMAN *is seated on the sofa, crocheting. She is an elderly lady of coldly aristocratic appearance, with a stiff demeanour and immobile features. Her rich hair is heavily streaked with grey. Delicate, transparent hands. She is wearing a thick, dark, silk dress, which was once elegant but is now somewhat worn and tired-looking. A woollen shawl covers her shoulders. For a few moments she sits upright and motionless at her crocheting. Then the sound of bells is heard from a sleigh passing outside.* MRS BORKMAN *listens.*

MRS BORKMAN: Erhart! At last! (*She gets up and peers out through the curtains. Looks disappointed, sits down again on the sofa, and resumes her work. A few moments later, the* MAID *comes in through the door with a visiting-card on a small tray.*)

MRS BORKMAN (*quickly*): Was that Mr Erhart?

MAID: No, madam. But there's a lady out in the—

MRS BORKMAN (*puts down her work*): Oh, Mrs Wilton—

MAID: No, it's a strange lady.

MRS BORKMAN (*reaches out her hand for the card*): Let me see. (*Reads it, rises quickly to her feet and looks coldly at the* MAID) Are you sure it's me she wants to speak to?

MAID: Yes, I understood she meant you, madam.

MRS BORKMAN: Did she ask to speak with Mrs Borkman?

MAID: Oh yes, madam.

MRS BORKMAN: Very well. Tell her I am at home.

The MAID *opens the door for the visitor, and goes out.* MISS ELLA RENTHEIM *enters the room. In appearance she resembles her sister, but her face bears evidence of suffering rather than of hardness. It still retains traces of her early beauty, strong and full of character. Her abundant and once black hair is combed up in natural waves from her forehead, and is completely white. She is dressed in black velvet, with hat and fur-lined coat of the same material. For a moment the two sisters stand in silence looking searchingly at each other. Each seems to be waiting for the other to speak first.*

ELLA (*remaining near the door*): I know you're surprised to see me, Gunhild.

MRS BORKMAN (*stands rigidly upright between the sofa and table, pressing her fingers against the cloth*): You've made a mistake. The bailiff lives in the side wing, you know.

ELLA: It's not the bailiff I've come to see today.

MRS BORKMAN: You want to speak to me?

ELLA: Yes. I must have a few words with you.

MRS BORKMAN (*moves towards her*): Well, sit down, then.

ELLA: Thank you, I'll stand.

MRS BORKMAN: As you please. Unfasten your coat, anyway.

ELLA (*unbuttoning her coat*): Yes, it's very hot in here.

MRS BORKMAN: I am always cold.

ELLA (*stands for a moment and looks at her, her arms resting on the back of the armchair*): Yes, Gunhild; it's nearly eight years now since we saw each other last.

MRS BORKMAN (*coldly*): Since we spoke, at any rate.

ELLA: Since we spoke, yes. You must have seen me when I had to come out here on my annual visit to the bailiff.

MRS BORKMAN: Once or twice, perhaps.

ELLA: I have caught a glimpse of you, too, once or twice. In that window.

MRS BORKMAN: You must have sharp eyes to see through the curtains, Ella. But the last time we spoke was in here—

ELLA: Yes, I know.

MRS BORKMAN: The week before they let him out.

ELLA: Oh, don't, Gunhild, don't!

MRS BORKMAN: It was the week before John—before Borkman was released from prison.

ELLA (coming towards her): I haven't forgotten. But I can't bear to think about it.

MRS BORKMAN: And yet one is never allowed to think about anything else—ever. I don't believe it—I can't—I cannot understand that anything so terrible could happen to a family. And to our family. Such a noble family as ours!

ELLA: Oh, Gunhild—it wasn't only our family that suffered. There were so many others.

MRS BORKMAN: Oh yes—but I don't care so much about them. All they lost was money or some pieces of paper— but we—I—and Erhart! Only a child at the time! The shame he brought on us, who were innocent—the disgrace, the terrible disgrace! And we were utterly ruined!

ELLA (carefully): Tell me, Gunhild. How does he take it?

MRS BORKMAN: Erhart, you mean?

ELLA: No. He. How does he take it?

MRS BORKMAN: Do you think I ask him?

ELLA: Ask? Surely you don't need to ask him—?

MRS BORKMAN: Do you think I talk to him? Or see him?

ELLA: Don't you even see him?

MRS BORKMAN: A man who spent five years in prison? Oh, the disgrace! And remember what the name of John Gabriel Borkman meant once! No, no, no—I shall never see him again, never!

ELLA: You are hard, Gunhild.

MRS BORKMAN: Towards him, yes.

ELLA: But he is your husband.

MRS BORKMAN: Didn't he tell the court that I had started him on the path to ruin? That I spent too much money—

ELLA: Wasn't there some truth in that?

MRS BORKMAN: But he wanted it that way! He wanted everything to be so absurdly luxurious—

ELLA: I know. But shouldn't you have restrained him?

MRS BORKMAN: Was I to know it wasn't his own money he was giving me to squander? And wasn't he ten times as extravagant as I?

ELLA (*quietly*): Well, I suppose he had to keep up his position.

MRS BORKMAN: Oh yes! He always said we had to "put on a show"! Oh, he put on a show all right! Drove a four-in-hand, as though he were a king. Made people bow and scrape to him, the way they would to a king. (*Laughs*) And they called him by his Christian names—throughout the country—just as though he *was* the King. "John Gabriel." Oh, he was a great man in their eyes, was John Gabriel.

ELLA: He *was* a great man then, Gunhild.

MRS BORKMAN: So it seemed. But he never said one word to me about his real position. He never hinted where he took his money from.

ELLA: I don't suppose any of the others suspected.

MRS BORKMAN: Oh, the others! But it was his duty to tell me the truth. And he never did. He simply lied—lied to me endlessly—

ELLA: No, Gunhild. He may have concealed the truth from you. But he didn't lie.

MRS BORKMAN: Call it what you like. It comes to the same thing. But then it all crashed about our ears. The whole magnificent edifice.

ELLA (*to herself*): Yes, everything crashed—for him—and for others.

MRS BORKMAN: But I tell you, Ella, I shall not give up. I shall find redress somehow. You can be sure of that.

ELLA: Redress? What do you mean?

MRS BORKMAN: Redress for our name, our honour, our

fortunes. For the wreck that's been made of my life. I've got a trick up my sleeve. You'll see. Someone who will redeem everything that *he* defiled!

ELLA: Gunhild!

MRS BORKMAN: Someone who will right all the wrongs his father did to me.

ELLA: You mean Erhart?

MRS BORKMAN: Yes, Erhart—my son. He will know how to restore our family, our house, our name. Everything that *can* be restored.

ELLA: How do you expect him to achieve this?

MRS BORKMAN: It'll happen some way. I don't quite know how. But it must and shall happen sometime. Tell me, Ella—honestly—hasn't this been in your mind ever since Erhart was a child?

ELLA: No, I can't say it has.

MRS BORKMAN: Then why did you take him and look after him?

ELLA: You weren't able to, Gunhild.

MRS BORKMAN: Oh, no. I wasn't able to. And his father— the law wouldn't let him—oh, he was nicely tucked away from all responsibility.

ELLA: Oh—how can you?

MRS BORKMAN: And you? How could *you* bring up the child of a—John Gabriel's child? Just as though he were your own son—take him away from me—and keep him with you, till he was nearly grown up? Why did you do it, Ella?

ELLA: I grew to love him so dearly.

MRS BORKMAN: More than I—his mother?

ELLA: That I can't judge. And Erhart was rather a weak child—

MRS BORKMAN: Erhart—weak?

ELLA: I thought so—at the time, anyway. And the air over there on the west coast is so much milder than it is here, as you know.

MRS BORKMAN (*smiles bitterly*): Hm. Is it? Oh yes, you've certainly done a great deal for Erhart. Well, you've been able to afford it. You were lucky, Ella. You managed to get back everything you'd invested.

ELLA: Not because of anything I did. I didn't know until years later that my investments in the bank had been saved.

MRS BORKMAN: Well, I don't understand these things. I merely point out that you were lucky. But when you took it on yourself to bring up Erhart for me—what was your motive then?

ELLA: My motive—?

MRS BORKMAN: Yes, you must have had some motive. What did you want to make of him? What did you want to turn him into?

ELLA: I wanted to give Erhart a chance to find happiness.

MRS BORKMAN (scornfully): Psh. People in our position have more important things to do than bother about happiness.

ELLA: What do you mean?

MRS BORKMAN: Erhart's first duty is to shine so bright that no one in this land will remember the shadow his father cast over me—and my son.

ELLA: Tell me, Gunhild—is that the aim to which Erhart has pledged his life?

MRS BORKMAN: I sincerely hope so.

ELLA: Or isn't it rather an aim to which you have pledged him?

MRS BORKMAN: I and Erhart always have the same aims.

ELLA: You are very sure of your son, aren't you, Gunhild?

MRS BORKMAN: Yes, I thank God I am.

ELLA: Then you must be happy, in spite of everything.

MRS BORKMAN: I am, as far as that goes. But then, every moment, Ella, those memories blow into my heart like a bitter wind.

ELLA: Gunhild, I might as well come to the point. There's something I have to talk to you about.

MRS BORKMAN: Yes?

ELLA: Erhart doesn't live out here with you and . . . with you, does he?

MRS BORKMAN: Obviously Erhart cannot live out here with me. He has to live in town.

ELLA: Yes, he has told me so in his letters.

MRS BORKMAN: He has to, for his studies. But he comes out to me for a while every evening.

ELLA: Yes—well, could I talk with him, now, then?

MRS BORKMAN: He hasn't come yet. But I expect him any moment.

ELLA: But, Gunhild, he must be here. I can hear him upstairs.

MRS BORKMAN (*with a quick glance*): Up in the great room?

ELLA: Yes. I've heard him walking up there ever since I arrived.

MRS BORKMAN: That isn't Erhart, Ella.

ELLA: Not Erhart? (*Beginning to suspect*) Who is it, then?

MRS BORKMAN: He.

ELLA (*quietly*): Borkman. John Gabriel Borkman.

MRS BORKMAN: He walks up and down like that. From morning till night. Day after day.

ELLA: I had heard rumours, of course—

MRS BORKMAN: I daresay people talk a good deal about us.

ELLA: Erhart hinted in his letters that his father spends most of his time alone up there, and you down here.

MRS BORKMAN: Yes. That's how we've lived, Ella. Ever since they let him out, and sent him home to me. Eight years.

ELLA: But—I didn't think it could be possible—

MRS BORKMAN: That is how it is. And it can never be otherwise.

ELLA: It must be a terrible existence, Gunhild.

MRS BORKMAN: I don't think I can stand it much longer.

ELLA: I can imagine—

MRS BORKMAN: Hearing his footsteps up there the whole time. From early morning until late at night. They sound so loud down here.

ELLA: Yes.

MRS BORKMAN: I often feel as though I had a sick wolf padding in a cage up there in the great room. Right above my head. (*Listens and whispers*) Listen, Ella! Listen! To and fro, to and fro, the wolf pads.

139

ELLA (*gently*): Couldn't you do something about it, Gunhild?

MRS BORKMAN: He has never made any move towards me.

ELLA: Couldn't you make the first move?

MRS BORKMAN: I? After all he has done to me? No, thank you. Let the wolf pad in his cage.

ELLA: It's too hot for me in here. I will take my coat off after all.

MRS BORKMAN: Well, I did ask you. (ELLA *takes off her hat and coat*).

ELLA: Don't you ever meet him outside the house?

MRS BORKMAN (*laughs bitterly*): At parties, you mean?

ELLA: I mean when he goes for a walk.

MRS BORKMAN: He never goes out.

ELLA: Not even when it's dark?

MRS BORKMAN: No. His cape and hat hang there in the cupboard. In the hall—you know—

ELLA (*to herself*:) The cupboard we used to play in as children—

MRS BORKMAN (*nods*): Sometimes—late at night—I hear him come down to put them on and go out. But he always stops halfway down the stairs—and turns—and goes back to his room.

ELLA (*quietly*:) Don't any of his old friends ever come to see him?

MRS BORKMAN: He has no old friends.

ELLA: He had so many.

MRS BORKMAN: Ha! He rid himself of them all right. He was dear to his friends, was John Gabriel Borkman.

ELLA: Yes, I suppose so.

MRS BORKMAN (*vehemently*): Though I must say it's mean and paltry and contemptible of people to attach so much importance to the little loss they sustained through him. After all, it was only money.

ELLA: So he lives up there, completely alone.

MRS BORKMAN: I have heard there's an old copyist or bank clerk who visits him now and again.

ELLA: Ah, yes. That must be Foldal. I know they've been friends since boyhood.

MRS BORKMAN: I believe so. I don't know anything else about him. He never mixed with us. In the days when we mixed with people.

ELLA: But now he comes to see Borkman?

MRS BORKMAN: Yes, he can't afford to be particular. Of course, he only comes after dark.

ELLA: Foldal—wasn't he one of the people who lost their money when the bank failed?

MRS BORKMAN: I seem to remember he did lose some money. Nothing to talk about.

ELLA: It was all he had.

MRS BORKMAN (*smiles*): Oh, but dear God, what he had! It was nothing—only a few pounds. Not worth mentioning.

ELLA: It wasn't mentioned, either, was it, at the trial? By Foldal, I mean.

MRS BORKMAN: Anyway, I can tell you Erhart has more than compensated him for the little he lost.

ELLA: Erhart! How did he manage to do that?

MRS BORKMAN: He's taken Foldal's youngest daughter under his wing. Helped her with her reading, so that she'll be able to make something of herself, and support herself when she's older. You see! That's a great deal more than her father could ever have done for her.

ELLA: Yes, her father must be having a hard time of it now.

MRS BORKMAN: And Erhart's arranged for her to study music. She's already become so good at it that she's able to come up—go upstairs and play for him.

ELLA: So he still likes music?

MRS BORKMAN: I suppose he does. And he has the piano you sent out here when—before he came back.

ELLA: And she plays to him?

MRS BORKMAN: Yes, now and again. In the evenings. Erhart arranged that, too.

ELLA: But doesn't that mean the poor girl has to walk all the way from town and back again?

MRS BORKMAN: No, Erhart's arranged for her to lodge with a lady who lives near here. A Mrs Wilton—

ELLA (*suddenly alert*): Mrs Wilton?

141

MRS BORKMAN: A very rich lady. You don't know her.

ELLA: I've heard her name. Mrs Fanny Wilton, isn't it?

MRS BORKMAN: Yes, that's right.

ELLA: Erhart's mentioned her several times in his letters. Does she live out here now?

MRS BORKMAN: Yes, she's rented a villa here. She moved out of town some while ago.

ELLA: They say—she's said to be divorced.

MRS BORKMAN: I believe her husband died several years ago.

ELLA: Yes, but they were divorced. He divorced her.

MRS BORKMAN: He left her. It wasn't her fault.

ELLA: Do you know her well, Gunhild?

MRS BORKMAN: Yes, quite well. She lives nearby and calls occasionally.

ELLA: And you like her?

MRS BORKMAN: She's a woman of very shrewd judgment. She understands Erhart. All his thoughts, all his feelings. And of course she's come to idolise him—as one must.

ELLA. Perhaps she knows Erhart even better than she knows you?

MRS BORKMAN: Yes, he used to meet her quite often in town. Before she came to live out here.

ELLA (*involuntarily*): And yet she moved away from town?

MRS BORKMAN (*looks sharply at her*): Yet—? What do you mean?

ELLA: Mean? Why, good heavens, I—!

MRS BORKMAN: You said that in such a curious way. You meant something, Ella.

ELLA: Yes, Gunhild. I did mean something.

MRS BORKMAN: Well?

ELLA: First I want to tell you that I think I, too, have a kind of claim on Erhart. Perhaps you don't agree?

MRS BORKMAN: I am hardly in a position to disagree. After all the money you have spent on him—

ELLA: Oh, not because of that, Gunhild. Because I love him.

MRS BORKMAN (*smiles*): Can you really love my son? In spite of everything.

ELLA: Yes, in spite of everything, I do. I love Erhart. As dearly as I can love any human being, now that I am old.

MRS BORKMAN: Yes, yes, but—

ELLA: So, you see, as soon as I feel that anything threatens him I become worried.

MRS BORKMAN: Threatens Erhart? What threatens him? Or—who threatens him?

ELLA: You, for one. In your way.

MRS BORKMAN: I!

ELLA: And this Mrs Wilton—I'm afraid of her, too—

MRS BORKMAN: *You* can believe such a thing of Erhart! Of my own son! He has a great mission to fulfil—(*looks at her, speechless*).

ELLA (*contemptuously*): Mission!

MRS BORKMAN: How dare you refer to it in that tone!

ELLA: Do you think a healthy, gay young man of Erhart's age is going to sacrifice himself for any mission?

MRS BORKMAN: Erhart will. I know it. I am sure.

ELLA: You don't know it. You don't even believe it, Gunhild.

MRS BORKMAN: *I* don't believe it?

ELLA: It's simply something you dream of, because if you didn't have that hope to cling to you know you would despair utterly.

MRS BORKMAN: Yes, Then I would utterly despair. Perhaps that's what you really want, Ella dear.

ELLA: Yes—if you can't find peace except by making Erhart suffer.

MRS BORKMAN: You want to come between us. Between mother and son. You!

ELLA: I want to get him out of your clutches.

MRS BORKMAN: You can't do that any longer. You had him in your clutches till he was fifteen. But now I've won him back.

ELLA: Then I will win him again. We two have fought for a man before, Gunhild.

MRS BORKMAN: Yes, and I won.

ELLA: Do you still think you gained by your victory?

MRS BORKMAN: My God, no.

ELLA: You won't gain anything this time, either.

MRS BORKMAN: No gain—to keep a mother's hold over her son?

ELLA: No. It's only the power you want.

MRS BORKMAN: What about you?

ELLA: I want his heart—his mind—his whole soul—

MRS BORKMAN: That you will never have again.

ELLA: You've seen to that, have you?

MRS BORKMAN (*smiles*): Couldn't you tell from his letters?

ELLA (*nods slowly*): I recognised your hand in those last letters of his.

MRS BORKMAN: I have used these eight years while I have had him under my eyes, you may be sure.

ELLA: What have you told Erhart about me? Dare you tell me?

MRS BORKMAN: Oh, yes, I am not afraid to tell you. I have simply told him the truth.

ELLA: Well?

MRS BORKMAN: I have continually impressed upon him that it is you we have to thank for the fact that we are able to live as comfortably as we do. That we are able to live at all.

ELLA: But Erhart knew this already.

MRS BORKMAN: He used to be under the impression that you had done it all simply out of kindness. He doesn't believe that any longer, Ella.

ELLA: What does he believe now?

MRS BORKMAN: The truth. I asked him how he could explain why Aunt Ella never came to visit us.

ELLA: He already knew.

MRS BORKMAN: He knows better now. You'd led him to believe that you'd stayed away to spare my feelings and—those of that man who walks upstairs.

ELLA: So I did.

MRS BORKMAN: Erhart doesn't believe that any longer.

ELLA: What have you got him to believe about me now?

MRS BORKMAN: He believes the truth—that you're ashamed of us—that you despise us. Or don't you? Didn't you once consider taking him away from me for good? Think, Ella. You haven't forgotten.

ELLA: That was when the scandal was at its height. When the case was before the court. I don't want that any longer.

MRS BORKMAN: It wouldn't be any good if you did. Erhart needs me, not you. As far as you're concerned, he's dead; and as far as he's concerned, you're dead.

ELLA: We shall see. I have decided to stay here.

MRS BORKMAN: In this house?

ELLA: Yes.

MRS BORKMAN: Overnight, you mean?

ELLA: For the rest of my life, if need be.

MRS BORKMAN: Yes, yes, Ella. The house is yours, of course.

ELLA: Oh, Gunhild—

MRS BORKMAN: Everything here is yours. The chair I am sitting on is yours. The bed in which I toss sleeplessly at night belongs to you. The food we eat comes to us by your good grace.

ELLA: It can't be done any other way. Borkman can't own anything. Someone or other would very quickly come and claim it.

MRS BORKMAN: Yes, I know. We have to exist on your charity, and be grateful.

ELLA: If you want to look at it that way, I can't stop you.

MRS BORKMAN: No, you can't. When do you want us to move out?

ELLA: Move out?

MRS BORKMAN: Yes. You don't imagine for a moment, do you, that I will live under the same roof as you? I'd rather go to the workhouse, or tramp the roads.

ELLA: Very well. Then let Erhart come with me.

MRS BORKMAN: Erhart! My son! My own child!

ELLA: Yes. If you do, I shall go straight home again.

MRS BORKMAN: Erhart shall choose between us.

ELLA: Dare you let him, Gunhild?

MRS BORKMAN (laughs): Dare I let my own son choose between his mother and you?

ELLA (listening): Is someone coming? I think I can hear—

MRS BORKMAN: It must be Erhart!

There is a sharp rap on the door leading from the hall, and it is at once opened. MRS WILTON, *in evening dress and overcoat, enters. Behind her the* MAID, *who has not had time to announce her, stands confused. The door remains half open.* MRS WILTON *is a strikingly handsome woman in her thirties, with a fine figure, broad, red smiling lips, playful eyes and rich, dark hair.*

MRS WILTON: Dear Mrs Borkman, good evening.

MRS BORKMAN (*drily*): Good evening. (*To* MAID, *pointing to garden room*) Take that lamp out, and light it.

      MAID *takes lamp and goes out.*

MRS WILTON (*noticing* ELLA): Oh, forgive me—I see you have a visitor—

MRS BORKMAN: Only my sister. She's come to visit me—

ERHART BORKMAN *throws the half-open door wide, and rushes in. He is a young man with shining, gay eyes. Elegantly dressed. The beginnings of a moustache.*

ERHART (*joyfully, as he stands in the doorway*): Has Aunt Ella come? (*Runs to her. and seizes her hand*) Aunt Ella? It can't be possible! Are you here?

ELLA (*embracing him*): Erhart! My dear, dear boy! How tall you've grown! Oh, how good it is to see you again!

MRS BORKMAN: What does this mean, Erhart? Have you been hiding in the hall?

MRS WILTON: Erhart—Mr Borkman came with me.

MRS BORKMAN: I see, Erhart. You visit other people before your mother?

ERHART: I had to call in on Mrs Wilton for a few minutes to collect Frida.

MRS BORKMAN: Is—Miss Foldal with you too, then?

MRS WILTON: Yes, she's standing out in the porch.

ERHART (*speaking through the open door*): You can go upstairs now, Frida.

Pause. ELLA *watches* ERHART. *He seems embarrassed and rather impatient. His face has become tense and colder. The* MAID *brings the lighted lamp into the garden room, goes out, and closes the door behind her.*

MRS BORKMAN (*with forced politeness*): Well, Mrs Wilton—
if you'd care to join us for the evening, please—

MRS WILTON: Thank you so much, dear Mrs Borkman.
We have another engagement—we are going to visit Mr
Hinkel, the lawyer.

MRS BORKMAN: We? Whom do you mean by we?

MRS WILTON (*smiling*): Well, I only really mean myself.
But Mrs Hinkel and her daughters made me promise to
bring your son with me if I should happen to meet him.

MRS BORKMAN: As you apparently have done.

MRS WILTON: Yes, as luck would have it—since he was so
kind as to look in on me—on little Frida's account.

MRS BORKMAN (*drily*): Erhart, I wasn't aware you knew these
people, the—Hinkels.

ERHART: I don't really know them. You know best, mother,
whom I know or don't know.

MRS WILTON (*laughs*): There is no formality in that house.
They are gay, friendly, hospitable people. Plenty of young
ladies.

MRS BORKMAN: If I know my son, that is hardly the right
company for him, Mrs Wilton.

MRS WILTON: But, good heavens, dear Mrs Borkman, he is
young, too.

MRS BORKMAN: Yes, I am glad to say, he is young.

ERHART (*concealing his impatience*): Oh, all right, mother.
Of course I won't visit the Hinkels this evening. I'll stay
with you and Aunt Ella.

MRS BORKMAN: I knew you would, Erhart dear.

ELLA: No, Erhart—please don't put it off for my sake.

ERHART: Yes, Aunt Ella, of course I will. (*Glances uncertainly
at* MRS WILTON) But will it be all right? Can we get out
of it? You've already accepted on my behalf.

MRS WILTON: What nonsense you talk! "Can we get out of
it?" When I come down to those bright, festive rooms,
alone, abandoned—think of it!—I shall simply say: "No"
—on your behalf.

ERHART (*reluctantly*): Oh well, if you think it'll be all right—

MRS WILTON: I'm quite used to saying "No" to people; as

I am to saying "Yes". And how can you think of abandoning your aunt now, just when she's arrived? Shame on you, Monsieur Erhart—is that a way to behave towards your mother?

MRS BORKMAN: Mother?

MRS WILTON: Foster-mother, I should have said, Mrs Borkman.

MRS BORKMAN: That would be more correct.

MRS WILTON: Oh, I think one has more reason to be grateful to a good foster-mother than to one's real mother. *I* think.

MRS BORKMAN: Is that your own experience?

MRS WILTON: Heaven bless you, no, I hardly knew my mother. But if I had had such a wonderful foster-mother as Erhart, I might not have become such a wicked woman as they say I am. (*Turns to* ERHART) You stay at home with your mother and aunt and have a nice cup of tea, young man. (*To the* LADIES) Goodbye, goodbye, dear Mrs Borkman. Goodbye, Miss Rentheim.

They bow silently. She goes towards the door.

ERHART (*going after her*): Let me see you on your way.

MRS WILTON (*at the door*): Not a yard. I am quite used to finding my way alone. But, be careful, Master Borkman—I am warning you.

ERHART: Why should I be careful?

MRS WILTON: Because while I am going down the road—alone and abandoned—I shall try to cast a spell on you.

ERHART (*laughs*): Are you going to try that again?

MRS WILTON: Yes; so take care. While I walk down to the house, I shall say to myself, with all the magic I can command; "Master Erhart Borkman, put on your hat".

MRS BORKMAN: And you think he will?

MRS WILTON (*laughing*): Bless you, yes—he'll pick it up at once. Then I shall say: "Put on your overcoat, Erhart Borkman! And your galoshes. Please don't forget your galoshes. And come after me. Obey. Obey. Obey."

ERHART: I shall do as you command me.

MRS WILTON (*with raised forefinger*): Obey! Obey! Goodnight! (*Laughs, nods to the ladies, and closes the door behind her*).

MRS BORKMAN: Does she really practise such tricks?

ERHART: No, how can you think that? It was only a joke. Don't let's talk about Mrs Wilton, now.

He indicates to ELLA to seat herself in the easy chair by the stove, and stands for a moment looking at her.

So you've really come all the way to see us, Aunt Ella? And in winter!

ELLA: I had to in the end, Erhart.

ERHART: Had to? Why?

ELLA: I had to come and have a word with the doctors.

ERHART: Well, that's good.

ELLA (*smiles*): Good?

ERHART: Yes, that you finally made up your mind to see them.

MRS BORKMAN (*on the sofa, coldly*): Are you not well, Ella?

ELLA: You know I'm not well.

MRS BORKMAN: Well, you've been ailing for years—

ERHART: When I was staying with you, I told you you ought to see a doctor.

ELLA: Oh, there isn't anybody I have any faith in out there. Besides, I didn't feel too bad in those days.

ERHART: Are you worse now, Aunt Ella?

ELLA: Yes, my boy. I am rather worse now.

ERHART: Not dangerously?

ELLA: It depends on what you think of as dangerous.

ERHART: Then you mustn't go home too soon.

ELLA: No, I don't think I shall.

ERHART: You must stay here in the town. Here you have all the best doctors to choose from.

ELLA: Yes, I had that in mind when I left home.

ERHART: And you must take care to find yourself somewhere really nice to stay—some hotel where it's cosy and peaceful.

ELLA: I booked in this morning at that old hotel I used to stay at.

149

ERHART: Yes, you'll enjoy it there.

ELLA: Well, I don't think I shall be staying there after all.

ERHART: Oh? Why not?

ELLA: I changed my mind when I came out here.

ERHART: You—changed your mind?

MRS BORKMAN (*crocheting, without looking up*): Your aunt wants to live here, on her estate, Erhart.

ERHART: Here? With us? With *us*? Is this true, Aunt Ella?

ELLA: Yes. I have decided to do that now.

MRS BORKMAN: It all belongs to your aunt, you know.

ELLA: Yes. So I shall be staying out here, Erhart. For a while. I shall manage for myself. Over in the bailiff's wing—

ERHART: What a good idea! Your things are still there, aren't they? But, I say, Aunt Ella, aren't you very tired after your journey?

ELLA: Well, yes, I am a little.

ERHART: Then I think you ought to go to bed early. Really early.

ELLA (*looks at him, smiling*): Yes, I think I shall.

ERHART: Then we can have a real talk tomorrow—or some time. About everything. You and mother and I. That would be much better, wouldn't it, Aunt Ella?

MRS BORKMAN (*rising from the sofa*): Erhart, you want to leave me, don't you?

ERHART: What do you mean?

MRS BORKMAN: You want to go down to the Hinkels.

ERHART: Oh, that. Well, you don't want me to keep Aunt Ella up half the night, do you? She's ill, mother. Remember that.

MRS BORKMAN: You want to go to the Hinkels, Erhart?

ERHART (*impatiently*): But, good heavens, Mother, I don't see how I can not go. Or what do you think, Aunt Ella?

ELLA: You must do what you want to, Erhart.

MRS BORKMAN: You want to get him away from me!

ELLA (*rising*): Yes, Gunhild. If it's possible.

Music is heard from above.

ERHART: I can't stand this any longer. Where is my hat? (*To* ELLA) Do you recognise that music from upstairs?

ELLA: No. What is it?

ERHART: It is the danse macabre. The dance of death. Don't you recognise the dance of death, Aunt Ella?

ELLA (*smiles sadly*): Not yet, Erhart.

ERHART: Mother—I beg you, please—let me go.

MRS BORKMAN: You want to leave your mother?

ERHART: I'll be back again. Tomorrow, perhaps.

MRS BORKMAN: You want to leave me! You prefer to be with strangers! With—no, I won't think about it!

ERHART: There are lights down there, and young faces, happy faces—and music, mother.

MRS BORKMAN (*pointing up to the ceiling*): There is music up there too, Erhart.

ERHART: Yes, and that music is driving me out of the house.

ELLA: Do you grudge your father his few moments of forgetfulness?

ERHART: I don't grudge him anything. Let him enjoy his music. As long as I don't have to listen to it.

MRS BORKMAN: Be strong, Erhart! Strong, my son. Never forget that you have a mission in life. A great mission.

ERHART: Oh, mother, stop preaching. I wasn't made to be a missionary. Goodnight, Aunt Ella. Goodnight, mother. (*Runs quickly out through the door*).

MRS BORKMAN (*after a short silence*): You got him back quickly, didn't you, Ella?

ELLA: I wish I could believe that.

MRS BORKMAN: But you won't keep him for long. You'll see.

ELLA: Because of you?

MRS BORKMAN: Because of me. Or—her.

ELLA: I'd rather she had him than you.

MRS BORKMAN (*nods slowly*): That I can understand. I say the same. I'd rather she had him that you.

ELLA: However it might end for him?

MRS BORKMAN: I hardly think I care about that any longer.

ELLA (*takes her overcoat over her arm*): For the first time in our lives, we twins agree. Goodnight, Gunhild. (*Goes out through the hall*).

The music sounds louder from upstairs.

MRS BORKMAN: The wolf howls again. The sick wolf. (*Stands for a moment, then throws herself to the floor, and moans softly*) Erhart, Erhart! Be loyal to me. Come home and help your mother. I can't bear this life any longer.

ACT TWO

The great drawing-room—or rather, what was formerly the drawing-room—upstairs in the Rentheim house. The walls are covered with old tapestries, portraying hunting scenes, shepherds and shepherdesses, all in faded colours. In the left-hand wall are folding doors. Downstage a piano. In the corner of the rear wall, left, a concealed door flush with the wall. In the middle of the right-hand wall, a large, carved oak desk, covered with many books and papers. Further downstage right is a sofa, with table and chairs. All the furniture is severe Empire style. On the desk and the table stand lighted lamps.

JOHN GABRIEL BORKMAN *stands with his hands behind his back by the piano, listening to* FRIDA FOLDAL *who, seated, is playing the last bars of the* danse macabre.

BORKMAN *is of medium height, trimly and strongly built, in his sixties. Distinguished appearance, finely carved profile, sharp eyes and grey-white, curling hair and beard. He is dressed in a black, rather old-fashioned suit, with a white cravat.* FRIDA FOLDAL *is a pretty, pale girl of fifteen, with a somewhat tired and strained expression, cheaply dressed in a light-coloured frock.*

The music ends. Silence.

BORKMAN: Can you guess where I first heard music like that?
FRIDA (*looking up at him*): No, Mr Borkman.
BORKMAN: Down in the mines.
FRIDA (*not understanding*): Really? Down in the mines?
BORKMAN: I am a miner's son, as you know. Or perhaps you didn't know that?

FRIDA: No, Mr Borkman.

BORKMAN: A miner's son. And sometimes my father took me down with him into the mines. Down there, the iron ore sings.

FRIDA: It sings?

BORKMAN (*nods*): When it is broken loose. The hammer-blows that loosen it are the midnight bell that sets it free. And then, in its own way, the iron sings—for joy.

FRIDA: Why does it do that, Mr Borkman?

BORKMAN: It wants to be taken up into the daylight, and serve humanity.

He walks up and down the floor of the room, keeping his hands behind his back.

FRIDA (*sits for a moment, waiting; glances at her watch, and gets up*): If you'll excuse me, Mr Borkman, I'm afraid I must go now.

BORKMAN (*stops in front of her*): Are you going already?

FRIDA (*putting her music in her portfolio*): Yes, I have to. (*Embarrassed*) I've been engaged to play somewhere else this evening.

BORKMAN: At a party?

FRIDA: Yes.

BORKMAN: And you are to play for the guests?

FRIDA: No. I'm to provide the dance music.

BORKMAN: Only dance music?

FRIDA: Yes—they want to dance after supper.

BORKMAN (*stands gazing at her*): Do you like that—playing dance music in peoples' houses?

FRIDA (*putting on her overcoat*): Well, yes, when I can get an engagement. They always pay me something.

BORKMAN: And that is what you think about while you play and they dance?

FRIDA: No, most of the time I think how nice it would be if I could join in the dance, too.

BORKMAN (*nods*): I thought as much. (*Begins to walk restlessly across the floor again*) Yes, yes, yes. Not be able to join in oneself—that is the heaviest burden of all. (*Stops*)

But there is one thought that should compensate you, Frida.

FRIDA: What's that, Mr Borkman?

BORKMAN: The fact that you have ten times more music in you than all the dancers put together.

FRIDA (*smiles*): Oh, I'm not so sure about that.

BORKMAN (*points his finger at her*): Don't be foolish, girl. Never doubt yourself.

FRIDA: Even if nobody else believes in you?

BORKMAN: As long as you yourself are sure, that is enough. Where are you to play this evening?

FRIDA: Over at Mr Hinkel's.

BORKMAN (*looks sharply at her*): Hinkel—the lawyer?

FRIDA: Yes.

BORKMAN: Do people visit that man's house? Does he have guests?

FRIDA: Yes, a lot of people are going to be there, I heard Mrs Wilton say.

BORKMAN: But what kind of people? Can you tell me that?

FRIDA: No, I don't really know. Oh, yes—I know young Mr Borkman will be there this evening.

BORKMAN: Erhart? My son?

FRIDA: Yes. He's going.

BORKMAN: Where did you hear that?

FRIDA: He said so himself. An hour ago.

BORKMAN: Is he out here today?

FRIDA: Yes, he's been at Mrs Wilton's all afternoon.

BORKMAN: Do you know if he has been here, too? I mean, if he has come to speak to anyone downstairs?

FRIDA: Yes, I think he looked in on Mrs Borkman.

BORKMAN: Aha. I see.

FRIDA: But she had a strange lady with her, I think.

BORKMAN: Had she? Indeed. Oh well, I suppose people visit her now and then.

FRIDA: If I meet Mr Erhart this evening, shall I tell him to come up here and see you too?

BORKMAN (*gruffly*): No. Don't tell him any such thing. If anyone wants to visit me, let him come. I ask favours of no one.

FRIDA: Oh, well then, I won't say anything. Goodnight, Mr Borkman.

BORKMAN (*starts walking again, growling to himself*): Goodnight.

FRIDA: May I run down the back stairs? It's quicker.

BORKMAN: Great heavens, run down what staircase you like. Goodnight to you.

FRIDA: Goodnight, Mr Borkman.

Goes out through the small concealed door upstage left. BORKMAN *goes meditatively over to the piano and makes to close it, but does not bother. Looks at the emptiness around him, and begins again to pace up and down the floor from the corner by the piano to the corner upstage right. Restless and uneasy the whole time. At length he goes to the desk, cocks an ear towards the folding doors, picks up a hand-mirror quickly, looks in it and arranges his cravat. There is a knock on the door.* BORKMAN *listens, gives a quick glance towards the door, but remains silent. After a moment, the knock is repeated, more loudly.*

BORKMAN (*standing at the desk, his left hand resting on the desk top and his right hand thrust into the breast of his coat*): Come in.

VILHELM FOLDAL *cautiously enters the room. He is a bent, worn-out man with mild blue eyes and long, thin grey hair which hangs down over his coat collar. He carries a portfolio under his arm, a soft felt hat in his hand, and big horn spectacles pushed up on to his forehead.*

BORKMAN (*changes position, and gives the newcomer a disappointed yet friendly look*): Oh, it's you.

FOLDAL: A good evening to you, John Gabriel. Yes, indeed it's me.

BORKMAN: Anyway, you're very late.

FOLDAL: Well, it's quite a distance. Especially on foot.

BORKMAN: But why do you always walk, Vilhelm? The tram goes practically by your door.

FOLDAL: Walking's healthier. And saves twopence. Well, has Frida been up to play for you this evening?

BORKMAN: She left this very moment. I'm surprised you didn't meet her outside.

FOLDAL: No. I haven't seen her for a long time. Ever since she went out to live with Mrs Wilton.

BORKMAN (*sits on the sofa and waves his hand towards a chair*): Do take a chair, Vilhelm.

FOLDAL (*sits on the edge of a chair*): Thank you very much. (*Looks gloomily at him*) You can't imagine how lonely I've been since Frida left home.

BORKMAN: What nonsense. You've still got all the others.

FOLDAL: God knows I have. Five of them. But Frida was the only one who understood me a little. (*Shakes his head miserably*) None of the others understand me at all.

BORKMAN (*darkly, looks into space and drums his fingers on the table*): Yes. That is the curse, the burden we chosen men have to bear. The masses, the mediocre millions—they do not understand us, Vilhelm.

FOLDAL: I could do without being understood. If one's patient, that may come. But there's something worse.

BORKMAN: Nothing can be worse than that.

FOLDAL: Well, I don't agree with you, John Gabriel. I've had a dreadful scene at home, just before I came here.

BORKMAN: Indeed? Why?

FOLDAL: My family—they despise me.

BORKMAN: Despise you?

FOLDAL (*wipes his eyes*): I've been aware of it for some time. But today it all came out.

BORKMAN (*is silent for a moment*): You didn't make a very good choice when you married, did you, Vilhelm?

FOLDAL: I didn't have much choice. Besides, one wants to get married when one's getting on in years. Especially when you're in such straitened circumstances as I was—

BORKMAN (*springs up in anger*): What is this? An accusation? A reproach?

FOLDAL: Oh no, for God's sake, John Gabriel—

BORKMAN: You're harping on the bank disaster, aren't you?

FOLDAL: But I don't blame you for that. God forbid—

BORKMAN (*sits down again, growling*): Well, I'm glad to hear it.

FOLDAL: You mustn't think it's my wife I complain about. She hasn't much education, poor thing, I must admit. But she's a good soul. No, it's the children—

BORKMAN: I might have known.

FOLDAL: The children—they're educated, you see. They expect more from life.

BORKMAN (*looks at him sympathetically*): So your children despise you, Vilhelm?

FOLDAL (*shrugs his shoulders*): Well, I haven't made much of a career, I must admit.

BORKMAN (*leans closer and places his hand on* FOLDAL'S *arm*): Don't they know that you wrote a play when you were young—a tragedy?

FOLDAL: Yes, of course they know, but that doesn't seem to impress them very much.

BORKMAN: Then they lack judgment, Vilhelm. Your tragedy is good. I believe that sincerely.

FOLDAL: Yes, there is quite a lot of good stuff in it, don't you think, John Gabriel? Oh dear, if I could only get it put on! (*Opens the portfolio and fumbles eagerly in it*) Look! I want to show you a change I've made—

BORKMAN: You have it with you?

FOLDAL: Yes, I brought it along. It's so long since I read it to you, I thought it might entertain you to listen to an act or two—

BORKMAN (*getting up*): No, no, some other time.

FOLDAL: Well, well. As you like.

BORKMAN *walks to and fro across the floor.* FOLDAL *puts the manuscript back into the portfolio.*

BORKMAN (*stops in front of him*): You were right just now, when you said you hadn't made a career. But this I promise you, Vilhelm—the day I am rehabilitated—

FOLDAL (*begins to rise*): Oh thank you very much.

BORKMAN (*with a wave of his hand*): Sit down, please, Vilhelm. The day I am rehabilitated—when they realise they cannot do without me—when they come up to me in this room and get down on their knees and implore me to take over control of the bank again—the new bank they have founded—but cannot run—(*Stops by the desk as before, and strikes his chest*) I shall stand *here* to receive them. And throughout the land men will ask and learn what conditions John Gabriel Borkman lays down—(*Pauses suddenly and stares at* FOLDAL) You look doubtingly at me. Perhaps you don't believe they will come? They must—must—must come to me—some time. You do believe that, don't you?

FOLDAL: Yes, yes, God knows I do, John Gabriel.

BORKMAN (*sits on the sofa again*): I am sure of it. Absolutely certain—that they will come. Were I not certain—I should have put a bullet through my head long ago.

FOLDAL: No, for heaven's sake—

BORKMAN: But they will come! Oh, they will come! You'll see. I expect them any day, any hour. And as you see, I hold myself perpetually in readiness to receive them.

FOLDAL (*with a sigh*): If only they would come soon.

BORKMAN (*restlessly*): Yes, Vilhelm. Time passes; the years pass; life—no, I dare not think of it. (*Looks at him*) Do you know how I sometimes feel?

FOLDAL: How?

BORKMAN: Like a Napoleon, maimed in his first battle.

FOLDAL (*puts his hand on his portfolio*): Ah—I know that feeling.

BORKMAN: You can hardly compare the two situations.

FOLDAL: My little world of poetry means much to me, John Gabriel.

BORKMAN: Yes, but I—I could have created millions! Think of all the mines I could have brought under my control, the shafts I could have sunk. I would have harnessed cataracts—hewn quarries. My ships would have covered the world, linking continent to continent. All this I would have created alone.

FOLDAL: Yes, I know. Nothing was too big for you.

BORKMAN: And now I have to sit here like a wounded eagle, watching other men sneak in and steal it from me, piece by piece.

FOLDAL: It's just the same for me.

BORKMAN: I was so close to my goal. I only needed eight days to consolidate my position. Every deposit would have been redeemed. All the money I had used so boldly would have been back in its place. All the stupendous enterprises I had planned were within a hair's breath of being realised. No one would have lost a penny.

FOLDAL: My word, yes, how nearly you succeeded.

BORKMAN: And then, in those last crucial days, I was betrayed. (*Looks at* FOLDAL) Do you know what I hold to be the ultimate treachery a man can commit?

FOLDAL: No, tell me.

BORKMAN: Not murder. Not robbery or perjury. Those are crimes one commits against people one hates or is indifferent to.

FOLDAL: What is it then, John Gabriel?

BORKMAN: The ultimate crime is to abuse the trust of a friend.

FOLDAL: Yes, but wait a moment—

BORKMAN: You don't have to say it—I can see it in your face. But you're wrong. All those who had their money in the bank would have got it back. To the last farthing. No, Vilhelm—the ultimate crime a man can commit is to abuse the trust of a friend, publish his letters to the world, letters written in confidence, to be read by one person only, like a whisper in an empty, dark, locked room. The man who can stoop to such means is poisoned through and through, and rotted by evil. But such a friend I had. And it was he who broke me.

FOLDAL: I think I know whom you mean.

BORKMAN: There wasn't a detail of my affairs I didn't reveal to him. And then, when the moment was ripe, he turned against me the weapon I had placed in his hand.

FOLDAL: I've never been able to understand why he—of course, there was a rumour at the time.

BORKMAN: Rumour! What rumour? Tell me. I never heard anything. I was—confined at once. What was this rumour, Vilhelm?

FOLDAL: I heard they wanted to make you a Cabinet Minister.

BORKMAN: It was offered to me. But I refused.

FOLDAL: Then you didn't stand in his way there?

BORKMAN: Oh, no. That wasn't why he betrayed me.

FOLDAL: Well, then I simply don't understand.

BORKMAN: I may as well tell you. There was a woman, Vilhelm.

FOLDAL: A woman? But, John Gabriel—?

BORKMAN: A stupid business. Finished—we won't say any more about it. (*Sardonically*) Neither of us became a Cabinet Minister in the end.

FOLDAL: But he climbed.

BORKMAN: And I sank.

FOLDAL: Yes, what a tragedy—

BORKMAN: Yes. When I think about it, it seems almost as tragic as your play.

FOLDAL (*innocently*): Quite as tragic.

BORKMAN (*laughs quietly*): But if you look at it another way, it is really a kind of comedy.

FOLDAL: A comedy?

BORKMAN: You didn't meet Frida when you came this evening?

FOLDAL: No.

BORKMAN: While we two sit here, she is sitting down there playing dance music for the man who betrayed and ruined me.

FOLDAL: Believe me, John Gabriel, I had no idea.

BORKMAN: Yes. She gathered up her music and left me—for that fine house.

FOLDAL (*apologetically*): Yes, yes, poor child—

BORKMAN: And can you guess for whom she will be playing there?

FOLDAL: Who?

BORKMAN: My son, Vilhelm.

FOLDAL: What?

BORKMAN: Yes, Vilhelm; what do you think of that? My son is dancing in his house tonight. Is not that a comedy?

FOLDAL: Yes, but—he doesn't know, surely.

BORKMAN: What doesn't he know?

FOLDAL: He doesn't know how he—how this man—er—

BORKMAN: You may use his name. I can endure it now.

FOLDAL: I'm sure your son doesn't know what happened between you, John Gabriel.

BORKMAN: He knows, Vilhelm. As surely as I sit here.

FOLDAL: If he did, do you think he'd go there?

BORKMAN: I don't suppose my son sees things with my eyes. I dare swear he sides with my enemies. Doubtless he believes, as they do, that Hinkel only did his damned duty as a lawyer when he came forward and betrayed me.

FOLDAL: But, John Gabriel, who could have put that idea into his head?

BORKMAN: Who? You forget who brought him up. First his aunt—from the time when he was six or seven years old. And now his mother.

FOLDAL: I think you're being unjust.

BORKMAN: I am never unjust. Both those women have turned him against me, I tell you!

FOLDAL (*meekly*): Yes, yes, if you say so.

BORKMAN: Women! They corrupt and pervert our lives. They deflect us from our destinies, rob us of our triumphs.

FOLDAL: Not all women.

BORKMAN: Indeed? Name me one who is worthy.

FOLDAL: No, it's true. The few I know aren't worth much.

BORKMAN: What's the use then—if such women exist, but one does not know them?

FOLDAL: Yes, John Gabriel, it makes a world of difference. It's a rare and blessed thought that somewhere on earth, far away perhaps, there lives the true woman.

BORKMAN: Oh, spare me your poet's twaddle.

FOLDAL: Do you call my most sacred belief poet's twaddle?

BORKMAN: I do! That's why you've never got anywhere. If you would only forego all this nonsense, I could still help you back on to your feet again—help you to make a career.

FOLDAL: Oh, you couldn't do that.

BORKMAN: I can. Once I am returned to power.

FOLDAL: But that's a very remote prospect.

BORKMAN: Perhaps you think the time will never come? Answer me!

FOLDAL: I don't know what to say.

BORKMAN (*rises, cold and aloof, and waves his hand towards the door*): Then I have no further use for you.

FOLDAL (*rising from his chair*): No use—?

BORKMAN: If you do not believe that my fortunes will change—

FOLDAL: But that would be against all reason—you'd have to be rehabilitated first—

BORKMAN: Go on. Go on.

FOLDAL: I never sat for my degree, I admit, but I've read enough to know—

BORKMAN: You think it's impossible?

FOLDAL: There's no precedent.

BORKMAN: Precedents are for ordinary people.

FOLDAL: The law doesn't discriminate.

BORKMAN (*with harsh finality*): You are no poet, Vilhelm.

FOLDAL: Do you really mean that?

BORKMAN: We are simply wasting each other's time. You had better not come again.

FOLDAL: You want me to go, then?

BORKMAN (*without looking at him*): I have no further use for you.

FOLDAL (*humbly, taking his portfolio*): No, no. As you wish.

BORKMAN: In other words, you have been lying to me all these years.

FOLDAL: Never lied, John Gabriel.

BORKMAN: Haven't you sat here and built up my hopes and beliefs with lies?

FOLDAL: It wasn't a lie, as long as you believed in my vocation. As long as you believed in me, I believed in you.

BORKMAN: Then we have deceived each other. And perhaps we have deceived ourselves too.

FOLDAL: But isn't that what friendship really is, John Gabriel?

BORKMAN: Yes. To deceive; that is friendship. You are right there. I have had this experience once before.

FOLDAL: No poet. That you could be so brutal.

BORKMAN (*more gently*): Well, I am no expert.

FOLDAL: More than you realise, perhaps.

BORKMAN: How?

FOLDAL: I have had doubts myself—now and again. A horrible doubt—that I have frittered away my life for the sake of an illusion.

BORKMAN: If you doubt yourself, you stand on feet of clay.

FOLDAL: You believed in me. That's why it was so comforting for me to come here. (*Takes his hat*) But now you are a stranger to me.

BORKMAN: And you to me.

FOLDAL: Goodnight, John Gabriel.

BORKMAN: Goodnight, Vilhelm.

FOLDAL *exits left.* BORKMAN *stands for a moment, staring at the closed door. He makes a movement as though he would call* FOLDAL *back, but thinks better of it and begins to pace up and down the floor with his hands behind his back. Then he stops by the sofa table and extinguishes the lamp. The room becomes half dark. Shortly afterwards, there is a knock on the concealed door.*

Who's that knocking?

No answer. There is another knock.

Who is it? Come in.

ELLA RENTHEIM, *with a lighted candle in her hand, appears in the doorway. She is wearing the same dress as before, with her coat thrown over her shoulders.*

BORKMAN (*staring at her*): Who are you? What do you want?

ELLA (*closes the door behind her and walks towards him*): It is I, Borkman. (*She sets the candle down on the piano and remains standing there*).

BORKMAN (*stares at her and whispers*): Is it—is it Ella? Is it Ella Rentheim?

ELLA: Yes. It is "your" Ella—as you used to call me. Once. Many, many years ago.

BORKMAN: Yes, it is you, Ella—I see it now.

ELLA: Can you recognise me?

BORKMAN: Yes—now I begin to—

ELLA: The years have been unkind to me, Borkman. Don't you think so?

BORKMAN: You have changed somewhat. At first sight, I didn't—

ELLA: I don't have dark curls now, falling over my shoulders. Do you remember how you loved to twist them round your fingers?

BORKMAN: That's it! You wear your hair differently. I see it now, Ella.

ELLA (*smiles sadly*): Exactly. I wear it differently.

BORKMAN: I didn't know you were in this part of the country.

ELLA: I've only just come.

BORKMAN: Why have you come here—now, in winter?

ELLA: I'll tell you.

BORKMAN: Is there something you want from me?

ELLA: From you too, yes. But if we are going to talk about that, I shall have to begin at the beginning—a long time ago.

BORKMAN: You must be tired.

ELLA: Yes, I am tired.

BORKMAN: Won't you sit down?

ELLA: Thank you. I need to sit down.

Goes right, and seats herself on the corner of the sofa. BORKMAN stands by the table with his hands behind his back, looking at her. Short silence.

It's a long time since we met face to face, Borkman.

BORKMAN: A long, long time.

ELLA: A whole lifetime has passed. A wasted life.

BORKMAN: Wasted?

ELLA: Yes. For both of us.

BORKMAN: I do not regard my life as wasted—yet.

ELLA: But my life? What about that?

BORKMAN: You have only yourself to blame for that, Ella.

ELLA: *You* say that?

BORKMAN: You could have been happy without me.

ELLA: Do you think so?

BORKMAN: If you'd wanted to.

ELLA: Oh, yes; I knew of course that there was someone else ready to receive me—

BORKMAN: But you turned your back on him.

ELLA: Yes.

BORKMAN: Again and again you rejected him. Year after year—

ELLA: Year after year I rejected happiness. Is that what you mean?

BORKMAN: You could have been as happy with him. And I would have been saved.

ELLA: You—?

BORKMAN: Yes. You would have saved me, Ella.

ELLA: How?

BORKMAN: He thought you had rejected him because of me. So—he took his revenge. It was easy for him. He had all my secret and confidential letters in his care. He used them—and that was the end of me, for the time being. You see; that is your fault, Ella.

ELLA: Why, yes, Borkman—when we look at it closely, perhaps it is I who have betrayed you, and stand in your debt.

BORKMAN: If you like. I know well enough what I have to thank you for. At the auction you bought the estate, and gave me and—and your sister the use of this house. You took Erhart, and cared for him in every way—

ELLA: For as long as I was allowed to.

BORKMAN: Allowed by your sister, yes. I have never interfered in domestic matters. As I was saying—I know the sacrifices you have made for me and for your sister. But remember, it was I who put you in a position to make those sacrifices, Ella.

ELLA: You're wrong, Borkman! It was love that forced me to act as I did—my devotion to Erhart—and to you too.

BORKMAN: My dear, let's not drag our emotions into this. I mean of course that when you acted as you did, it was I who had provided you with the means to do so.

ELLA (*smiles*): Hm. The means—

BORKMAN: Yes, exactly, the means! When the time came for the decisive battle—when I could spare neither family

166

nor friend—when I had to *take*, and took, the millions which had been entrusted to me—I spared everything that was yours, everything you had—though I could have taken that too, and used it—like everything else.

ELLA (*cold and calm*): That is perfectly true, Borkman.

BORKMAN: It is. But when they came and took me, everything of yours lay there untouched, in the vaults of the bank.

ELLA (*looks at him*): I've so often wondered about that—why did you spare everything that belonged to me? And nothing else?

BORKMAN: Why?

ELLA: Yes, why? Tell me that.

BORKMAN (*scathingly*): You think I wanted something to fall back on, if everything should fail?

ELLA: Oh, no. You never feared that. In those days.

BORKMAN: No, never! I was so unshakably certain of victory.

ELLA: Exactly; then why—?

BORKMAN (*shrugs his shoulders*): Great heavens, Ella—it isn't so easy to remember one's motives of twenty years ago. I only remember that, as I walked there alone, wrestling with all the great projects I intended to launch, I felt—almost like an aeronaut. Walking the sleepless nights—filling, as it were, some giant balloon in which I was about to sail across an uncharted and perilous ocean.

ELLA (*smiles*): You, who never doubted victory.

BORKMAN (*impatiently*): People are like that, Ella. They doubt and believe in the same breath. (*To himself*)That was why I did not want to have you and your money with me in the balloon.

ELLA: Why? Tell me why?

BORKMAN (*without looking at her*): One does not take what one loves most dearly on such a journey.

ELLA: But you had what you loved most dearly on board with you. Your future. Your own life.

BORKMAN: Life is not always the most precious thing.

ELLA: Is that how you felt then?

BORKMAN: Yes. So it seems to me now.

ELLA: I was dearer to you than your life?

BORKMAN: I—seem to remember—I felt—something of the kind.

ELLA: But this was years after you had betrayed me, and married—someone else!

BORKMAN: Betrayed you, you say? You know quite well that it was higher motives—well, other motives, that compelled me. Without him, I could get nowhere.

ELLA (*controlling herself*): So you betrayed me from—higher motives?

BORKMAN: I could not do without his help. And you were the price he named.

ELLA: And you paid. In full; without bargaining.

BORKMAN: There was no choice. I had to conquer or be destroyed.

ELLA: And yet you can truthfully say that to you I was the most precious thing in the world!

BORKMAN: Yes, and afterwards too. Long, long afterwards.

ELLA: And yet you bartered me! Traded your love to another man! Sold my love for the chairmanship of a bank.

BORKMAN (*dark, bowed*): It was an absolute necessity, Ella.

ELLA (*rises passionately from the sofa, trembling*): You criminal!

BORKMAN: I have heard that word before.

ELLA: Oh, don't think I'm talking about your crimes against the law. Do you think I care what use you made of those stocks and bonds? If I had been beside you when everything collapsed—

BORKMAN: Yes?

ELLA: I would have borne it all so gladly with you. The shame, the ruin, everything, everything—and helped you to bear it too.

BORKMAN: Would you have done that? Could you?

ELLA: I could and would have done it. Because then I didn't know about the monstrous crime you had committed.

BORKMAN: Which crime? What do you mean?

ELLA: I mean the crime for which there is no forgiveness—

168

BORKMAN: You must be out of your mind.

ELLA (*moving closer to him*): You are a murderer! You have committed the mortal sin!

BORKMAN (*retreats towards the piano*): You are raving, Ella.

ELLA: You have killed love in me! (*Goes towards him*) Do you understand what that means? The Bible speaks of a mysterious sin for which there is no forgiveness. I've never understood what that meant before. Now I understand. The sin for which there is no forgiveness is to murder love in a human being.

BORKMAN: And—*that* you say I have done?

ELLA: You have. I never really understood what had happened to me until this evening. That you betrayed me and turned to Gunhild instead I just accepted as male inconstancy on your part—a result of callous tricks on hers. And I think I despised you a little—in spite of everything. But now I see it! You betrayed the woman you loved! Me, me, me! The thing you held most precious in the world, you were willing to dispose of at a profit. You are guilty of double murder. The murder of your own soul, and mine.

BORKMAN (*cold and controlled*): How well I recall your passionate nature, Ella. It is only natural for you to see it like that. You are a woman. Consequently, nothing else in the whole world matters to you. You can only think about this one thing.

ELLA: Exactly. Only this one thing.

BORKMAN: Only what is nearest to your own heart.

ELLA: Only that! Only that!

BORKMAN: But you must remember that I am a man. As a woman, you were, to me, the most precious thing in the world. But if need be, one woman can be replaced by another—

ELLA (*smiles*): Did you find that out after you had married Gunhild?

BORKMAN: No. But my mission in life helped me to bear that too. I wanted all the sources of power in this country to serve me. The earth, the mountains, the forests, the sea.

So that I might create a kingdom for myself, and prosperity for thousands and thousands of others.

ELLA: I know. The evenings we spent talking about your plans—

BORKMAN: Yes. I was able to talk to you, Ella.

ELLA: I used to make fun of your dreams, and ask if you wanted to release the spirits that slumber in the mines.

BORKMAN (*nods*): I remember that phrase. (*Slowly*) The spirits that slumber in the mines.

ELLA: But you took it seriously. You said: "Yes, yes, Ella, that is exactly what I want to do."

BORKMAN: So it was. I only needed to get my foot on the ladder, and that depended on this one man. He was able and willing to obtain for me the key position in the bank —provided that I on my part—

ELLA: Renounced the woman you loved—and who was so consumingly in love with you.

BORKMAN: I knew how insatiable his passion for you was. I knew no other condition would induce him to—

ELLA: So you struck the bargain.

BORKMAN: Yes, Ella, I did! My lust for power was so overwhelming, can't you understand? So I—struck the bargain. I had to. And he helped me up towards the heights—halfway towards the heights that drew me—and I climbed and climbed—year after year I climbed—

ELLA: And I passed out of your life.

BORKMAN: But he threw me back into the abyss. Because of you, Ella.

ELLA: Borkman—don't you feel as if our relationship had been cursed in some way?

BORKMAN: Cursed?

ELLA: Yes. Don't you think so?

BORKMAN (*uneasily*): Yes. But why? Oh, Ella—I don't know any longer who is right—you or I.

ELLA: You are the one who sinned. You destroyed my capacity for love.

BORKMAN: Don't say that, Ella.

ELLA: At least you made it impossible for me to love as a woman. From the time your image began to fade, I have lived as though under an eclipse. All these years it has become more and more difficult, until finally it became impossible for me to love any living thing. People, animals, flowers—only this one person—

BORKMAN: Who?

ELLA: Erhart, of course.

BORKMAN: Erhart?

ELLA: Your son, Borkman.

BORKMAN: Has he really meant so much to you?

ELLA: Why else do you suppose I took him to live with me? And kept him for as long as I could? Why else?

BORKMAN: I thought it was simply out of charity. Like all the other things you've done.

ELLA: Charity, did you say? (*Laughs*) I've never felt charity towards anyone, not since you betrayed me. If a poor, starving child came into my kitchen, frozen and crying, and asked for a little food, I told the cook to see to it. I never felt any compulsion to take the child into my own room, warm it at my own fire, enjoy watching it eat its fill. And I was never like that when I was young—I remember so well—it's you who've created this emptiness and sterility in me, and all around me.

BORKMAN: But not towards Erhart.

ELLA: No. Not towards your son. But towards all other living things. You cheated me of the joy of being a mother —and of the sorrow and tears of motherhood, too. And that is perhaps the cruellest thing you've done to me, Borkman.

BORKMAN: Ella!

ELLA: Who knows? Perhaps the sorrow and tears were what I needed most. But I couldn't accept that loss. So I took Erhart—and won his confidence, his love—until—

BORKMAN: Until what?

ELLA: Until his mother took him from me again.

BORKMAN: Well, he had to come back and live in town.

ELLA: Yes, but I can't stand the desolation—the emptiness —the loss of Erhart's love.

BORKMAN: Hm! I don't think you've lost him, Ella. It isn't easy to lose one's heart to anyone downstairs.

ELLA: I have lost him. And she has won him back. Or some-one else has. I can tell that from the letters he writes to me.

BORKMAN: Did you come here to take him away with you?

ELLA: If only I could—

BORKMAN: Certainly you can, as far as I'm concerned. You have the greater claim on him.

ELLA: Claim, claim! If he doesn't come of his own free will, he won't belong to me. And that's what I must have! I must have my child—he must belong to me. I won't share him with anyone.

BORKMAN: Well, we must remember that Erhart is a grown man. You couldn't expect to retain his undivided affections for long.

ELLA: It needn't be for long.

BORKMAN: Oh? I thought when you want anything, you want it for life.

ELLA: I do. But that needn't be very long.

BORKMAN: What do you mean?

ELLA: You know I have been ill these last years?

BORKMAN: Have you?

ELLA: Didn't you know?

BORKMAN: No, I don't think so.

ELLA: Hasn't Erhart told you?

BORKMAN: Not that I remember.

ELLA: Perhaps he doesn't talk about me to you?

BORKMAN: Oh, I'm sure he's mentioned you. I hardly ever see him. There is someone downstairs who keeps him away from me. Well away—you understand?

ELLA: Are you sure of that, Borkman?

BORKMAN: I am sure. But—you said you have been ill, Ella?

ELLA: Yes, I have. This autumn it became so bad that I've had to come over here and see a specialist.

BORKMAN: And you have talked to him?

ELLA: Yes. This morning.

BORKMAN: What does he say?

ELLA: He confirmed what I had long suspected—

BORKMAN: Yes?

ELLA (*calmly*): I shan't live for long, Borkman.

BORKMAN: You mustn't believe that, Ella.

ELLA: It's a disease for which the doctors know no cure. They can only let it run its course. And reduce the pain a little, perhaps. That at least is something.

BORKMAN: Oh, but—it may be a long time yet, I'm sure—

ELLA: I may get through the winter, they say.

BORKMAN (*without thinking*): Well, the winters are long here.

ELLA (*quietly*): Long enough for me, anyway.

BORKMAN: But what on earth can have been the cause of this disease? You've always lived such a healthy life.

ELLA (*looks at him*): The doctor suggested that perhaps I had at some time gone through some violent emotional crisis.

BORKMAN: Oh, I understand. *I* am to blame for this?

ELLA: It's too late to talk about that now. But I must have my child again, before I go. It's so hateful for me to think that I must lose everything, leave the sunshine and light and air, without leaving behind me a single person who will remember me and love me and be sad that I have gone—the way a son remembers a mother he has lost.

BORKMAN (*after a brief pause*): Take him, Ella—if you can win him.

ELLA: You agree?

BORKMAN: Yes. But it's not much of a sacrifice. He isn't mine to give away.

ELLA: Thank you—thank you. But there is another thing I want to ask you. Something that means very much to me, Borkman.

BORKMAN: Name it.

ELLA: You will probably think it childish of me.

BORKMAN: Name it. Name it.

ELLA: When I die, I shall leave a considerable fortune—

BORKMAN: Yes. It must be considerable.

ELLA: I intend to leave it all to Erhart.

BORKMAN: I don't suppose you have anyone closer.

ELLA: No. No one closer.

BORKMAN: There are no other members of your family left. You are the last.

ELLA: Yes. When I die, the name of Rentheim will die too. I hate that thought. To be obliterated so utterly that even one's name will die.

BORKMAN: Ah! I see what you want!

ELLA: Don't let it happen. Let Erhart bear my name after me.

BORKMAN: I understand you. You want to free my son from the burden of his father's name. That's it, isn't it?

ELLA: No. I would gladly and defiantly have borne your name with you. But when a mother is about to die—a name binds her to her son more closely than you know, Borkman.

BORKMAN (*coldly and proudly*): It shall be as you wish, Ella. I am man enough to bear my name alone.

ELLA (*seizes his hands*): Thank you, thank you. All debts are paid between us, now. Yes, yes! You have made amends as far as you could. When I am dead, Erhart Rentheim will live.

The concealed door is thrown open. MRS BORKMAN, *her big shawl over her head, stands in the doorway.*

MRS BORKMAN: Never! Erhart shall never bear that name!

ELLA: Gunhild!

BORKMAN: No one has leave to come up here!

MRS BORKMAN (*takes a step into the room*): I have given myself leave.

BORKMAN: What do you want with me?

MRS BORKMAN: I want to fight for you—protect you!

ELLA: It is you he needs to be protected against, Gunhild.

MRS BORKMAN: I hardly think so. I tell you he shall bear his father's name. And restore it to honour. And I alone shall be his mother! My son's love shall belong to me, and to no one else.

She goes out through the concealed door and closes it behind her.

ELLA: Borkman—this will destroy Erhart. You and Gunhild *must* come to an understanding. We must go down to her. At once.

BORKMAN: We? You mean I should go down there?

ELLA: You and I, together.

BORKMAN (*shakes his head*): She is hard, Ella. As hard as the iron I once dreamed of quarrying out of the mountains.

ELLA: Try. Try now.

BORKMAN *does not reply. He stands looking at her uncertainly.*

ACT THREE

Mrs Borkman's *sitting room. The lamp is still burning on the sofa table. Inside the garden room the lamp is out and it is dark.* Mrs Borkman, *her shawl over her head, enters through the hall door, greatly agitated. She goes to the window and pushes the curtain slightly to one side. Then she moves away and sits by the stove. but soon jumps to her feet again, walks across the room and pulls the bell-rope. Stands by the sofa and waits a moment. Nobody comes. Then she rings again, this time more violently. A few seconds later, the* Maid *comes in from the hall. She looks bad-tempered and sleepy and has obviously dressed in a hurry.*

Mrs Borkman (*impatiently*): Where have you been, Malene? I've rung for you; twice.

Maid: Yes, madam, I heard you.

Mrs Borkman: Well, why didn't you come?

Maid: I had to get some clothes on first, didn't I?

Mrs Borkman: Now dress yourself warmly and run down and fetch my son at once.

Maid (*surprised*): You want me to fetch Mr Erhart?

Mrs Borkman: Yes. Tell him to come at once, I want to speak to him.

Maid (*sulkily*): Well! I suppose I'd better go across to the bailiff's and wake the coachman.

Mrs Borkman: Why should you do that?

Maid: So that he can harness the sleigh. There's a terrible snowstorm outside tonight.

Mrs Borkman: Oh, never mind that. Hurry up and run down there. It's only just round the corner.

Maid: No, but madam, it's not just round the corner.

MRS BORKMAN: Of course it is. Don't you know where Mr Hinkel lives?

MAID (*maliciously*): Oh, that's where he is this evening, is it?

MRS BORKMAN: Where else?

MAID (*smirks*): No, no. I only thought he'd be in the usual place.

MRS BORKMAN: Where do you mean?

MAID: At that Mrs Wilton's, or whatever her name is.

MRS BORKMAN: Mrs Wilton? But my son doesn't go there very often.

MAID: I've heard he's there every day.

MRS BORKMAN: That is just gossip, Malene. Now run down to Mr Hinkel's and get hold of him.

MAID (*tosses her head*): Very good, madam. I'll go, I'll go. (*Terrified, clasps her hands*): Oh, Jesus!

She is about to go out through the hall, but at that moment the door opens and ELLA RENTHEIM *and* BORKMAN *appear in the doorway.*

MRS BORKMAN (*whispers to the* MAID): Tell him to come at once.

MAID: Yes, madam.

ELLA *and, after her,* BORKMAN, *enter the room. The* MAID *sidles behind them through the door, and closes it after her. There is a short silence.*

MRS BORKMAN (*turns to* ELLA): What does he want down here?

ELLA: He wants to try to come to an understanding with you, Gunhild.

MRS BORKMAN: He has never tried to do so before.

ELLA: He wants to now.

MRS BORKMAN: The last time we stood facing each other was in the court. When I had been summoned to defend myself—

BORKMAN: And tonight it is I who shall defend myself.

MRS BORKMAN: You?

177

BORKMAN: Not against the charge I was convicted on. I did what they said I did.

MRS BORKMAN: Yes. All the world knows that.

BORKMAN: But they do not know why I did it. Why I had to do it. People don't understand that I had to because I was myself—because I was John Gabriel Borkman—and no one else. That's what I want to try to explain to you.

MRS BORKMAN: It's no use explaining what drove you to it. That won't acquit you.

BORKMAN: It can, in my own eyes.

MRS BORKMAN: Oh, let us leave the subject. I have brooded long enough over these things.

BORKMAN: So have I. Five endless years in the prison cell, and three before the trial, gave me time. And during the eight years in the room upstairs, I have had even more time to brood. Again and again I have gone through the trial, re-trying it—before myself. I have been my own prosecutor, my own counsel, and my own judge. I have been more impartial than anyone else could have been. I think I may say that. I have walked up there on the floor of that room, turning every one of my actions inside out, and upside down. I have examined them from every angle as ruthlessly and mercilessly as any advocate. And the verdict I reach is always the same; that the only person against whom I have committed any crime is myself.

MRS BORKMAN: What about me? And your son?

BORKMAN: I include my family when I say myself.

MRS BORKMAN: What about the hundreds of others whom you ruined?

BORKMAN: I had the power! And the irresistible calling within me! The buried millions lay there all over the country, deep in the mountains, crying out to me, crying to be released. But no one else heard them. I alone.

MRS BORKMAN: Yes, and branded the name of Borkman with shame for ever.

BORKMAN: If the others had had the power, wouldn't they have acted exactly as I did?

178

MRS BORKMAN: No one but you would have done it.

BORKMAN: Then it was because no one had my ability. And if they had done as I did, it would have been for selfish reasons. The case would have been quite different. In short, I have acquitted myself.

ELLA: Dare you say that so confidently, Borkman?

BORKMAN (*nods*): I have dismissed the charges that were brought against me. But now comes the great and dreadful charge I bring against myself.

MRS BORKMAN: What is that?

BORKMAN: Up there, I have wasted eight precious years of my life! The day I was released, I should have walked out into reality—reality hard as iron, free of dreams. I should have begun from the bottom and worked myself up to the heights again—higher than ever before—in spite of all that had happened.

MRS BORKMAN: Oh, you would only have done it all over again, believe me.

BORKMAN (*shakes his head and looks magisterially at her*): Nothing new happens. But equally, that which has happened never happens in quite the same way again. The vision transforms the deed. The new vision transforms the old deed. No, you don't understand that.

MRS BORKMAN: No, I don't understand that.

BORKMAN: No, that is the curse upon me—I have never been understood by anyone.

ELLA: Never, Borkman?

BORKMAN: Except once, perhaps. Long ago. When I didn't think I needed it. Since then I have never had anyone at my side, vigilant enough to keep me continually alert and urge me forward, challenging me to take up my work again, with renewed strength. To assure me that I have not failed irrevocably.

MRS BORKMAN: So you need to be assured about that?

BORKMAN: Yes. The whole world proclaims that I am finished, and there are moments when I almost believe it. But then a voice within me reminds me who I am. And that acquits me.

MRS BORKMAN: Why did you never come to me and ask for—understanding?

BORKMAN: Would it have been any use?

MRS BORKMAN: You have never loved anything outside yourself—that is the real truth.

BORKMAN (*proudly*): I have loved power—

MRS BORKMAN: Power, yes.

BORKMAN: The power to create happiness all around me.

MRS BORKMAN: Once you had the power to make me happy. Why did you never use it?

BORKMAN (*without looking at her*): In a shipwreck, casualties cannot always be avoided.

MRS BORKMAN: And your own son! Have you used your power to create happiness for him?

BORKMAN: I do not know him.

MRS BORKMAN: No. You don't even know him.

BORKMAN: His mother saw to that.

MRS BORKMAN: If you only knew what I have seen to!

BORKMAN: Well, tell me.

MRS BORKMAN: I have seen to your epitaph.

BORKMAN (*with a short, dry laugh*): My epitaph! Listen to her! She speaks as though I were dead.

MRS BORKMAN: You are.

BORKMAN (*slowly*): Yes, perhaps you're right. No! Not yet! I came very close, so close to dying. But now I am awake. I am well again. Life still lies ahead of me. I can see it— my new life—waiting for me—new and shining. And you shall see it too. You too!

MRS BORKMAN (*raising her hand*): Never dream of life again! Rest in peace where you lie!

ELLA: Gunhild! Gunhild!

MRS BORKMAN: I shall raise a monument over your grave.

BORKMAN: Suitably inscribed, no doubt.

MRS BORKMAN: Oh, no. It won't be any monument of stone or metal. And no one shall carve any scornful inscription on the monument I shall raise. There shall be planted as it were a living screen of trees and bushes, over the dead man walking in his tomb, shrouding his shame; consigning for ever to oblivion the name of John Gabriel Borkman.

BORKMAN: And you will perform this labour of love?

MRS BORKMAN: No. I cannot. But I have brought up someone who will dedicate his life to this work. And he shall be so clear and bright and shining that your dark life of the pit will be obliterated and forgotten.

BORKMAN: Is it Erhart you mean?

MRS BORKMAN: Yes, Erhart. My son, whose name you are willing to sacrifice as a penance for your own misdeeds.

BORKMAN (*with a glance at* ELLA): As a penance for my greatest sin.

MRS BORKMAN: That was a sin against a stranger. What about your sin against me? But he won't obey you. When I cry to him in my need, he will come! Because it's with me he wants to live! With me, and no one else. (*Listens suddenly and cries*) There he is—there he is! Erhart!

ERHART BORKMAN *flings open the door and enters the room. He is wearing an overcoat and a hat.*

ERHART (*pale and worried*): Mother—what in God's name—? (*He sees* BORKMAN *standing in the doorway of the garden room, stops, and takes off his hat. Is silent for a moment, then asks*) Why do you want me, mother? What has happened here?

MRS BORKMAN (*stretches out her arms towards him*): I want to see you, Erhart. I want to keep you with me—always.

ERHART: Always? What do you mean?

MRS BORKMAN: Keep you, keep you, that's what I want! Because there's someone who wants to take you away from me.

ERHART: Ah—you know that?

MRS BORKMAN: Yes. Do you know it too?

ERHART: Do I know it? Yes, of course—

MRS BORKMAN: Ah, you've been plotting! Behind my back! Erhart, Erhart!

ERHART: Mother, tell me what you know.

MRS BORKMAN: I know everything. I know your aunt has come here to take you away from me.

ERHART: Aunt Ella!

ELLA: Please listen to what I have to say first, Erhart.

MRS BORKMAN: She wants me to give you to her. She wants to take your mother's place, Erhart. From now on, she wants you to be her son, and not mine. Wants you to inherit everything when she dies—to renounce your name and take her name instead.

ERHART: Aunt Ella, is this true?

ELLA: Yes, it's true.

ERHART: I had no idea. Why do you want me to come back and live with you again?

ELLA: Because I feel I'm losing you.

MRS BORKMAN: Yes, to me. And that is as it should be.

ELLA: Erhart, I can't be without you. I am a—lonely, dying woman.

ERHART: Dying?

ELLA: Yes, dying. Will you stay with me till the end? As though you were my own child—?

MRS BORKMAN: And betray your mother and perhaps your mission in life?

ELLA: I haven't much time left, Erhart.

ERHART: Aunt Ella—you have been so wonderfully good to me. You gave me as happy a childhood as anyone could have—

MRS BORKMAN: Erhart!

ELLA: You still remember—!

ERHART: —but I can't give up my life to you now. I can't— I can't possibly put everything aside and try to be a son to you—

MRS BORKMAN: I knew it! You won't get him! You won't get him, Ella!

ELLA: No. You have won him back.

MRS BORKMAN: Yes, yes! He is mine, and he'll always be mine. Erhart—it's true, isn't it?—we two shall stay together for a while yet!

ERHART: Mother. I'd better tell you now—

MRS BORKMAN: Yes?

ERHART: You and I won't be together for much longer.

MRS BORKMAN: What are you trying to tell me?

ERHART: Good God, mother, I'm young! I'm suffocating in this house! I can't breathe here!

MRS BORKMAN: Here? Living with me?

ERHART: Yes, living with you, mother.

ELLA: Oh, Erhart, come with me!

ERHART: No, Aunt Ella, it's no better with you. It's different —but no better. It's roses and lavender—it's airless, the same as here.

MRS BORKMAN: Airless, did you say?

ERHART (*with rising impatience*): Yes—I don't know what else to call it. Your sickly pampering, and—I don't know how to put it—the way you idolise me—I can't stand it any longer.

MRS BORKMAN: Have you forgotten what you have dedicated your life to, Erhart?

ERHART (*explosively*): You mean, what *you* have dedicated it to! You, mother, you've been my will—I've never been allowed to have any of my own. But now—I can't bear this straitjacket any longer! I'm young! Remember that, mother! (*With a respectful glance at* BORKMAN) I can't dedicate my life to atoning for what someone else has done. Whoever it may be.

MRS BORKMAN: Erhart! Who has made you change your mind?

ERHART (*stung*): Who—? Couldn't I have done it myself?

MRS BORKMAN: No, no, no! You are not under your mother's influence any longer. Nor your foster-mother's. There is someone else.

ERHART (*trying to seem confident*): I stand on my own feet now, mother. I have a will of my own.

BORKMAN (*takes a step towards* ERHART): Then perhaps my turn has come at last.

ERHART (*distantly respectful*): What do you mean by that, father?

MRS BORKMAN: Yes, that I should like to know.

183

BORKMAN: Listen, Erhart—will you come with your father? You cannot redeem another man's failure. That is only an empty dream, which has been instilled into you in this airless room. Even if you were to live like all the saints put together, it would not help me one whit.

ERHART (*respectfully*): Yes. That is true.

BORKMAN: Nor would it help if I were to moulder up there, contrite and penitent. All these years I have tried to keep alive on hopes and dreams. Now I want reality.

ERHART (*with a slight bow*): And where—what will you do, father?

BORKMAN: I shall rehabilitate myself. I shall start at the bottom again. It is only through his present and his future that a man can redeem his past. Through work; untiring work for the ideal that inspired me when I was young, and inspires me a thousand times more strongly today. Erhart—will you come with me, and help me with this new life?

MRS BORKMAN: Don't do it, Erhart!

ELLA (*warmly*): Yes, yes, Erhart, help him!

BORKMAN: Will you?

ERHART: Father—I can't now. It's impossible.

BORKMAN: Well, Erhart. What do you propose to do?

ERHART: I'm young! I want to live! I want to live my own life!

ELLA: And you won't sacrifice a few short months to brighten the last days of my life?

ERHART: Aunt Ella, I can't. I'd gladly do it, but I can't.

MRS BORKMAN: And you feel no duty towards your mother any longer?

ERHART: I shall always love you, mother. But I can't live just for you.

BORKMAN: Then come with me. Life is work, Erhart! Come; we two will go out into life and work together.

ERHART (*passionately*): Yes, but I don't want to work now! I'm young! I never knew what it was to be young before. But now—I feel it in my veins. I don't want to work! I just want to live, live, live!

184

MRS BORKMAN (*sensing the truth*): Erhart—what do you want to live for?

ERHART: For happiness, mother.

MRS BORKMAN: And where do you expect to find it?

ERHART: I have found it!

MRS BORKMAN (*with a cry*): Erhart—!

ERHART *goes quickly to the hall door and opens it.*

ERHART (*calls*): Fanny, you can come in now.

MRS WILTON, *wearing her overcoat, appears in the doorway.*

MRS BORKMAN (*clasping her hands*): Mrs Wilton!

MRS WILTON (*shyly, with a questioning glance at* ERHART): May I—?

ERHART: Yes, you can come in now. I have told them everything.

MRS WILTON *comes into the room.* ERHART *closes the door behind her. She bows respectfully to* BORKMAN, *who acknowledges her greeting silently. Short pause.*

MRS WILTON: You have heard the news, then. I fear I am the cause of much unhappiness in this house.

MRS BORKMAN: You have destroyed the little I had left to live for. But this is all utterly impossible!

MRS WILTON: I appreciate how impossible it must seem to you, Mrs Borkman.

MRS BORKMAN: Surely you yourself must admit that it is impossible.

MRS WILTON: Incredible is the word I would use. Nevertheless it is true.

MRS BORKMAN: Do you mean this seriously, Erhart?

ERHART: This is the happiness I have found, mother. That is all I can say.

MRS BORKMAN (*to* MRS WILTON): You have infatuated and seduced my unfortunate son!

MRS WILTON (*tosses her head proudly*): I have not.

MRS BORKMAN: Do you dare to deny it?

MRS WILTON: Yes. I have neither infatuated nor seduced

185

him. Erhart has come to me of his own free will. And I have met him halfway, of my free will.

MRS BORKMAN: Oh yes. I can well believe that.

MRS WILTON: Mrs Borkman—there are forces in life of the existence of which you seem to be unaware.

MRS BORKMAN: What forces, if I may ask?

MRS WILTON: Those forces which command two human beings to join their lives together regardless of other people.

MRS BORKMAN (*smiles*): I thought you were already joined to someone else.

MRS WILTON: He left me.

MRS BORKMAN: But he is still alive, I am told.

MRS WILTON: He is dead to me.

ERHART: Yes, mother, as far as Fanny is concerned he is dead. And he's no concern of mine.

MRS BORKMAN: Then you know about him?

ERHART: Yes, mother, of course I know about him.

MRS BORKMAN: And yet you say he's no concern of yours?

ERHART: I tell you I want happiness, mother! I'm young! I want to live, live, live!

MRS BORKMAN: Yes, you are young, Erhart. Much too young for—this.

MRS WILTON: Don't think I haven't told him so, Mrs. Borkman. I've told him everything about myself. I have continually reminded him that I am a full seven years older than he—

ERHART: Oh, Fanny, I knew that from the beginning.

MRS WILTON: But nothing—nothing could make him change his mind.

MRS BORKMAN: Indeed? Nothing? Why didn't you tell him to stop seeing you? Keep your doors closed to him? That is what you should have done while there was still time.

MRS WILTON: I couldn't do that, Mrs Borkman.

MRS BORKMAN: Why not?

MRS WILTON: Because my happiness, too, depended on it.

MRS BORKMAN (*scornfully*): Hm—happiness!

MRS WILTON: I have never known till now what happiness

186

is. And I cannot turn back on it, merely because it comes so late.

MRS BORKMAN: And how long do you suppose this happiness will last?

ERHART: A few months or a lifetime, mother—what does it matter?

MRS BORKMAN: Oh, you are blind! Don't you see where all this is going to end?

ERHART: I don't want to think about the future. I only want the chance to live.

MRS BORKMAN: And you call that living, Erhart?

ERHART: Yes—don't you see how beautiful she is?

MRS BORKMAN: Now I shall have to bear the shame of this too.

BORKMAN: Well, you are used to that, Gunhild.

ELLA: Borkman—

ERHART: Father—

MRS BORKMAN: I shall have to live here and see my son every day together with a—

ERHART: You won't have to see anything, mother. You needn't worry about that. I shall not be staying here.

MRS WILTON: We are going away, Mrs Borkman.

MRS BORKMAN: Together?

MRS WILTON: Yes, I am going south. I'm taking a young girl abroad. And Erhart is coming with us.

MRS BORKMAN: With you—and a young girl?

MRS WILTON: Yes. Little Frida Foldal, whom I have had living with me. I want her to go abroad and study music.

MRS BORKMAN: And so you are taking her with you?

MRS WILTON: Yes, I can't let the child go abroad alone.

MRS BORKMAN (repressing a smile): What do you have to say to that, Erhart?

ERHART (a little embarrassed, shrugs his shoulders): Why, mother, if that's what Fanny wants—

MRS BORKMAN (coldly): When do you intend to leave, if I may ask?

MRS WILTON: Now. Tonight. My sleigh is waiting down there, on the road—outside the Hinkels' house.

MRS BORKMAN: Of course. The party.

MRS WILTON (*smiles*): Yes, Erhart and I were the only guests. And little Frida, of course.

MRS BORKMAN: And where is she now?

MRS WILTON: Sitting in the sleigh waiting for us.

ERHART: Mother, you do understand—? I wanted to spare you and—and everybody—all this.

MRS BORKMAN: You wanted to leave me without saying goodbye?

ERHART: Yes, I thought it would be better. Better for both of us. Everything was arranged—I'd packed my clothes— but then you sent for me, so—(*He makes to stretch out his hands towards her*) Goodbye, mother.

MRS BORKMAN: Don't touch me!

ERHART (*quietly*): Is that your last word?

MRS BORKMAN: Yes.

ERHART (*turning*): Goodbye, Aunt Ella.

ELLA (*clasping his hands*): Goodbye, Erhart! Live your life —and be happy—as happy as you can.

ERHART: Thank you, Aunt Ella. (*Bows to* BORKMAN) Goodbye, father. (*Whispers to* MRS WILTON) Let's get away, now.

MRS WILTON: Yes.

MRS BORKMAN: Mrs Wilton—do you think you are being wise in taking this young girl with you?

MRS WILTON: Men are so unpredictable, Mrs Borkman. And women too. When Erhart is tired of me, and I of him, it will be good for both of us that he should have someone to fall back on, poor boy.

MRS BORKMAN: And what will you do?

MRS WILTON: Oh, I shall manage, I promise you. Goodbye, everybody!

She inclines her head and goes out into the hall. ERHART *stands for a moment as though hesitating : then he turns and follows her.*

MRS BORKMAN (*with lowered, folded hands*): Childless!

BORKMAN (*as though awakening to a decision*): Then out into the storm alone! My hat! My cape! (*He rushes towards the door*).

ELLA (*stops him, frightened*): John Gabriel, where are you going?

BORKMAN: Out into the storm of life! Let me go, Ella!

ELLA (*holding him tightly*): No, no, I won't let you go. You're ill!

BORKMAN: Let me go, I tell you! (*Tears himself loose and goes out through the door into the hall*).

ELLA (*in the doorway*): Help me to stop him, Gunhild!

MRS BORKMAN (*cold and hard, standing in the middle of the room*): I'm not keeping anyone. Let them all leave me. All of them. Let them go—as far as they like. (*Suddenly, with a rending scream*) Erhart, don't go!

She rushes with outstretched arms towards the door. ELLA *stops her.*

ACT FOUR

An open courtyard outside the house, which stands on the right. A corner of it, with the front door and a flight of stone steps, juts out. Upstage, close behind the courtyard, stretches a line of steep hills covered with pine trees. On the left can be seen the edge of the forest, with young trees and scattered undergrowth. The snow has stopped, but the ground is covered with a deep layer of freshly fallen snow. The pines are heavily bowed with it. Dark night sky, with driving clouds. The moon can be vaguely glimpsed from time to time. The only illumination comes from the light reflected from the snow.

BORKMAN, MRS BORKMAN and ELLA stand outside on the steps. BORKMAN, faint and tired, is leaning against the wall of the house. He has an old-fashioned cape thrown over his shoulders, and holds a soft grey felt hat in one hand and a thick thorn stick in the other. ELLA has her coat on her arm. MRS BORKMAN's big shawl has fallen down over her shoulders, leaving her head bare.

ELLA (*barring* MRS BORKMAN's *path*): Don't run after him, Gunhild!

MRS BORKMAN: Let me go, Ella. He mustn't leave me.

ELLA: I tell you it's no use. You won't catch him.

MRS BORKMAN: Let me go! I want to run down the road and scream after him. Surely he must hear his mother's screams!

ELLA: He can't hear you. The windows of the sleigh will be closed.

MRS BORKMAN: No, no. He can't have got to the sleigh yet.

ELLA: He reached it ages ago, believe me.

MRS BORKMAN: If he's in the sleigh she will be there with him.

BORKMAN (*laughs grimly*): And he won't hear his mother's screams, then, will he?

MRS BORKMAN: No, he won't hear them. (*Listens*) Ssh! What's that?

ELLA (*listens too*): It sounds like sleigh bells—

MRS BORKMAN (*softly*): It's her sleigh!

ELLA: It might be someone else's.

MRS BORKMAN: No, no, it's Mrs Wilton's sleigh. I know those silver bells. Listen! Now they're driving past the house—down at the bottom of the hill.

ELLA: Gunhild, if you're going to cry after him do it now. Perhaps he might still—

The bells sound very close, in the forest.

Quickly, Gunhild! They're right below us.

Short silence.

MRS BORKMAN: No. I shall not cry after him. Let Erhart Borkman drive past me—to what he calls life and happiness.

The sound dies away in the distance.

ELLA (*after a moment*): I can't hear the bells any longer.

MRS BORKMAN: They sounded to me like funeral bells.

BORKMAN (*laughs drily*): Not yet. They haven't tolled for me yet.

MRS BORKMAN: But for me they have. And for him who has left me—

ELLA: Perhaps they ring in life and happiness for him, Gunhild.

MRS BORKMAN: Life and happiness, did you say?

ELLA: For a while, at least.

MRS BORKMAN: Can you really wish him happiness—with her?

ELLA: Yes, with all my heart!

MRS BORKMAN: Then your love must be stronger than mine.

ELLA: Perhaps it is want of love that gives my love strength.

MRS BORKMAN: In that case, mine will soon be as strong as yours. (*She turns and goes into the house*).

ELLA (*stands for a moment, looking anxiously at* BORKMAN. *Then she puts her hand gently on his shoulder*): John, you must go in now.

BORKMAN (*as though awakening*): Me?

ELLA: Yes. The winter air is too cold for you. I can see that, John. Come now, come in with me. Into the warmth.

BORKMAN: Upstairs again?

ELLA: No; downstairs to her.

BORKMAN: I shall never again set foot under that roof.

ELLA: Where will you go? It's night-time, and late, John—

BORKMAN (*puts his hat on*): First of all I shall go out and look over my buried treasures.

ELLA: John—I don't understand you.

BORKMAN (*with a coughing laugh*): Oh, I don't mean hidden loot. You needn't be afraid of that, Ella. (*Stops and points*) Over there! Who is it?

VILHELM FOLDAL, *in an old jacket covered with snow, the brim of his hat turned down and a big umbrella in his hand, enters downstage past the corner of the house, plodding laboriously through the snow. He limps badly on his left foot.*

Vilhelm! Are you here again? What do you want?

FOLDAL (*looks up*): Good God! Are you out of doors, John Gabriel! (*Bows*) And Mrs Borkman, too, I see.

BORKMAN: This is not my wife.

FOLDAL: Oh, I beg your pardon. You see, I've lost my glasses in the snow. But you never go out—

BORKMAN (*recklessly hilarious*): It's time I returned to life in the open air, you see. Nearly three years before the trial; five in the cell; eight upstairs; sixteen years in prison—

ELLA: Borkman, Borkman—

FOLDAL: Ah, yes, yes, yes—

BORKMAN: But tell me, what do you want?

FOLDAL (*still standing below the steps*): I felt I wanted to come up and see you, John Gabriel. I felt I *had* to come up and talk to you in your room. Dear God, that room, John Gabriel!

BORKMAN: You wanted to come, even after I had shown you the door?

FOLDAL: Oh, that doesn't matter now.

BORKMAN: What have you done to your foot? You're limping.

FOLDAL: You'll never guess. I've been run over.

ELLA: Run over!

FOLDAL: Yes, by a sleigh—

BORKMAN: Ha!

FOLDAL: With two horses. They came galloping down the hill. I couldn't get out of the way quickly enough, and so—

ELLA: And so they ran over you?

FOLDAL: They drove right at me, Mrs—er—or Miss. They drove right at me, so that I rolled over in the snow, and lost my glasses and got my umbrella broken. (*Rubs himself*) And my foot got hurt a little, too.

BORKMAN (*laughs*): Do you know who was sitting in that sleigh, Vilhelm?

FOLDAL: No, how could I? It was all closed, and the curtains were drawn. And the driver didn't stop when he saw me lying there. But that doesn't matter because—oh, I'm so happy!

BORKMAN: Happy?

FOLDAL: I don't know whether that's the right word. But I—I think it must be. The most extraordinary thing's happened. So I had to come up and share my happiness with you, John Gabriel.

BORKMAN (*roughly*): Well, give me my share, then.

ELLA: Take your friend inside first, Borkman.

BORKMAN: I've told you I won't enter that house again.

ELLA: But you've just heard he's been run over.

BORKMAN: We all get run over some time in life. The only thing to do is to get up again and behave as though nothing had happened.

FOLDAL: Those are wise words, John Gabriel. But I can easily tell you out here.

BORKMAN (*more gently*): Do me that favour, Vilhelm.

193

FOLDAL: Listen. Can you imagine what I found when I came home from seeing you this evening? A letter. And you'll never guess who it's from.

BORKMAN: Little Frida, perhaps?

FOLDAL: Yes! How did you guess? Yes, it was a long—well, quite a long letter from Frida. Brought by a servant. And can you guess what was in the letter?

BORKMAN: A farewell to her parents, perhaps?

FOLDAL: Right again! How clever of you to guess! Yes, she writes that Mrs Wilton has become so fond of her that she's taking her abroad to carry on with her music, she writes. And Mrs Wilton's managed to find a clever tutor to go with them, and coach Frida. Her education's been a little neglected, you see.

BORKMAN (*chuckles*): Yes, yes. I understand it all so well, Vilhelm.

FOLDAL (*continues eagerly*): And imagine, she wasn't told about it until tonight! At the party, you know—the—er—yes. And even so she managed to find time to write. And such a warm and tender and loving letter it was, too. No suggestion that she despises me any longer. And what a delicate gesture, to say goodbye to us in writing! (*Laughs*) But I'm not going to be satisfied with that!

BORKMAN: How do you mean?

FOLDAL: She writes that they're off tomorrow. Very early.

BORKMAN: Indeed, indeed! Tomorrow? Is that what she says?

FOLDAL (*laughs and rubs his hands*): Yes, but I'm too clever for her. I'm going straight up to Mrs Wilton's—

BORKMAN: Now? Tonight?

FOLDAL: Good heavens, yes, it's not too late. And if the house is shut up, I'll ring. Without hesitation. For I must and shall see Frida before she goes. Goodnight, goodnight. (*Begins to go*)

BORKMAN: My poor Vilhelm, you can save yourself that long walk.

FOLDAL: Ah, you're thinking of my foot—

BORKMAN: Yes, and you won't get into Mrs Wilton's house, anyway.

FOLDAL: Indeed I shall. I'll ring and ring till someone opens. I must see Frida.

ELLA: Your daughter has gone, Mr Foldal.

FOLDAL (*thunderstruck*): Has she gone already? Are you sure? Where did you hear that?

BORKMAN: We heard it from her tutor—

FOLDAL: Oh? Who is he?

BORKMAN: A student by the name of Erhart Borkman.

FOLDAL (*overjoyed*): Your son, John Gabriel! Is he going too?

BORKMAN: Yes; he's the one who's going to help Mrs Wilton to educate little Frida.

FOLDAL: God be praised! The child's in the best possible hands, then. But are you quite sure they've gone?

BORKMAN: They were in the sleigh which ran you down.

FOLDAL (*claps his hands*): My little Frida in that magnificent sleigh!

BORKMAN: Yes, yes, Vilhelm. Your daughter is doing very well for herself. And Erhart Borkman too. Did you notice the silver bells?

FOLDAL: Oh yes, I— *Silver* bells did you say? Were they silver bells? Real, solid silver bells?

BORKMAN: You can be sure of that. Everything there was real. Inside and out.

FOLDAL: Isn't it strange the way things work out? My—my little talent for poetry has resulted in Frida being musical. So I haven't been a poet for nothing after all. For now she's able to go out into the great world and see all the things I longed to see once. Little Frida drives out into the world in a closed sleigh! With silver bells on the harness—

BORKMAN: And runs over her father.

FOLDAL (*joyfully*): Oh, that! What does it matter about me, as long as the child—? Well, I've come too late. I'll go home and console her mother, who's sitting in the kitchen crying.

BORKMAN: Is she crying?

FOLDAL: Yes. Imagine it! She was crying her heart out when I left.

BORKMAN: And you laugh, Vilhelm?

FOLDAL: I, oh yes! But, she, poor thing, she doesn't know

195

any better. Well, goodbye! It's lucky I haven't far to go to the tram. Goodbye, goodbye, John Gabriel. Goodbye, Miss. (*Waves and plods painfully out the way he came*).

BORKMAN: Goodbye, Vilhelm. It's not the first time in your life you have been run over, old friend.

ELLA (*controlling her concern as she watches him*): You're so pale, John, so pale—

BORKMAN: That is because of the prison air upstairs.

ELLA: I've never seen you like this.

BORKMAN: No. You've never seen an escaped prisoner before, have you?

ELLA: Come inside with me, John.

BORKMAN: It's no good trying to wheedle me. I've told you I—

ELLA: I beg you—for your own sake.

The MAID *comes out on to the steps.*

MAID: Excuse me, madam says I'm to lock the front door now.

BORKMAN (*quietly, to* ELLA): Listen to that! They want to shut me in again.

ELLA (*to the* MAID): The master is not feeling well. He wants a little fresh air.

MAID: Yes, but Mrs Borkman *said*—

ELLA: I shall lock up. Leave the key in the door.

MAID: Very good, madam, I'll do as you say. (*She goes back into the house*).

BORKMAN (*stands still for a moment listening, then goes quickly down to the courtyard*): I'm outside the wall now, Ella! They'll never catch me now!

ELLA (*down with him*): But you're free in there too, John. You can come and go as you please.

BORKMAN (*quietly, as though frightened*): I shall never go under a roof again. Out here in the night air, it's good! If I were to go up to that room now, the walls and ceiling would shrink and crush me, crush me like a fly—

ELLA: But where will you go?

BORKMAN: I shall go on, and on, and on. See if I can find my way back to freedom and life and humanity. Will you go with me, Ella?

ELLA: I? Now?

BORKMAN: Yes, yes. At once.

ELLA: But—how far—?

BORKMAN: As far as I can go.

ELLA: But, John—it's a winter night—it's wet and cold—

BORKMAN: Ah! You're concerned for your health, are you, madam? Yes, yes, it's very frail, isn't it?

ELLA: It's your health I'm concerned for.

BORKMAN (*laughs*): A dead man's health! You make me laugh, Ella. (*He goes on*).

ELLA (*goes after him and holds him back*): What did you say you were?

BORKMAN: A dead man. Don't you remember, Gunhild said I should rest in peace where I lay?

ELLA (*wrapping her coat purposely around her*): I shall go with you, John.

BORKMAN: Yes, we two belong together, Ella; you and I. Come.

They enter the trees on the left, and gradually disappear from sight. The house and courtyard fade away, and the landscape, rugged and mountainous, slowly changes, becoming wilder and wilder.

ELLA'S VOICE (*from within the forest, right*): Where are we going, John? I don't know where I am.

BORKMAN'S VOICE (*higher up*): Follow my footprints!

ELLA'S VOICE: But why must we climb so high?

BORKMAN'S VOICE (*nearer*): We must follow the winding path.

ELLA'S VOICE (*she is still hidden*): I haven't the strength to go on much longer!

BORKMAN (*at the edge of the forest, right*): Come, Ella, come! We are not far from the prospect now. There was a seat here—

ELLA (*coming into sight through the trees*): Do you remember?

BORKMAN: There you can rest.

197

They have reached a small clearing high up in the forest. The mountain rises steeply behind them. To the left, far down, can be seen a vast landscape, with fjords, and high distant peaks rising one behind another. To the left of the clearing is a dead pine tree with a seat beneath it. Snow lies deep on the ground. BORKMAN, *with* ELLA *following him, wades heavily through the snow.*

BORKMAN (*stops by the precipice, left*): Come, Ella, and I shall show you!

ELLA (*joining him*): What will you show me, John?

BORKMAN (*pointing*): See how the country stretches out before us, open and free—far, far away.

ELLA: We used to sit on that seat, and stare into the distance.

BORKMAN: It was a country of dreams we gazed into.

ELLA (*nods heavily*): The country of our dreams, yes. Now it is covered with snow. And the old tree is dead.

BORKMAN (*not listening to her*): Can you see the smoke from the great steamers out on the fjord?

ELLA: No.

BORKMAN: I can. They come and go. They create a sense of fellowship throughout the world. They bring light and warmth to the hearts of men in many thousands of homes. That is what I dreamed of creating.

ELLA (*quietly*): But it remained a dream.

BORKMAN: Yes. It remained a dream. (*Listens*) Listen. Down there by the river the factories hum. *My* factories. Listen how they hum. The night shifts are working. They work both night and day. Listen, listen! The wheels whirl and the pistons thud, round and round, in and out. Can't you hear them, Ella?

ELLA: No.

BORKMAN: I hear them.

ELLA (*frightened*): No, John, you can't.

BORKMAN: Ah, but these are only the outworks surrounding the kingdom.

ELLA: What kingdom?

BORKMAN: My kingdom! The kingdom I was about to take possession of when I died.

198

ELLA: Oh, John, John!

BORKMAN: And there it lies, defenceless, masterless, abandoned to thieves and robbers. Ella! Do you see those mountains far away? Range beyond range, rising and towering. That is my infinite and inexhaustible kingdom.

ELLA: Ah, but it's a cold wind that blows from that kingdom, John.

BORKMAN: To me it is the breath of life. It is a greeting from the spirits that serve me. I feel them, those buried millions. I see those veins of iron ore, stretching their twisting, branching, enticing arms towards me. I've seen you all before, like shadows brought to life—that night when I stood in the vaults of the bank with the lantern in my hand. You wanted to be freed. And I tried to free you. But I failed. Your treasure sank back into the darkness. (*Stretching out his hands*) But let me whisper this to you now, in the stillness of the night. I love you where you lie like the dead, deep down in the dark. I love you, treasures that crave for life, with your bright retinue of power and glory. I love you, love you, love you.

ELLA: Yes, your love is still buried down there, John. It always has been. But up here, in the daylight, there was a warm, living heart beating for you, and you broke it. Worse, you sold it—for—

BORKMAN (*a cold shiver seems to go through him*): For the kingdom—and the power—and the glory, you mean?

ELLA: That is what I mean. And therefore I prophesy, John Gabriel Borkman, that you will never get the price you demanded for that murder. You will never ride triumphant into your cold kingdom.

BORKMAN (*staggers to the seat and sits down heavily*): I fear you are right, Ella.

ELLA: You must not fear that, John. It will be better for you.

BORKMAN (*clutches his chest with a cry*): Ah! (*Weakly*) Now it let go of me.

ELLA: What was it, John?

BORKMAN (*sinks back on the seat*): A hand of ice that gripped my heart.

ELLA: John! *You've* felt that hand of ice now?

BORKMAN (*mumbles*): No. Not a hand of ice. A hand of iron. (*He slides down upon the seat*).

ELLA (*tears off her coat and covers him with it*): Rest quietly, John. I'll go for help.

She goes a few paces right. Stops, goes back and feels his pulse and his face.

ELLA: No. Better so, John Borkman. Better so; for you.

She wraps her coat more tightly round him and sits down in the snow in front of the seat. MRS BORKMAN, in her greatcoat, enters through the forest on the right. In front of her goes the MAID with a lighted lantern.

MAID (*shining the lantern on the snow*): Yes, yes, madam. Here are their footprints.

MRS BORKMAN (*peering round*): Yes, there they are. Over on that seat. Ella!

ELLA (*rises*): Are you looking for us?

MRS BORKMAN: What else could I do?

ELLA: Here he is, Gunhild.

MRS BORKMAN: Asleep?

ELLA: A long, deep sleep, I am afraid.

MRS BORKMAN: Ella! (*Controls herself, and asks quietly*) Was it—deliberate?

ELLA: No.

MRS BORKMAN (*relieved*): Not by his own hand, then?

ELLA: No. A hand of iron gripped his heart.

MRS BORKMAN (*to MAID*): Go for help. Get some people from the farm.

MAID: Very good, madam. (*To herself*) God in Heaven! (*Goes out right, through the forest*).

MRS BORKMAN (*behind the seat*): So the night air killed him.

ELLA: So it seems.

MRS BORKMAN: That strong man.

ELLA (*goes in front of the seat*): Won't you look at him, Gunhild?

MRS BORKMAN: No, no! (*Quietly*) John Gabriel Borkman was a miner's son. He couldn't live in the fresh air.

ELLA: I think it was the cold that killed him.

MRS BORKMAN: The cold? That killed him long ago.

ELLA: And turned us into shadows.

MRS BORKMAN: Yes.

ELLA: One dead man and two shadows. See what the cold has done.

MRS BORKMAN: Yes. The coldness of the heart. And now I think we two can join hands, Ella.

ELLA: I think we can, now.

MRS BORKMAN: We twin sisters—over the man we both loved.

ELLA: We two shadows—over the dead man.

MRS BORKMAN *behind the seat, and* ELLA *in front of it, join hands.*

When We Dead Awaken

INTRODUCTION

When We Dead Awaken, Ibsen's last play, is the least known in
England of all his mature works. It has never been adequately
staged in London, though Michael Elliot directed it memorably
in Edinburgh in 1968 (see p.214). William Archer did not
understand it, and thought it evidenced senility.[1] C. E.
Montague also found it bewildering. "The play as a whole
affected us like a large complicated machine working in a dark
room; one peered in here and there, and saw part of a wheel
going round with apparent purpose, or a piece of belting that
seemed to imply coherence in the whole apparatus, but the next
moment it whirled on undistinguishably, and even that small
clue was lost. However," he added, "likely enough, when we
stupid awaken, we shall find the queer, tough play a big thing,
and even a clear one."

Two people at least, had already found it big. "It shews no
decay of Ibsen's highest qualities," wrote Bernard Shaw.
"His magic is nowhere more potent. It is shorter than usual;
that is all." And the young James Joyce, writing in the
Fortnightly Review in 1900, proclaimed: "On the whole,
When We Dead Awaken may rank with the greatest of the
author's work if, indeed, it be not the greatest."

It is significant that *When We Dead Awaken* should so
have appealed to Joyce, for, although Ibsen sub-titled it
"A Dramatic Epilogue", he took pains to make clear that
he intended it, not as his final word, but as a declaration that
he had now finished with the realistic type of drama through
which he had won international recognition, and was

[1] "It is scabrous to a degree—if it weren't like deserting the Old Man,
'pon my soul I'd let someone else translate it." (Letter to Charles Archer,
14 December 1899).

intending to break out into new and experimental fields. When, a few days before the publication of the play in December 1899, the Danish newspaper *Politiken* assumed from the sub-title that "with this play the author will have said his last word, and will thereby have written *finis* to his dramatic work," the correspondent of another newspaper, *Verdens Gang*, asked Ibsen if this were true. Ibsen replied:

"No, that conclusion has been too hastily reached. The word 'epilogue' was not meant by me to have any such implications. Whether I write any more is another question, but all I meant by 'epilogue', in this context, was that the play forms an epilogue to the series of plays which began with *A Doll's House* and which now ends with *When We Dead Awaken.* . . . It completes the cycle, and makes of it an entity, and now I am finished with it. If I write anything more, it will be in quite another context; perhaps, too, in another form."

Within a month, on New Year's Day 1900, he told Ernst Motzfeldt that he wanted to begin work on a new play; and on 5 March he wrote to his French translator, Moritz Prosor: "If it be granted to me to retain the strength of body and spirit which I still enjoy, I shall not be able to absent myself for long from the old battlefields. But if I return, I shall come forward with new weapons, and with new equipment."

I do not think there is much doubt that, by these remarks, Ibsen meant that he was finished with orthodox realism and was intending to move, as Strindberg had recently done, back towards poetry and symbolism. This tendency had already found expression in the final act of *John Gabriel Borkman*, which he had completed in 1896. In 1898 Strindberg had sent Ibsen a copy of his new and highly symbolic drama, *To Damascus*, and although Ibsen seldom read books ("I leave them to my wife", he once said, and most of the presentation copies in his library remain uncut) it is known that he read both volumes of *To Damascus*. Nor, surely, is it without significance that, at this time, he had an oil-painting of Strindberg on his study wall. He had bought it, he explained, not because of any sympathy or friendship with either the painter or Strindberg, but because "I am now not able to write a word without having that madman staring down at me!" One can only speculate on what Ibsen would have written if illness had not struck him down and rendered him helpless for the last years of his life; but *When We Dead Awaken* gives us a hint, and one may speculate on its possible influence on Joyce, who was to make the same decision to abandon realism in favour of symbolism barely a dozen years later.

Theatrically, the chief difficulties that *When We Dead Awaken* offers are not, as Montague suggested, difficulties of staging; snow-peaks and avalanches, which Montague thought it impossible to present, pose no insuperable problems to an imaginative director, as the 1959 London performance of *Brand* proved. The real trouble with *When We Dead Awaken* is that it is one of those plays, like *King Lear* and *Brand*, which, unless they are played big, had better not be played at all. Ibsen's realistic plays, such as *Ghosts*, can be presented as domestic melodramas with the subtleties and overtones ironed out, and can still be reasonably successful, just as a performance of *Hamlet* on a thriller level can be. One cannot do either of these things with *When We Dead Awaken*. Although it exists on a realistic level, it exists much more powerfully on a symbolic one; Rubek and Irene are the shadows of mighty archetypal creatures moving near the sun.

A vital factor in any discussion or presentation of *When We Dead Awaken* is Irene's age. This is not specified anywhere in the play, and although Ibsen once told Gunnar Heiberg that she should be twenty-eight, and then grudgingly allowed that she might be forty, I am sure Mr Casper Wrede is right in suggesting that, for the play to seem plausible and achieve its full effect, she should be played as a woman of sixty-five and Rubek as a man of seventy. A mad woman of forty who complains that her life has been wasted arouses limited sympathy; a deranged woman of sixty-five who makes the same complaint is a much more tragic figure. The love affair that never was then becomes something dimly remembered from long ago. It is not a dozen years but half a century of wasted life that they are looking back on; and, at the end, as Maja and Ulfhejm, the young and the strong, descend to the valley of what they call life, the two old people climb upwards to what they have come to believe is the only real life, the kind that is attained through the death of the body.

When We Dead Awaken is not only Ibsen's most experimental play; it is also his final account with himself. He had portrayed different facets of himself in most of his plays: the unsatisfactory husband preoccupied with his work (Tesman in *Hedda Gabler*, Allmers in *Little Eyolf*,) the uncompromising idealist who brings unhappiness to those he loves most (Brand, Gregers Werle in *The Wild Duck*, Dr Stockmann in *An Enemy of the People*), the egoistic artist (Ejnar in *Brand*, Hjalmar Ekdal in *The Wild Duck*, Lyngstrand in *The Lady from the Sea*), the ruthless old man who despises the world and neglects his wife (Solness in *The Master Builder*, John Gabriel Borkman). But nowhere do we find so complete and merciless a self-portrait as the character of Rubek in *When We Dead Awaken*. The aging artist, restless in his married life, restless in the homeland to which he has returned after a long sojourn abroad, restless in his art, shocked, like Brand, near the top of a mountain, into the realisation that to reject love is to reject life; such is Ibsen's Portrait of the Dramatist as an Old Man, painted at the age of seventy-one.

Ibsen wrote *When We Dead Awaken* in Christiania in 1899. Although for the past eight years he had been living in Norway, after twenty-seven years in Italy and Germany, he had never really settled down there. In a letter to Georg Brandes dated 3 June 1897 (eight months after he had completed *John Gabriel Borkman*) he wrote: "Can you guess what I am dreaming of, and planning, and picturing to myself as delightful? It is to settle somewhere in the Sound, between Copenhagen and Elsinore, in a free, open place, where I shall be able to see all the deep-sea ships coming from afar and going afar. Here I can't do that. Here every sound is locked (in both senses); every channel of understanding is stopped. Oh, my dear Brandes, one does not live for twenty-seven years out in the great, free, liberating world of culture for nothing. Here among the fjords is my native land. But—but—but—where shall I find my home? The sea is what draws me most. I live here alone and plan some new dramatic work. But I can't yet see clearly what shape it will take."

It was Ibsen's routine to begin a new play two summers after he had completed the previous one, but he was much distracted during 1898 by celebrations in honour of his seventieth birthday, not only in Norway, but also in Sweden and Denmark. At the banquet given for him in Christiania he spoke of his wish "to dispel the misconception which in many ways has hampered me—I mean, the idea that un-alloyed happiness must naturally have resulted from the unusual fortune which has been granted to me in winning reputation and fame in foreign lands. I have also found friendship and understanding there; which is much more impor-tant. But inward happiness, real happiness; that is not some-thing which one just finds, or receives like a gift. It must be earned, at a price which often seems heavy. For the truth is that a man who has won for himself a home in many foreign lands feels in his heart of hearts nowhere truly at home, hardly even in his own fatherland."

He then surprised his hearers by announcing his intention of writing a non-dramatic autobiographical work: "a book which will knit my life and my work into a comprehensible whole. Yes; for I think I have by now reached a sufficiently ripe age to be granted a short breathing-space—to take a year's holiday—for the writing of such a book would be a holiday in comparison with the vexatious and exhausting business of writing plays. I have never taken a real holiday since I left Norway thirty-four years ago; and I think I could do with one now. But, ladies and gentlemen, you must not therefore assume that I intend to lay down my dramatic pen. No; I intend to take it up again, and to hold on to it tightly until the end. I have, you see, a few crazy ideas left in my head which I have not yet found occasion to express. Not until I have rid myself of them will it be time for me to lay down my pen."

In Copenhagen that spring (1898) Ibsen for the first time saw *Brand* performed. The actress Oda Nielsen, who sat next to him during the performance (her husband was playing the title-role) related that when it was over Ibsen said to her: "This moves me. This is—all my youth. I haven't thought about *Brand* for thirty years." We are told that he lay awake most of that night, thinking about the play he was going to write. As he lay there, he may have remembered, consciously or unconsciously, that thirty years before, just after *Brand* had brought him the recognition from his countrymen that he had longed for, he had remarked to Georg Brandes (26 June 1869) that Brand "could as well have been a sculptor or a politician as a priest." The chief character in his new play was to be a sculptor, of the same uncompromising ruthlessness as Brand; and, like Brand, he was to die in an avalanche near the top of a mountain, his pride crushed, with a Latin blessing cried out to him as though from a forgiving deity at the moment of death.

Later that month he visited Stockholm, and attended a dinner given for him at Skansen by two Swedish women's organizations. To entertain their guest they had arranged an exhibition of folk dancing, and among the dancers was a young girl who especially attracted his attention. Her name was Rosa Fitinghoff; he talked to her several times during the evening, and asked her to see him off at the station next day. On his return to Christiania he sent her his photograph, with an accompanying note:

"When I received your beautiful postcard, it was as though you had entered my house yourself with a spring greeting to warm my heart. There was music and dance in what you wrote; and it was through dance and music that we met. That is the happy part of the story. The sad part is that we did not meet until my last evening. Parties are often like life; people do not meet until they have to say goodbye. But go on writing to me."

During the past ten years Ibsen had entered into relationships of close affection with several young girls; Emilie Bardach, an eighteen-year-old Viennese girl; Helene Raff, a German painter; and Hildur Andersen, a Norwegian pianist. None of these relationships seems to have developed into an affair. Helene Raff in a letter written in 1927 said: "Ibsen's relations with young girls had in them nothing whatever of infidelity in the usual sense of the term, but arose solely out of the needs of his imagination; as he himself said, he sought out youth because he needed it for his poetic production". His farewell message to Emilie Bardach, inscribed in her album on 20 September 1889, has a pathetic ring about it: "*Hohes, schmerzliches Glück—um das Unerreichbare zu ringen*"—"High and painful joy—to struggle for the unattainable."

In 1895 Georg Brandes had sent Ibsen an essay he had written about the young Marianne von Willemer's infatuation for Goethe, when the latter was sixty-six, and its stimulating effect on the poetry of his old age. This essay had greatly interested Ibsen; in a letter dated 11 February 1895 he wrote to Brandes: "I cannot forbear to send you especial thanks for your *Goethe and Marianne von Willemer*. I didn't know anything about the episode you describe in it. I may have read about it years ago, in Lewes's book, but if so I had forgotten it, because at that time the affair held no particular interest for me. But now things are somewhat different. When I think of the quality that characterises Goethe's work during that period, I mean the sense of renewed youth, I ought to have guessed that he must have been graced with some such revelation, some such reassurance of beauty, as his meeting with Marianne von Willemer. Fate, Providence, Chance, can be genial and benevolent powers now and then."

In July 1898, three months after their meeting in Stockholm, Ibsen invited Rosa Fitinghoff to visit him in Christiania that summer. She did not come that year, but they continued to correspond; the following April we find him thanking her for a blue anemone she had sent him to mark the anniversary of their first meeting. He told her that he always glanced at where her letters lay before starting work. He had begun his new play that winter (an unusual time for him), or had at any rate written down his title page—*The Day of Resurrection* he called it at first—and his cast list, for these are dated 20 February 1899; but spring came, and summer, and still he, who normally wrote so rapidly, had not finished the first act. With the summer, however, Rosa came to Christiania, with her mother, the authoress Laura Fitinghoff; and her visit thawed his inspiration. On 31 July he finished the first act. On 2 August he began the second act, and finished it on 23 August; and on 25 August he began the third act, which he finished on 21 September. By this time he had altered the title to *When The* [sic] *Dead Awaken*.

It was, however, a further two months before the final fair copy was ready to go to the printer. The most notable piece of revision concerns the ending. In his original draft Rubek and Irene reach their mountain-peak, and the closing lines of the play read as follows:

RUBEK (*to* IRENE): Up above the mists I glimpse the mountain-peak. It stands there, glittering in the sunrise. That is where our path lies. Through the mists of night, up into the light of morning.

The mist closes down more quickly over the scene. RUBEK *and* IRENE *step down into the veil of mist, and gradually disappear from sight. The* NUN'S *head appears in a rift in the mist, searching for them. High up above the sea of mist the mountain peak shines in the morning sun.*

The Nun, one supposes, like the house in *Rosmersholm* and the crutch in *Little Eyolf*, symbolizes the past that stands in the way of happiness. But Ibsen changed this ending. In the final version Rubek and Irene are killed by the descending avalanche, the Nun's voice whispers a blessing on them, and the last sound as the curtain falls, is Maja singing triumphantly as she descends into the valley. I think we must assume that, by this revision, Ibsen wanted to point the contrast between the two different ideas of what is meant by life. Maja and Ulfhejm return to what they think is life, but what Rubek and Irene regard as death, while Rubek and Irene climb upwards to what the others regard as death but they regard as life. As long as people remain imprisoned in flesh, Ibsen seems to say, they are dead; it is only when the body dies that the dead awaken.

Ibsen completed his revision of the play on 21 November 1899, and sent it to the printer the following day. *When We Dead Awaken* (as he finally entitled it, as though wishing to identify himself conclusively with the choice made by Rubek and Irene) was published on 22 December simultaneously in Copenhagen, Christiania and Berlin, and received its first performance proper at the Hoftheater, Stuttgart, on 26 January 1900.[1] Within a month it had been played at many other theatres throughout Germany, as well as in Copenhagen, Helsinki, Christiania and Stockholm. In 1902 a notable production was given at the Deutsches Theater in Berlin, with Albert Basserman and Irene Triesch. London saw the play in 1903 and New York in 1905, at the Knickerbocker Theatre, with Frederick Lewis as Rubek and Florence Kahn (later the wife of Max Beerbohm) as Irene.

In the spring of 1900 Ibsen had a stroke, and he spent the summer in a sanatorium at Sandefjord undergoing a cure for erysipelas. The following year he spoke again of his intention to write a new play, but then he had a second stroke which left him unable to walk or write, and he remained virtually paralysed until his death on 23 May 1906.

MICHAEL MEYER

[1] As with all of his plays from *Hedda Gabler* onwards, however, a special edition of twelve copies in Norwegian, identical with the Copenhagen edition except for the title-page, had been published in London by William Heinemann three days earlier to secure copyright, since Denmark did not join the Berne Convention until 1903. A public reading of the play in Norwegian had already been given at the Theatre Royal, Haymarket, on 16 December (at 10 a.m., a formidable hour at which to listen to such a work) to secure performing copyright.

CHARACTERS

PROFESSOR ARNOLD RUBEK, a sculptor
MAJA, his wife
THE INSPECTOR (at the Baths)
ULFHEJM, a country squire
A LADY TRAVELLER
A NUN
WAITERS, GUESTS AND CHILDREN.

The action takes place in Norway—the first act at a coastal watering place, the second and third acts in the grounds and vicinity of a mountain health resort.

This translation of When We Dead Awaken *was first performed on 9 February 1961 at the Gate Theatre, Dublin. The cast was:*

RUBEK	Anew McMaster
MAJA	Barbara Chilcott
INSPECTOR	Desmond O'Neill
ULFHEJM	William Marshall
IRENE	Madalena Nicol
NUN	Maureen Halligan

Directed by Cyril Frankel

On 26 August 1968, it was performed at the Assembly Hall, Edinburgh. The cast was:

RUBEK	Alexander Knox
MAJA	Irene Hamilton
INSPECTOR	Roger Swaine
ULFHEJM	Brian Cox
IRENE	Wendy Hiller
NUN	Brenda McGuinne

Directed by Michael Elliott

This production was televised on 12 February 1970 by the B.B.C., with the same cast and director.

ACT ONE

Outside the Spa Hotel at a watering place on the Norwegian coast. It is an open, park-like space, with fountains, shrubs, and clumps of large old trees. On the left stands a little pavilion, covered with ivy and wild vine. In the background the fjord is visible, stretching right out to sea, with tongues of land and small islets in the distance. It is a still, hot summer morning.

PROFESSOR RUBEK and his wife, MAJA, are seated in basket chairs beside a laid table on the lawn outside the hotel. They have just lunched; now they are drinking champagne and seltzer, and each has a newspaper. The PROFESSOR is an elderly, distinguished-looking man wearing a black velvet jacket; apart from this he is in light summer clothes. MAJA RUBEK looks youthful, and has a lively face and bright, provocative eyes; yet there is a hint of tiredness about her. She is dressed in elegant travelling clothes.

MAJA (*sits for a moment as though waiting for the PROFESSOR to say something. Then she lowers her newspaper, and sighs*).
RUBEK (*looks up from his newspaper*): Well, Maja, what's the matter with you?
MAJA: Just listen to the silence!
RUBEK (*smiles indulgently*): Can you hear it?
MAJA: Hear what?
RUBEK: The silence.
MAJA: I certainly can.
RUBEK: Perhaps you're right, my dear. One really can hear the silence.
MAJA: God knows one can. When it's as deafening as it is here—
RUBEK: Here at the baths, you mean?
MAJA: Everywhere in Norway. Oh, down in the city it

215

was noisy enough. But even there, I thought all that noise and bustle had something dead about it.

RUBEK (*looks hard at her*): Aren't you happy to be home again, Maja?

MAJA: Are *you*?

RUBEK: I?

MAJA: Yes. You've been abroad so much, much longer than I. Are you really happy to be home again?

RUBEK: No, to be perfectly honest. Not really happy.

MAJA: There, you see. I knew it.

RUBEK: Perhaps I have been abroad too long. This northern provincial life seems foreign to me.

MAJA (*eagerly, pulling her chair towards him*): Let's go away again! As quickly as possible.

RUBEK (*a trifle impatiently*): Well, we *are* going, Maja. You know that.

MAJA: Why not now, right away? We could be so comfortable down there, in our lovely new house—

RUBEK (*smiles indulgently again*): Shouldn't you rather say "our lovely new home"?

MAJA (*curtly*): I prefer to say "house." Let's use that word.

RUBEK (*gives her a long look*): You're a funny little creature, really.

MAJA: Am I so funny?

RUBEK: Yes, I think so.

MAJA: Why? Because I don't want to stay pottering around up here?

RUBEK: Who was it who was so insistent that we should come north this summer?

MAJA: I suppose it was I.

RUBEK: Well it certainly wasn't I.

MAJA: But, good God, how could I have known everything would have changed so dreadfully? And in such a short time! I mean, it's only just four years since I went away—

RUBEK: Since you got married, you mean.

MAJA: Married? What's that got to do with it?

RUBEK (*continues*): Since you became Mrs Arnold Rubek, and the mistress of a beautiful home—oh, I beg your pardon,

I should have said a handsome house. And a villa on the Taunitzer See—surrounded by all the best people. And it *is* very fine and handsome, Maja, there's no denying that. And very spacious. We don't have to sit in each other's laps all the time—

MAJA (*passing it off lightly*): No, no—we've got all the room we need—

RUBEK: Exactly; you've grown used to a more spacious and luxurious way of life. And a more gracious society than you'd been accustomed to at home.

MAJA: Oh, so you think it's I who've changed?

RUBEK: Yes, Maja. I do.

MAJA: Not the people here?

RUBEK: Oh, yes, they've changed too, a little, no doubt. And not for the better. That I'm prepared to concede.

MAJA: I'm glad to hear it.

RUBEK (*changing the subject*): Do you know what I'm reminded of when I look at the people here and the way they live?

MAJA: No. What?

RUBEK: It reminds me of that night we spent in the train, when we were coming up from the Continent—

MAJA: You were asleep the whole time.

RUBEK: Not the whole time. I noticed how silent it was at all the little places we stopped at. I—heard the silence— like you, Maja—And then I realized we had crossed the frontier. Now we were home. I knew it, because at every one of these little roadside halts, the train stopped, and stood quite still—though nothing ever happened.

MAJA: Why did it stop if there was no one there?

RUBEK: Don't know. No one got off, no one got on—and yet the train stood there, absolutely silent, for minute after minute—as it might have been eternity. And at every station I heard two men walking down the platform—one of them had a lantern in his hand—and they muttered to each other, softly, tonelessly, meaninglessly in the night.

MAJA: Yes, you're right. There are always two men who walk and talk together—

Rubek: About nothing. (*Changes his tone, and speaks more cheerfully*) Never mind, we only have to wait until to-morrow. Then the liner will put into harbour; and we shall go on board, and sail along the coast, northwards, as far as we can go—right up into the Arctic.

Maja: Yes, but then you won't see anything of the country, and the people. And that's what you came for.

Rubek (*curtly and irritably*): I've seen more than enough.

Maja: Do you think a sea-voyage'll be better for you?

Rubek: Well, it's always a change.

Maja: All right, if you think it'll be good for you—

Rubek: Good for me? For me? There's nothing the matter with me.

Maja (*gets up and goes over to him*): Yes, there is, Rubek. And you know it.

Rubek: But, my dear, what should be the matter with me?

Maja (*behind him, leaning over the back of his chair*): You tell me. You've begun to wander round restlessly, as though you couldn't find peace, at home or anywhere else. And you've begun to avoid people lately.

Rubek (*with a touch of sarcasm*): Really? You've noticed that?

Maja: No one who knows you could help noticing it. And I think it's such a pity you've lost your passion for work—

Rubek: That, too?

Maja: You used to work all the time. Day and night—

Rubek: Used to.

Maja: But ever since you finished your masterpiece—

Rubek (*nods reflectively*): "The Day of Resurrection."

Maja: The masterpiece which has been exhibited all over the world, and has made you famous—

Rubek: Perhaps that's where it began to go wrong, Maja.

Maja: What do you mean?

Rubek: When I completed my masterpiece—(*makes a passionate gesture with his hand*)—For "The Day of Resurrection" is a masterpiece. Or was, when I first— No, it still is! It must, must, *must* be a masterpiece!

Maja (*stares at him surprised*): Yes, Rubek. The whole world knows that.

RUBEK: The world knows nothing. It understands nothing.

MAJA: At least they can sense *something*—

RUBEK: Something that isn't there, oh yes! Something I've never imagined. And that is what they all go mad about! (*Growls to himself*) What's the use of working oneself to death to please the masses—the mob—"the whole world"?

MAJA: Are you better occupied nowadays, churning out these portrait busts? Do you really think they're worthy of you?

RUBEK (*smiles forbearingly*): They are not ordinary portrait busts, Maja.

MAJA: Oh, yes they are. These last two or three years—ever since you got that big group finished and out of the house—

RUBEK: Nevertheless, they are not ordinary portraits. Believe me.

MAJA: What are they, then?

RUBEK: There is something hidden within those faces. A secret meaning which people cannot see.

MAJA: Oh, really?

RUBEK: Only I can see it. And I find it intensely amusing. Superficially, there are these "striking likenesses" as they call them, at which people gape, entranced. But deep within, I have sculpted the righteous and estimable faces of horses, the opinionated muzzles of donkeys, the lop ears and shallow brows of dogs, the overgorged chaps of swine, and the dull and brutalised fronts of oxen.

MAJA (*indifferently*): All nice, domestic animals, poor dears.

RUBEK: Just nice, domestic animals, Maja. All the animals which man has corrupted in his own image. And which have corrupted him in return. (*Empties his champagne glass and smiles*) And these disingenuous works of art are what our honest burghers commission from me—and pay for, in good faith and solid cash. Oh, they are almost literally worth their weight in gold.

MAJA (*fills his glass*): Shame on you, Rubek. Drink, and be happy.

RUBEK (*wipes his brow several times, and leans back in his chair*): I am happy, Maja. Really happy. In a way. (*Is silent for a moment*) I mean, there is a certain happiness in feeling absolutely free and independent—in having everything one could possibly wish for. Everything material, I mean. Don't you agree, Maja?

MAJA: Oh, yes, I suppose so. It's not to be despised. (*Looks at him*) But do you remember what you promised me that day when we agreed on this arrangement—?

RUBEK (*nods*): Agreed that we two should marry. It was a little difficult for you, wasn't it, Maja?

MAJA (*continues deliberately*): And I was to go abroad with you, and stay there, and enjoy myself, always. Can you remember what you promised me then?

RUBEK (*shakes his head*): I'll be damned if I can. What did I promise you?

MAJA: You said you would take me with you to the top of a high mountain, and show me all the glory of the world.

RUBEK (*starts*): Did I promise that to you, too?

MAJA (*looks at him*): Me too? Who else?

RUBEK (*casually*): No, no, I only meant, did I promise to show you—?

MAJA: All the glory of the world. Yes, that's what you said. And all that glory was to be mine, and yours, you said.

RUBEK: It was a phrase I used to be fond of.

MAJA: Only a phrase?

RUBEK: Yes. From my school days. I used to say it to the other children when I wanted to get them to come and play with me in the forest or up in the mountains.

MAJA: Perhaps that was all you wanted me for? To play games with?

RUBEK (*passing it off as a joke*): Well, it's been quite an enjoyable game, hasn't it, Maja?

MAJA (*coldly*): I didn't go away with you just to play games.

RUBEK: No, no, I dare say not.

MAJA: And you never took me with you up any mountain, to show me—

RUBEK (*irritated*): All the glory of the world? No, I didn't. The fact is, little Maja, you were not exactly made to climb mountains.

MAJA (*tries to control herself*): You seemed to think I was, once.

RUBEK: Four or five years ago, yes. (*Stretches in his chair*) Four or five years. That's a long, long time, Maja.

MAJA (*looks at him bitterly*): Has it seemed so long to you, Rubek?

RUBEK: It begins to seem a little long now. (*Yawns*) Just now and then.

MAJA (*goes back to her chair*): Well, I won't bore you any longer.

She sits in her chair, picks up her newspaper and turns the pages. Silence on both sides.

RUBEK (*leans across the table on his elbows and stares banteringly at her*): Is the Frau Professor offended?

MAJA (*coldly, without looking up*): Not in the least.

Visitors to the baths, mostly ladies, wander singly and in groups through the park from the right, and go out left. Waiters carry refreshments from the hotel out past the pavilion. The INSPECTOR, wearing gloves and carrying a stick, comes from his round of the park, meets the visitors, greets them respectfully, and exchanges a few words with some of them.

INSPECTOR (*comes forward to PROFESSOR RUBEK'S table and takes his hat off respectfully*): May I have the honour to wish you a good morning, madam? Good morning, Professor.

RUBEK: Good morning, good morning, Inspector.

INSPECTOR (*addressing himself to MAJA*): May I enquire whether you have spent a good night?

MAJA: Thank you, yes, excellent—as far as I'm concerned. I always sleep like a log.

INSPECTOR: I am delighted to hear it. One's first night in a strange bed can sometimes be a trying experience. And you, Professor?

RUBEK: Oh, I always sleep badly. Especially recently.

INSPECTOR (*looks sympathetic*): Ah, I am sorry to hear that. But a few weeks here with us, and things will be different.

RUBEK (*looks up at him*): Tell me, Inspector—have you a patient who is in the habit of bathing at night?

INSPECTOR: At night? No, I've never heard of such a thing.

RUBEK: You haven't?

INSPECTOR: No, I don't know of anyone here who's so ill as to require *that*.

RUBEK: Well, is there someone who takes a nightly walk in the park?

INSPECTOR (*smiles and shakes his head*): No, Professor—that would be against the regulations.

MAJA (*impatiently*): For heaven's sake, Rubek, I told you this morning. You've been dreaming.

RUBEK (*drily*): Really? Have I? Thank you. (*Turns to the* INSPECTOR) It so happens I couldn't sleep last night, so I got up. I wanted to see what kind of a night it was—

INSPECTOR: Yes, Professor? And—?

RUBEK: So I looked out of the window. And I saw a figure dressed in white over there among the trees.

MAJA (*smiles at the* INSPECTOR): And the Professor says this figure was wearing a bathing dress.

RUBEK: Or something of the sort, I said. I couldn't see closely enough. I could only tell it was something white.

INSPECTOR: Most remarkable. Was it a gentleman or a lady?

RUBEK: A lady, I'm almost sure. But behind walked another figure. And this second figure was quite dark—like a shadow—

INSPECTOR: A dark figure? Was it black?

RUBEK: Yes, it appeared so to me.

INSPECTOR (*beginning to understand*): And it walked behind the white figure? Close behind her?

RUBEK: Yes, a little way behind.

INSPECTOR: Ah! Then I may be able to explain this mystery for you, Professor.

RUBEK: Well, tell me—who was it?

MAJA (*simultaneously*): You mean he wasn't dreaming after all?

INSPECTOR (*whispers, and points upstage, right*): Ssh, Professor! Look over there! Lower your voices for a moment, please!

A slender LADY, *dressed in fine, cream cashmere, enters past the corner of the hotel, followed by a* NUN *dressed in black, with a silver cross hanging from a chain on her breast. She walks through the park towards the pavilion downstage left. Her face is pale and drawn, as though numbed; her eyelids droop, and her eyes seem not to see. Her dress reaches to her feet, falling in long even folds close to her body. Over her head, neck, breast, shoulders, and arms, she wears a large, white, crepe shawl. Her arms are folded across her breast. She carries her body stiffly, and her steps are measured and precise. The* NUN'S *demeanour is similarly precise, and suggests that of a servant. She watches the* LADY *ceaselessly with sharp brown eyes. Waiters with napkins on their arms come to the door of the hotel and stare curiously at the two strangers, who take no notice and, without looking round, enter the pavilion.*

RUBEK (*has risen slowly and involuntarily from his chair, and is staring at the closed pavilion door*): Who was that lady?

INSPECTOR: A visitor who has rented that little pavilion.

RUBEK: Is she foreign?

INSPECTOR: I think she must be. They arrived here from abroad, anyway. About a week ago. They've never been here before.

RUBEK: She is the one I saw in the park last night.

INSPECTOR: It must have been. The thought occurred to me at once.

RUBEK: What is this lady's name, Inspector?

INSPECTOR: She registered as Madame de Satow and companion. That's all we know.

RUBEK (*reflectively*): Satow? Satow?

MAJA: Do you know anyone of that name, Rubek? Hm?

RUBEK (*shakes his head*): No, no one. Satow? That sounds Russian; or Slavonic, anyway. (*To the* INSPECTOR) What language does she speak?

INSPECTOR: When the two ladies talk together, they use a language I don't understand, but at other times she speaks good honest Norwegian.

RUBEK: Norwegian? Are you sure you're not mistaken?

INSPECTOR: How could I be? I've talked to her several times. Only a few words, she's very reticent. But—

RUBEK: But she spoke Norwegian?

INSPECTOR: Good, pure Norwegian. Possibly with a slight northern intonation.

RUBEK (*to himself*): That too!

MAJA (*a little hurt and ill at ease*): Perhaps the lady has been your model at some time, Rubek. Think back, now.

RUBEK (*looks sharply at her*): Model?

MAJA (*teasingly*): Yes, when you were young. Think of all those models you used to have. In the old days, I mean.

RUBEK: No, little Maja; to tell the truth, I have only ever had one model. Only one—for everything I have created.

INSPECTOR (*who has turned and stands looking away to the left*): I am afraid I must ask you to excuse me now. I see someone coming whom I would rather not speak to. Especially when a lady is present.

RUBEK (*glances in the same direction*): Who's the hunter?

INSPECTOR: That is Squire Ulfhejm, from—

RUBEK: Oh, Squire Ulfhejm.

INSPECTOR: The bear-baiter, they call him.

RUBEK: I know him.

INSPECTOR: Yes, who doesn't?

RUBEK: Only slightly. Has he come here for treatment at last?

INSPECTOR: No, surprisingly enough, not yet. He just passes through once a year, on his way up to his hunting-grounds. Please excuse me. (*Turns to go into the hotel*).

ULFHEJM (*offstage*): Wait a minute! Wait a minute, damn your eyes! Why do you always scuttle away when I come?

INSPECTOR (*stops*): I was not scuttling, Squire Ulfhejm.

SQUIRE ULFHEJM *enters from the left, followed by a* SERVANT *leading a pack of hounds. The* SQUIRE *is in shooting costume, with high boots and a felt hat with a feather in it. He is a lean, tall, sinewy man, with matted hair and beard, and a loud voice. His age is difficult to judge from his appearance, but he is no longer young.*

ULFHEJM (*pouncing on the* INSPECTOR): What kind of a way's that to receive visitors, eh? Running away with your tail between your legs as though the Devil was on your heels!

INSPECTOR (*calmly, ignoring the question*): Have you—ah—come with the steamer, sir?

ULFHEJM (*growls*): Ain't had the pleasure of seeing any damn steamer. (*With his hands on his hips*) Don't you know I always sail in my own cutter? (*To the* SERVANT) Take good care of your fellow-creatures, Lars. Keep 'em ravenous, though. Fresh meat-bones—but not too much meat on 'em, mind! And be sure it's reeking raw, with plenty of blood in it. And get something in your own belly, too. (*Aims a kick at him*) Well, get to Hell out of here!

The SERVANT *goes out with the hounds past the corner of the hotel.*

INSPECTOR: Won't you go into the restaurant, sir?

ULFHEJM: What, among all those dead flies and half-dead people? No thank you, Inspector.

INSPECTOR: Well, well, just as you please.

ULFHEJM: Just get the housekeeper to fix me up as usual. No stinting with the food, mind; and bring out your best aquavit. You can tell her that I or Lars'll come and put the fear of God into her if she doesn't—

INSPECTOR (*interrupts*): We know that from your previous visits. (*Turns*) Can I tell the waiter to bring you anything, Professor? Or something for Mrs Rubek, perhaps?

RUBEK: No, thank you, nothing for me.

MAJA: Nor for me.

The INSPECTOR *goes into the hotel.*

ULFHEJM (*glares at them for a moment, then raises his hat*): Death and damnation! This is fine company for a yokel like me to stray into!

RUBEK (*looks up*): I beg your pardon?

ULFHEJM (*more quietly and politely*): Isn't it master-carver Rubek himself?

RUBEK (*nods*): We met once or twice socially, the last autumn I spent in this country.

225

ULFHEJM: Yes, but that was years ago; and you weren't as famous then as I hear you've become now, so that in those days even a dirty bear-baiter dared to come within range of you.

RUBEK (*smiles*): Well, I don't bite, even now.

MAJA (*looks with interest at* ULFHEJM): Do you really hunt bears?

ULFHEJM (*seats himself at the next table, nearer the hotel*): Bears for choice, ma'am. But if they're not to be had, I'll take any wild thing that crosses my path. Eagles, wolves, women, elks, reindeer—as long as it's fresh and juicy and has good red blood in its veins. (*Drinks from his hip-flask*).

MAJA (*looking at him intently*): But bears for choice?

ULFHEJM: For choice, yes. If they give any trouble you can use your knife. (*With a slight smile*) We both like tough material to work on, ma'am, your husband and I. He struggles with his blocks of—marble, I suppose it'd be— and I with the bear. And both of us conquer our material in the end; make ourselves masters over it. We don't give up till we've brought it to heel, however strongly it resists us.

RUBEK (*thoughtfully*): There's truth in that.

ULFHEJM: Yes; even stone's got something to fight for. It's dead, and'll do everything it can to save itself from being chiselled into life. Just like a bear when you creep up and prod it in its lair.

MAJA: Are you going up to shoot in the forests?

ULFHEJM: Yes, high up in the mountains. I dare say you've never been up to the top of a mountain, Mrs Rubek?

MAJA: No, never.

ULFHEJM: Death and damnation, then, make sure you go up this summer! Come along with me. I'll take you both, gladly.

MAJA: Thank you. But my husband is thinking of going on a sea voyage this summer.

RUBEK: Only along the coast, among the islands.

ULFHEJM: Why the devil do you want to waste your time in those tepid gutters? I never heard of such an idea—

226

frittering away the summer in that ditch water! Dishwater I call it!

MAJA: Do you hear that, Rubek?

ULFHEJM: No, come with me up to the mountains. It's clean up there; no people. You can't imagine what that means to me. But a little lady like you, Mrs—! (*He stops himself. The* NUN *comes out of the pavilion and goes into the hotel.* ULFHEJM *follows her with his eyes*) Look at her, eh? That black crow. Who's going to be buried today?

RUBEK: No one that I know of—

ULFHEJM: Well then, someone must be at death's door. People who don't know how to keep themselves healthy ought to have the decency to get themselves buried, and not waste time about it.

MAJA: Have you ever been ill, Squire Ulfhejm?

ULFHEJM: Never. If I had, I wouldn't be sitting here. Some of my best friends have, though.

MAJA: And what did you do for them?

ULFHEJM: Shot them, of course.

RUBEK (*stares at him*): Shot them?

MAJA (*pushes her chair back*): Shot them dead?

ULFHEJM (*nods*): I never miss, ma'am.

MAJA: But what could induce you to kill human beings?

ULFHEJM: Who's talking about human beings?

MAJA: You said your best friends.

ULFHEJM: I was referring to my dogs.

MAJA: Are they your closest friends?

ULFHEJM: None closer. Fine sense of honour—never let you down—hundred per cent loyal—grand sportsmen. As soon as one of 'em turns sick or starts to mope—bang! Off he goes. Into the next world.

The NUN *comes out of the hotel with a tray, on which milk and bread are set, and places it on the table outside the pavilion, which she then re-enters.*

ULFHEJM (*laughs scornfully*): Look at that! Call that food for human consumption? Watered milk, and soft, mushy

227

bread! Now you ought to see my fellows eat! Would you like to see 'em?

MAJA (*smiles at the* PROFESSOR *and gets up*): Yes, I'd love to.

ULFHEJM (*gets up too*): Spoken like a woman of spirit, ma'am. Come with me, then. Great red meat-bones—they swallow 'em whole—cough 'em up, and then gulp 'em down again. Does your heart good to watch 'em. Come along and I'll show 'em to you. And we'll talk some more about this trip up into the mountains—

He goes out round the corner of the hotel. MAJA *follows him. A moment later, the* STRANGE LADY *comes out of the pavilion and seats herself at her table. She raises the glass of milk and is about to drink when she sees* RUBEK. *She stops, and looks at him with empty, expressionless eyes.* RUBEK *remains seated at his table, staring earnestly and intently at her. At length, he rises, goes a few paces towards her, stops and says softly:*

RUBEK: I recognize you, Irene.

IRENE (*tonelessly, setting down her glass*): You've guessed, have you, Arnold?

RUBEK: And you recognize me too, I see.

IRENE: That's different.

RUBEK: Why is it different?

IRENE: You're still alive.

RUBEK: Alive?

IRENE (*after a short pause*): Who was the other person? The one you had with you at the table?

RUBEK: That? That was—my wife.

IRENE (*nods slowly*): Indeed? Good, Arnold. No concern of mine, then.

RUBEK (*uncertainly*): No, of course not.

IRENE: Someone you found after I died.

RUBEK: After you—? How do you mean, Irene?

IRENE: And the child? Our child is well? It has survived me, and become famous and honoured.

RUBEK (*smiles, as though at some distant memory*): Our child? Yes, that's what we called it. (*Trying to seem jovial*) Yes,

Irene, now our child has become famous all over the world. You've read about it, I suppose?

IRENE (*nods*): And has made its father famous. That was your dream.

RUBEK (*quietly, emotionally*): I owe everything to you, Irene, everything. Thank you.

IRENE (*sits silent for a moment*): If I had done as I should have, Arnold—

RUBEK: Yes?

IRENE: I should have killed that child.

RUBEK: Killed it, did you say?

IRENE (*whispers*): Killed it—before I left you. Smashed it, smashed it to pieces.

RUBEK: You could never have done that, Irene. You wouldn't have had the heart.

IRENE: No. I hadn't that kind of heart then.

RUBEK: But—afterwards?

IRENE: Since then I have killed it a thousand times. In the daylight and in the dark. Killed it in hatred, and revenge, and agony.

RUBEK (*goes close to her table, and asks softly*): Irene, tell me now, after all these years. Why did you leave me? Vanish without a trace—nowhere to be found?

IRENE: Oh, Arnold. Why should I tell you that now—when I am dead?

RUBEK: Was there someone else you had fallen in love with?

IRENE: There was someone who had no use for my love. Or my life. Any longer.

RUBEK: Let's not talk any more about the past. Where have you been, Irene? All my efforts to find you came to nothing?

IRENE: I passed into the darkness. While our child stood transfigured in the light.

RUBEK: Have you travelled?

IRENE: Yes. Travelled through many countries.

RUBEK (*gently*): And what have you been doing, Irene?

IRENE: Well, now, let me think. I have stood like a statue, naked on a revolving platform, in music halls. I made a lot of money. That was something I'd never done when I was with you, because you hadn't any. And I've been with men whom I could drive crazy. That was something I'd never been able to do to you, Arnold. You had such self-control.

RUBEK: You married, too, didn't you?

IRENE: Yes, I married one of them.

RUBEK: Who is your husband?

IRENE: He was a South American diplomat. (*With a cold smile*) I drove him crazy. He went mad; incurably, hopelessly mad. It was amusing while it lasted.

RUBEK: Where is he now?

IRENE: In a graveyard somewhere. With a fine big monument over him. And a lead bullet rattling in his skull.

RUBEK: Did he kill himself?

IRENE: Yes. He was kind enough to save me the trouble.

RUBEK: Aren't you sorry he's dead, Irene?

IRENE: Sorry who's dead?

RUBEK: Herr von Satow.

IRENE: He wasn't called Satow.

RUBEK: No?

IRENE: My second husband's name is Satow. He's a Russian—

RUBEK: And where is he?

IRENE: Far away in the Ural mountains. Among his gold mines.

RUBEK: He lives there?

IRENE (*shrugs her shoulders*): Lives? Lives? I think I've killed him, too.

RUBEK: Killed?

IRENE: Killed him with a fine, sharp dagger I always take to bed with me—

RUBEK: I don't believe you, Irene!

IRENE (*smiles gently*): It's true, Arnold, I promise you.

RUBEK (*sympathetically*): Have you never had any children?

IRENE: Yes, I have had many children.

RUBEK: And where are they now?

IRENE: I killed them.

RUBEK (*severely*): Now you are lying to me again.

IRENE: I killed them, I tell you! Without a moment's pity. As soon as they entered the world. No, long, long, before that. One after the other.

RUBEK: There is another meaning in everything you say.

IRENE: I can't help it. Every word I say to you is whispered in my ear.

RUBEK: I think I am the only person who can guess that meaning.

IRENE: You should be the only one.

RUBEK (*rests his hands on the table and looks deep into her eyes*): Some string inside you has broken.

IRENE (*gently*): Doesn't that always happen when someone dies?

RUBEK: Oh, Irene, forget these wild ideas! You are alive! Alive, alive!

IRENE (*rises slowly from her chair, trembling*): I was dead for many years. They came and tied me up, tied my arms together behind my back. Then they lowered me into a tomb, with iron bars across the door, and padded walls so that no one up above could hear the shrieks of the dead. But now, slowly, I am beginning to rise from the dead. (*She sits again*).

RUBEK (*after a moment*): Do you blame me for this? Do you hold me guilty?

IRENE: Yes.

RUBEK: Guilty of—of your death, as you call it?

IRENE: Guilty of leaving me no future but death. (*Changes her tone and says casually*) Why don't you sit down, Arnold?

RUBEK (*moves a chair and sits down at the table*): Look, Irene. Now we two are sitting together as we used to in the old days.

IRENE: A little apart; as in the old days.

RUBEK (*moving nearer*): That's how it had to be, then.

IRENE: Had to?

RUBEK: There had to be a distance between us.

IRENE: Was it so necessary, Arnold?

RUBEK: Do you remember what you said when I asked you if you would leave home and come with me out into the world?

IRENE: I raised three fingers in the air and promised that I would go with you to the end of the world; and to the end of life. And that I would serve you in all things—

RUBEK: As a model for my work.

IRENE: Free and naked—

RUBEK: And you did serve me, Irene—joyfully, gladly, unstintingly—

IRENE: Yes; with all the trembling blood of my youth.

RUBEK: Too true you did.

IRENE (*shakes her fist at him*): I knelt down at your feet, and served you, Arnold. But you—you—you—!

RUBEK: I never wronged you. Never, Irene.

IRENE: Yes, you did! You wronged my inmost being.

RUBEK: I?

IRENE: Yes, you. I stripped myself naked for you to gaze at me. (*More quietly*) And you never once touched me.

RUBEK: Irene, didn't you understand that your beauty often drove me almost out of my mind?

IRENE: And yet, if you had touched me, I think I would have killed you on the spot. I had a sharp needle always with me; I hid it in my hair. (*Wipes her forehead pensively*) Yes, but—but, no, no! How could you?

RUBEK: I was an artist, Irene.

IRENE: An artist. Yes.

RUBEK: Before all else, I was an artist. And I was sick—sick with a longing to create the one great work of my life. (*Loses himself in memory*) It was to be called: "The Day of Resurrection". I conceived it in the likeness of a young woman, awakening from the sleep of death—

IRENE: Our child, yes.

RUBEK: She, this awakening girl, was to be all that is noble, all that is pure; perfection in woman. Then I found you. In you I saw all the things I wanted to express. And you agreed so gladly, so willingly. You left your family and your home, and came with me.

232

IRENE: When you took me away, I felt just as though I had become a child again.

RUBEK: That was why I was able to use you. You, and no-one else. To me, you were something sacred and untouchable, fit only to be worshipped. I was still young then, Irene. And I was convinced that if I touched you, if I desired you sensually, my vision would be profaned so that I would never be able to achieve what I was striving after. And I still think there is some truth in that.

IRENE: The child of the mind first; the child of the body second.

RUBEK: Condemn me if you will. But—I was so completely dominated by my task. And so exultantly happy in it.

IRENE: And you accomplished your task, Arnold.

RUBEK: Thanks to you, bless you, yes, I accomplished my task. I wanted to create woman as she will appear when she wakes, pure and undefiled, on the day of resurrection. Not marvelling at what is new, the unknown, the unimagined, but filled with a holy joy at finding herself unchanged—she, a mortal woman!—in the higher, freer, happier kingdom, after the long and dreamless sleep of death. (*Quietly*) That is how I created her—I created her in your image, Irene.

IRENE (*places her hands flat on the table, and leans back in her chair*): And then you were finished with me—

RUBEK: Irene!

IRENE: You had no further use for me—

RUBEK: How can you say that?

IRENE: You began to look round for other ideals to inspire you—

RUBEK: I found none after you.

IRENE: No other models, Arnold?

RUBEK: You were not a model to me. You were my inspiration.

IRENE (*after a moment*): What have you created since then? In marble, I mean. Since the day I left you.

RUBEK: Nothing. I have wasted the years carving trivialities.

IRENE: And the woman you're living with now—?

RUBEK (*sharply*): Don't speak of her now.

IRENE: Where do you intend to go with her?

RUBEK (*inert, tired*): On a long, tedious trip up north along
the coast.

IRENE (*looks at him, smiles almost imperceptibly, and whispers*):
Go high up into the mountains; as high as you can go.
Higher, higher—always higher, Arnold.

RUBEK: Are you going up there?

IRENE: Dare you meet me again?

RUBEK: If only we could! Ah, if only we could!

IRENE: Why shouldn't we? If we want to. Come, come,
Arnold! Oh, please come up to me—!

MAJA, *flushed and happy, comes past the corner of the hotel,
and hurries over to the table where she and* RUBEK *were sitting
before.*

MAJA: You can say what you like, Rubek, but—(*stops as she
sees* IRENE) Oh, excuse me! You've made a new acquaintance, I see.

RUBEK (*curtly*): I have renewed an old acquaintance. (*Stands
up*) What were you saying?

MAJA: I was saying, you may do as you like, but I am not
going with you on that awful steamer.

RUBEK: Why not?

MAJA: I want to go up into the mountains, and the forests.
I'd so love to. (*Coaxingly*) Oh, you must let me, Rubek.
I'll be so good if you do.

RUBEK: Who's given you these ideas?

MAJA: He—that horrible man who kills bears. Oh, you can't
imagine what extraordinary things he's been telling me
about the mountains! And the life up there! He's been
making up the most horrible and frightening stories—I'm
sure they're only stories—but somehow he makes it all
sound wonderfully attractive. Oh, may I go up there with
him? Just to see if all he says is true? May I, Rubek?

RUBEK: Go by all means, as far as I'm concerned. Yes,
go up into the mountains, go as far as you please, stay

234

as long as you please. I may possibly be going up there myself.

MAJA (*quickly*): No, no, you needn't trouble to come. Not for my sake.

RUBEK: But I want to go up into the mountains. I've made up my mind to do it now.

MAJA: Oh, thank you, thank you! May I run and tell him at once?

RUBEK: Tell him anything you like.

MAJA: Oh, thank you, thank you! (*Tries to take his hand, but he withdraws it*) How sweet and kind you are today, Rubek!

She runs into the hotel. At the same instant, the door of the pavilion is slowly and silently pushed ajar. The NUN stands inside the doorway, watching them. They do not see her.

RUBEK (*turning to IRENE*): Shall we meet up there, then?

IRENE (*rises slowly*): Yes, we shall meet up there. I've been looking for you for such a long time.

RUBEK: When did you begin to look for me, Irene?

IRENE (*with an ironical smile*): From the moment I realized I had given you something I couldn't do without, Arnold. Something one should never part with.

RUBEK (*bows his head*): Yes, that is true. You gave me four years of your youth.

IRENE: More; I gave you much more than that. I was too prodigal.

RUBEK: Yes, you were prodigal, Irene. All your naked beauty you gave me—

IRENE: To gaze at.

RUBEK: And immortalize.

IRENE: For your own glory. And for the child.

RUBEK: For you, too, Irene.

IRENE: You've forgotten the most precious gift I gave you.

RUBEK: The most precious—? What gift was that?

IRENE: I gave you my soul—young and alive. And left myself empty; soulless. Don't you see? That's why I died, Arnold.

235

The NUN *opens the door wide, and stands aside for her. She goes into the pavilion.*

RUBEK (*stands staring after her; then he whispers*): Irene!

ACT TWO

*At a mountain health resort. The landscape, a vast treeless
plateau, stretches away towards a long mountain lake. Beyond
the lake towers a range of mountain peaks, with bluish snow in
their crevices. Downstage left, a stream, divided into rivulets,
ripples down a steep wall of rock and flows out smoothly across
the plateau towards the right. The stream is lined with brushwood, plants and boulders. Downstage right is a small hillock with
a stone bench on its top. It is a summer evening, just before
sundown.*

*In the distance, beyond the stream, a number of small children
sing, dance and play. Some wear town clothes, some country
clothes. Their merry laughter is heard faintly throughout the
scene.*

PROFESSOR RUBEK *is seated on the bench with a plaid over his
shoulders, looking down at the children playing. After a few
moments,* MAJA *enters through some bushes left centre, and gazes
with her hand shading her eyes. She is wearing a flat tourist
bonnet, a short skirt gathered halfway up her legs, and tall,
strong, laced boots. In her hand she carries a long vaulting-stick.*

MAJA (*sees* RUBEK *at last, and calls*): Hallo!

*She goes forward, vaults over the stream with the help of her
stick and climbs up the hill.*

(*out of breath*): Oh, I've been looking for you every-
where, Rubek.
RUBEK (*nods indifferently*): Have you come from the hotel?
MAJA: Yes, a moment ago. Ugh, that fly-trap.

237

RUBEK: You didn't come down to lunch, I noticed.

MAJA: No, we ate ours in the open. Under the sky.

RUBEK: We? Who are "we"?

MAJA: I and—and that awful bear-baiter.

RUBEK: Oh, him.

MAJA: Yes. And tomorrow we're going out again. At dawn.

RUBEK: After bears?

MAJA: Yes. Off to kill bruin.

RUBEK: Have you found any tracks?

MAJA (*superciliously*): One doesn't find bears as high up as this. Didn't you know?

RUBEK: Where, then?

MAJA: Far down. Down in the valleys, where the forests are thickest. Where people from the towns can't go

RUBEK: And you two are going down there tomorrow?

MAJA (*throwing herself down in the heather*): Yes, that's what we've decided. Or we may even go this evening. If you've no objection?

RUBEK: I? No, far from it.

MAJA (*quickly*): Lars'll be coming with us, of course. With the pack.

RUBEK: I'm not interested in Mr Lars and his pack. (*Changing the subject*) Won't you come and sit here beside me?

MAJA (*drowsily*): No, thank you. I'm so comfortable in this soft heather.

RUBEK: I can see you're tired.

MAJA (*yawns*): I think I'm beginning to be.

RUBEK: It always comes afterwards, when the excitement is over.

MAJA (*sleepily*): Yes. I think I'll close my eyes.

Short pause

(*suddenly, impatiently*): Oh, Rubek, how can you bear to sit here and listen to those children yelling and watch them jumping around?

RUBEK: There's a kind of harmony in their movements; almost like music. At isolated moments, amid all that clumsiness. It amuses me to sit and wait for those moments.

MAJA: Always the artist, aren't you?

RUBEK: Yes, please God.

MAJA (*turns on her side, so that she has her back to him*): There's nothing artistic about him.

RUBEK: About whom?

MAJA (*sleepy again*): Him. You know.

RUBEK: The bear-baiter, you mean?

MAJA: Yes. Nothing artistic about him. Nothing at all.

RUBEK (*smiles*): I don't doubt that for a moment.

MAJA: And he's so ugly! (*Picks a tuft of heather, and throws it away*) So ugly, so ugly! Ugh!

RUBEK: Is that why you're so delighted to be going off with him into the forests?

MAJA (*curtly*): I don't know. (*Turns towards him*) You're ugly, too, Rubek.

RUBEK: Have you only just discovered that?

MAJA: No, I've noticed it for a long time.

RUBEK (*shrugs his shoulders*): One grows older. One grows older, Maja.

MAJA (*resigned*): I don't mean that. There's something so tired about your eyes—when you deign to look at me, which isn't often.

RUBEK: You've noticed that, have you?

MAJA (*nods*): Little by little a kind of evil expression has crept into them. Almost as though you were plotting something against me.

RUBEK: Really? (*Friendly, yet serious*) Come here and sit beside me, Maja, and let us have a little talk.

MAJA (*raises herself half up*): May I sit on your knee, then? Like I used to?

RUBEK: No, you mustn't do that—people can see us from the hotel. (*Moves slightly*) Come and sit here on the bench beside me.

MAJA: No, thanks, in that case I'd rather stay where I am. I can hear you quite well from here. Well, what was it you wanted to talk about?

RUBEK: What do you think was my real reason for suggesting that we should come up to this place?

239

MAJA: Well, you said among other things that it'd be so good for me. But—

RUBEK: But?

MAJA: But now I don't believe that was the real reason.

RUBEK: Well, what do you think was?

MAJA: I think it was because of that pale lady.

RUBEK: Mrs von Satow?

MAJA: Yes, the one who follows us round all the time. Yesterday evening she turned up here too.

RUBEK: But why on earth—?

MAJA: Well, you knew her very well, didn't you? Long before you knew me.

RUBEK: I'd forgotten her, too, long before I knew you.

MAJA (*sits up*): Do you forget so quickly, Rubek?

RUBEK (*curtly*): Very quickly. (*Adds harshly*) When I want to.

MAJA: Even someone who's been your model?

RUBEK: When I no longer have any use for her.

MAJA: A woman who's stripped herself naked for you?

RUBEK: That means nothing. Nothing to us artists. (*With a change of tone*) Besides, how, if I may venture to ask, could I possibly have guessed she was in this part of the country?

MAJA: You could have read her name in a visitors' list. In a newspaper.

RUBEK: Yes, but I didn't know that name she uses now. I'd never heard of any Mr von Satow.

MAJA (*pretending to be bored*): Oh, Lord, well I suppose you must have had some other reason for wanting to come here, then.

RUBEK: Yes, Maja. I had another reason. Quite a different reason. That's what we've got to talk about sooner or later.

MAJA (*stifling a giggle*): Lord, how solemn you look!

RUBEK: Unnecessarily so?

MAJA: What do you mean?

RUBEK: It's probably just as well, for us both.

MAJA: You're beginning to make me curious, Rubek.

RUBEK: Only curious? Not just a little bit worried?

MAJA: Not in the least.

RUBEK: Good. Then listen. You said that day down at the Spa that you thought I'd become very nervous these past months—

MAJA: Yes, so you have.

RUBEK: Why do you suppose that is?

MAJA: How should I know? Perhaps you've grown tired of being continually together with me.

RUBEK: Continually?

MAJA: Yes. We've lived together down there for five whole years, just the two of us, and have hardly ever been away from each other for an hour. Just we two, all by ourselves.

RUBEK: Well?

MAJA: You don't like being with people, Rubek. You prefer to be by yourself, and think your own thoughts. And I can't talk properly to you about what interests you. About art and all that. God knows I don't care very much for it, either.

RUBEK: Poor Maja. So we spend most of our time sitting by the fire and talking about *your* interests.

MAJA: Lord, I've no interests to talk about.

RUBEK: Well, perhaps they are rather trivial. Still, time passes, Maja. Time passes.

MAJA: True enough. Time passes. It's running away from you, Rubek. I suppose it's that that makes you so uneasy.

RUBEK (*nods vigorously*): And so restless. (*Shifts on the bench*) No, I can't stand this miserable life much longer.

MAJA (*gets up and stands for a moment looking at him*): If you want to be rid of me, just say so.

RUBEK: What on earth are you talking about? Be rid of you?

MAJA: Yes. If you want to be finished with me, say so straight out. And I'll go; at once.

RUBEK (*smiles almost imperceptibly*): Is that meant to be a threat, Maja?

MAJA: What threat can there be in that for you?

RUBEK (*gets up*): No, you're perfectly right. (*After a moment*) You and I can't possibly go on living this kind of life together.

MAJA: Well, then obviously—

241

RUBEK: There is no "then obviously" about it. Because we two can't go on living together as we are, it doesn't necessarily follow that we have to get divorced.

MAJA (*smiles acidly*): Just separate, you mean?

RUBEK: That isn't necessary, either.

MAJA: Well? Out with it. What do you want to do with me, then?

RUBEK (*hesitantly*): What I feel so keenly—almost painfully —is the need of someone who is really close to me—

MAJA (*interrupts*): Aren't I, Rubek?

RUBEK: Not in that way. I must live with someone who can make me complete—supply what's missing in me— someone who is one with me in everything I strive for.

MAJA (*slowly*): Yes; in big things like that I can't be of any help to you. And God knows I haven't any desire to be either!

RUBEK: I know that only too well. That wasn't what I had in mind when I married you.

MAJA: I can see you're thinking of someone else.

RUBEK: Indeed? I didn't know you were clairvoyant.

MAJA: Oh, I know you so well, Rubek. Too well.

RUBEK: Then perhaps you can also see of whom I am thinking?

MAJA: Indeed I can.

RUBEK: Well? Please tell me.

MAJA: You're thinking of that—that model you once used— (*Suddenly changes her thread of thought*) Do you know, the people down at the hotel think she's mad?

RUBEK: Oh? And what do the people down at the hotel think about you and our friend the bear-baiter?

MAJA: That has nothing to do with it. (*Returns to her previous thread of thought*) It was that pale lady you were thinking of, wasn't it?

RUBEK: Exactly; of her. When I no longer had any use for her—and anyway, she left me—vanished, just like that—

MAJA: You took me as a kind of makeshift?

RUBEK: More or less, yes, to be quite frank, Maja dear. For a year, or eighteen months, I had been alone, brooding in solitude. I had put the last touch—the absolutely final touch—to my work. "The Day of Resurrection" was exhibited all over the world. It brought me fame, and all the glory I could wish for. But I no longer loved my own work. The flowers and incense that were showered on me nauseated me, made me desperate; made me long to flee into the depths of the forest. Well, you are clairvoyant, can you guess what suddenly occurred to me?

MAJA: Yes, you decided to do portrait busts of ladies and gentlemen.

RUBEK (*nods*): On commission. With animal faces behind the masks. They got *them* thrown in; free, gratis. (*Smiles*) But that wasn't what I meant.

MAJA: Well, what did you mean?

RUBEK: I meant, it suddenly occurred to me that all this talk about the task of the artist and the vocation of the artist was empty, hollow and meaningless.

MAJA: Well, what do you want instead?

RUBEK: Life, Maja.

MAJA: Life?

RUBEK: Yes. Isn't life in sunshine and beauty far more worth while than wasting one's years in a raw, damp cellar, wearing oneself to death wrestling with lumps of clay and blocks of stone?

MAJA (*with a little sigh*): Yes, I've always thought so.

RUBEK: Well, then I became rich enough to live in luxury and idly quivering sunlight. To build myself a villa on the Taunitzer See, and a mansion in the capital, and all the rest of it.

MAJA: And to cap it all, you could afford to buy me. And gave me leave to share your wealth with you.

RUBEK: Didn't I promise to take you with me up a high mountain and show you all the glory of the world?

MAJA: You may have brought me up quite a high mountain, Rubek. But you haven't showed me all the glory of the world.

RUBEK (*laughs irritably*): How impossible you are to please Maja! Quite impossible! (*Angrily*) But can you guess what it really is that has driven me to despair?

MAJA: Yes; the fact that you've tied yourself to me for life.

RUBEK: I wouldn't have put it quite so heartlessly.

MAJA: That doesn't make the thought less heartless.

RUBEK: You don't understand what really goes on in an artist's mind.

MAJA: Good heavens, I haven't the faintest idea what goes on inside my own mind.

RUBEK: I live so fast, Maja. We live like that, we artists. I have lived through a whole lifetime in the few years we two have known each other. And I've come to realize that it's not within my power to find happiness in idleness and soft living. Life is not shaped like that for me and my kind. I must go on working, creating incessantly, until I die. (*With an effort*) That is why I can't go on with you any longer, Maja. Just you and I.

MAJA (*calmly*): Does that mean, in plain words, that you've grown tired of me?

RUBEK (*vehemently*): Yes, that is what it means! I've grown bored, intolerably bored and tired of living with you; it's drained all my vitality. Now you know! (*Controls himself*) Those are hard and ugly words. I know that well. And you are not to blame, I admit that willingly. It's only in me that this change, this revolution has occurred. (*Half to himself*) This awakening to the life that is really mine.

MAJA: Why in God's name can't we part, then?

RUBEK: Would you be willing?

MAJA (*shrugs her shoulders*): Ye-es, if there's no alternative—

RUBEK: But there is an alternative. There is a way—

MAJA: Now you're thinking of that pale lady again.

RUBEK: Yes. To be honest, my thoughts always return to her. Ever since I met her again. (*Moves closer to her*) I want to tell you a secret, Maja.

MAJA: Well?

RUBEK (*taps himself on the chest*): In here, Maja—in here I keep a small casket, with a lock that cannot be picked. In that casket, all my visions lie. But when she left me, and vanished from my life, the lock of that casket snapped shut. She had the key, and she took it with her. You, my poor Maja, you had no key. So everything in it lies unused. And the years pass—and all that wealth lies there—and I cannot touch it!

MAJA: Then get her to unlock it for you.

RUBEK (*puzzled*): Maja—?

MAJA: She's here. No doubt it's because of this little casket that she has been following us.

RUBEK: I never mentioned a word of this to her. Never.

MAJA (*innocently*): But, my dear Rubek, is it worth making all this fuss and bother about such a simple matter?

RUBEK: You call this a simple matter?

MAJA: Certainly I do. You go to whoever you need the most. I shall always be able to find somewhere.

RUBEK: Where?

MAJA: Well, I could move out to the villa if necessary. But it won't be. Our town house is very large; with a little give and take, there should be room enough in it for three.

RUBEK: Do you think that could work? In the long run?

MAJA: Lord, if it doesn't work, it doesn't. We won't get any further by discussing it.

RUBEK: But what shall we do if it doesn't work, Maja?

MAJA (*cheerfully*): Then you and I will simply go different ways. Part. I shall find something new, somewhere. A place where I can be free. Free, free! You needn't worry about me, Professor Rubek. (*Suddenly points away to the right*) Look! There she is!

RUBEK (*turning*): Where?

MAJA: Over there. Pacing along like a marble statue. She's coming this way.

RUBEK (*stands up and stares, his hand shading his eyes*): Isn't she the living image of "The Resurrection"? (*To himself*) Why did I ever let her go? Drive her into the darkness? Change her into a—? Fool that I was, fool!

MAJA: What does all that mean?

RUBEK: Nothing. Nothing that you would understand.

IRENE *comes across the plateau from the right. The playing children have already seen her and run to meet her. Now she is surrounded by the whole crowd of them; some of them seem gay and trusting, some shy and nervous. She speaks quietly to them, and indicates that they shall go down to the hotel; she herself wants to rest for a while by the stream. The children run off down the hill to the left. IRENE goes over to the rock face and lets the rivulets run coolingly over her hands.*

MAJA (*softly*): Go down and talk to her, Rubek. Alone.

RUBEK: Where will you go?

MAJA: From now on I shall go my own ways.

She goes down the hillside and swings herself across the stream with her vaulting-stick. She pauses beside IRENE.

Professor Rubek is up there waiting for you, madam.

IRENE: What does he want?

MAJA: He wants you to help him open a casket which has jammed shut.

IRENE: Can I help him with that?

MAJA: He says you're the only person who can.

IRENE: Then I'd better try.

MAJA: Yes, do, madam. Please do.

She goes down the path towards the hotel. A few moments later, PROFESSOR RUBEK descends to IRENE, but stops with the stream between them.

IRENE: She said you've been waiting for me.

RUBEK. I have been waiting for you. For years. Without knowing it.

IRENE: I couldn't come to you, Arnold. I was lying down there, asleep. A long, deep sleep, full of dreams.

RUBEK: Ah, but now you have awakened, Irene.

IRENE (*shakes her head*): The sleep is heavy in my eyes still.

RUBEK: The day will dawn and the sun will shine for both of us. You will see.

IRENE: Never believe that!

RUBEK: I do believe it! I know it! Now that I've found you again—

IRENE: Risen.

RUBEK: Transfigured!

IRENE: Only risen, Arnold. Not transfigured.

*He crosses to her on the stepping stones beneath the waterfall.
He sits down again. She sits on another stone near him.*

RUBEK: Where have you been all day, Irene?

IRENE (*points*): Far away, in the dead country yonder—

RUBEK (*trying to distract her*): You haven't your—your
friend with you today, I see.

IRENE (*smiles*): My friend keeps a close watch on me all the
time.

RUBEK: How can she?

IRENE (*glances around*): Oh, she can, she can! Wherever I go.
She never lets me out of her sight. (*Whispers*) Until, one
fine, sunny morning, I shall kill her.

RUBEK: Do you want to kill her?

IRENE: Oh, yes. If only I could.

RUBEK: Why?

IRENE: Because she's a witch. (*Furtively*) Do you know,
Arnold—she's turned herself into my shadow!

RUBEK (*trying to calm her*): Well, well, we all have to have a
shadow.

IRENE: I am my own shadow. (*Cries*) Can't you understand
that?

RUBEK (*heavily*): Yes, yes, Irene. I understand. (*He sits
down on a stone by the stream. She stands beside him, leaning
against the rock face*).

IRENE (*after a few moments*): Why do you sit there with your
eyes turned away from me?

RUBEK: I dare not—I dare not look at you.

IRENE: Why don't you dare to look at me any longer?

RUBEK: You have a shadow that torments you. And I a conscience.

IRENE (*with a happy cry, as though of liberation*): At last!

RUBEK (*leaps up*): Irene! What is it?

IRENE: Be calm, be calm! (*Takes a deep breath, and says, as
though relieved of a burden*) All right. Now they let go of

247

me. For a moment, anyway. Now we can sit down and talk. As we used to.

RUBEK: If only we could talk as we used to.

IRENE: Sit there where you were sitting before. Then I'll sit down here beside you.

He sits down again. She sits on another stone near him.

(*after a short silence*): Now I have come back to you from a far country, Arnold.

RUBEK: Yes; from an endless journey.

IRENE: Come home to my lord and master—

RUBEK: To ourselves; to our own selves, Irene.

IRENE: Have you waited for me every day?

RUBEK: How could I dare to wait for you?

IRENE (*with a sidelong glance*): No, I don't suppose you did. You never understood a thing.

RUBEK: Was it really not for someone else that you disappeared so suddenly?

IRENE: Couldn't it have been for you, Arnold?

RUBEK: But I don't understand—

IRENE: When I had served you with my soul and my body— and the sculpture stood there, finished—our child, as you called it—I laid at your feet the dearest sacrifice I could offer. I blotted myself out for ever.

RUBEK (*bows his head*): And left my life a desert.

IRENE: Exactly! I wasn't going to allow you to create again, ever! Once you had created this child of ours; our only child.

RUBEK: Was it jealousy that made you do this?

IRENE (*coldly*): No; hatred, I think.

RUBEK: Hatred? Hatred of me?

IRENE (*vehemently again*): Yes, of you! Of the artist who lightly and casually took a warm living body, a young human life, and tore the soul from it, because you needed it to create a work of art.

RUBEK: You say that? You, who shared my work so ardently, with such a high, holy passion? That work for which we met each morning as for an act of devotion?

IRENE (*coldly again*): There is one thing I must tell you, Arnold.

RUBEK: Yes?

IRENE: I never loved your work, before I met you. Nor afterwards.

RUBEK: But—as an artist, Irene?

IRENE: I hate the artist.

RUBEK: The artist in me, too?

IRENE: Most of all in you. When I stripped myself naked and stood there before you, I hated you, Arnold.

RUBEK (*violently*): That's not true, Irene! You didn't!

IRENE: I hated you, because you could stand there so unmoved—

RUBEK (*laughs*): Unmoved!

IRENE: Or so intolerably in control of yourself, then! And because you were an artist, only an artist, not a man! (*Changes her tone, and speaks warmly, intensely*) But that statue of wet and living clay, her I loved—as she rose out of that raw and formless mass, a human child, with a soul. She was *our* creation, *our* child. Mine, and yours.

RUBEK: It was. In spirit and in truth.

IRENE: It's for our child that I have made this long pilgrimage.

RUBEK: For that marble image?

IRENE: Call it what you will. I call it our child.

RUBEK (*uneasily*): And now you want to see it? Finished? In marble, which you always said was so cold? (*Eagerly*) Perhaps you do not know that it now stands far away in a great museum?

IRENE: I heard a story to that effect.

RUBEK: You always hated museums. You called them tombs.

IRENE: I want to make a pilgrimage to the place where my soul and the child of my soul lie buried.

RUBEK: You must never see that statue again! Do you hear, Irene? I beg you, never, never see it again!

IRENE: You think that I would die a second time?

RUBEK: I don't know what I think. How could I ever have known you would become so obsessed with this statue? You, who left me before it was complete!

IRENE: It *was* complete. That was why I was able to leave you. Leave you alone.

RUBEK (*sits with his elbows on his knees, rocking his head from side to side, his hands over his eyes*): In the end it—changed. Became—different, Irene.

IRENE (*quietly and swiftly, draws a thin, sharp knife from her bosom. She whispers*): Arnold, have you harmed our child?

RUBEK (*evasively*): Harmed? I'm not sure what you would call it.

IRENE: What have you done?

RUBEK: I'll tell you, if you promise to sit and listen calmly. And you mustn't look at me while I tell you.

IRENE (*hides the knife and moves across to a stone behind him*): I shall sit here, behind you. Now tell me.

RUBEK (*takes his hands from his eyes*): When I found you, I knew at once how I should use you. You were to be my masterpiece. I was young then. With no experience of life. I envisaged Resurrection as something perfect and beautiful—a pure young girl, unstained by life, awakening to light and glory without having to free herself from anything ugly or unclean.

IRENE: And that is how I stand there now?

RUBEK (*unwillingly*): Not—quite like that, Irene.

IRENE: Not quite—? Don't I stand there as I always stood before you?

RUBEK (*not replying*): In the years after you left me, Irene, I gained experience and knowledge. I began to envisage "The Day of Resurrection" as something bigger, something —something more complex. That small, round pedestal on which your statue stood erect and lonely—that was no longer big enough to hold all that I now wanted to express.

IRENE (*her hand moves towards the knife, but stops*): Well? Go on.

RUBEK: I portrayed what I saw with my own eyes in the world around me. I had to. I had no choice, Irene. I enlarged the pedestal, I made it broad and spacious. On it I set a small lump of our curved and fissured earth. And out of the fissures swarmed people, with the faces of beasts

250

beneath their human masks. Women and men, as I knew them, from life.

IRENE: But in the middle of the throng the young woman stands, with the light of happiness transfiguring her face? I do, don't I, Arnold?

RUBEK (*evasively*): Not quite in the middle. Unfortunately I had to move the statue back a little—for the sake of the composition, you understand. Otherwise it would have dominated it too much.

IRENE: But the light of wonder and joy still shines on my face?

RUBEK: Yes, Irene, it does. In a way, that is. A little subdued, perhaps. To accord with the changed vision I had of life.

IRENE (*rises silently*): And this new image—expresses life as you see it now, Arnold?

RUBEK: Yes, I suppose so.

IRENE: And in this image you have portrayed me as a background figure, in a crowd? (*She takes out the knife*).

RUBEK: No, no. Not a background figure. No, at the worst I'd call it a middleground figure—or thereabouts.

IRENE (*whispers*): Now you have pronounced judgment on yourself. (*Is about to strike him with the knife*).

RUBEK (*turns and glances up at her*): Judgment?

IRENE (*conceals the knife swiftly*): My whole soul—you and I—we, we, we and our child, were in that lonely figure.

RUBEK (*eagerly, tears off his hat and wipes the sweat from his forehead*): Yes, but listen how I have portrayed myself in this group. In the foreground, beside a spring, as it might be here, there sits a man weighed down by guilt; he cannot free himself from the earth's crust. I call him remorse—remorse for a forfeited life. He sits there dipping his fingers in the rippling water, to wash them clean; and he is gnawed and tormented by the knowledge that he will never, never succeed. He will never, in all eternity, free himself, and be granted resurrection. He must stay for ever in his Hell.

IRENE (*coldly*): Poet!

RUBEK: Why poet?

IRENE: Because you're soft and self-indulgent, and so ready to forgive all your own sins, everything you've ever done or thought. You killed my soul, and then you model yourself as a figure of penance and remorse. (*Smiles*) And in your eyes, that settles your account.

RUBEK: I am an artist, Irene. I am not ashamed of the frailty inherent in my nature. I was *born* to be an artist, you understand! And I shall never be anything else.

IRENE (*softly*): You are a poet, Arnold. (*Strokes his hair gently*) You dear, big, ageing child, can't you see it?

RUBEK: Why do you keep on calling me a poet?

IRENE: Because there is something condoning in that word, my friend. It is a word that condones all sins, and spreads a cloak over every weakness. (*Changes her tone suddenly*) But I was flesh and blood once. I, too, had a life to live, and a human destiny to fulfil. But I turned my back on it all, threw it away, to serve you. It was suicide; a mortal sin against myself. And that is a sin I can never expiate.

She sits down near him by the stream, keeping her eyes on him—though he does not see it. As though absentmindedly, she picks some flowers from the bushes around them.

IRENE: I should have borne children into the world. Many children. Real children; not the sort that are hidden away in tombs. That should have been my calling. I should never have served you—poet!

RUBEK (*lost in memories*): But those were wonderful times we had, Irene. Miraculous, wonderful times—now that I look back.

IRENE: Can you remember a little word you said to me when you had finished? Finished with me and with our child? Do you remember that little word, Arnold?

RUBEK: Did I say something you still remember now?

IRENE: Yes, you did. Can't you remember it any longer?

RUBEK (*shakes his head*): No, I can't say I do. Not at the moment, anyway.

IRENE: You took both my hands and pressed them warmly. I stood there, breathless, waiting. Then you said: "I am deeply grateful to you, Irene. This," you said, "this has been an inspiring episode in my life."

RUBEK: Episode? That's not a word I'm in the habit of using.

IRENE: "Episode" was the word you used.

RUBEK (*with attempted lightness*): Well, perhaps I may have—but so it was, really, an episode.

IRENE: At that word I left you.

RUBEK: You take everything to heart so, Irene.

IRENE (*wipes her forehead*): Yes. Perhaps you are right. Let's forget these things of the heart. (*Picks the petals from a mountain rose, and scatters them in the stream*) Look, Arnold. There are our birds swimming.

RUBEK: What kind of birds are they?

IRENE: Can't you see? They're flamingoes. Red like roses.

RUBEK: Flamingoes don't swim. They only wade.

IRENE: All right, they're not flamingoes, then. They're gulls.

RUBEK: Oh, yes, red-billed gulls, I expect. (*He plucks broad green leaves and throws them on the water*) Now I am sending my ships after them.

IRENE: But there mustn't be any huntsmen on board.

RUBEK: No, there are no huntsmen on board. (*Smiles at her*) Do you remember that summer when we sat like this outside the little farmhouse on the Taunitzer See?

IRENE (*nods*): On Saturday evenings, yes. When we'd finished our work for the week.

RUBEK: We went out there by train. And stayed over till Sunday.

IRENE: An episode, Arnold.

RUBEK (*as though he has not heard*): You made birds swim in the stream then, too. Water-lilies—

IRENE: White swans.

RUBEK: Yes, swans. And I remember I fastened a big hairy leaf to one of the swans. A dock-leaf, wasn't it?

IRENE: And it became Lohengrin's boat, with the swan drawing it.

RUBEK: How you loved that game, Irene.

IRENE: We played it so many times.

RUBEK: Every Saturday, I think. The whole summer through.

IRENE: You said I was the swan who was drawing your boat.

RUBEK: Did I say that? Yes, I may well have. (*Absorbed in the game*) Look, do you see how the gulls are swimming down the river, Irene?

IRENE (*smiles*): And all your ships have run aground.

RUBEK (*throws more leaves into the stream*): I have plenty of ships in reserve. (*Follows the leaves with his eyes, throws more. After a moment :*) Irene, I bought that little farmhouse on the Taunitzer See.

IRENE: Have you bought it? You often used to say you would if you could ever afford it.

RUBEK: Well, eventually I was able to. So I bought it.

IRENE (*glancing at him*): Do you live out there now, in our old house?

RUBEK: No, I had it pulled down long ago. And built myself a fine big villa in its place. With a park round it. That's where we—(*corrects himself*)—where I usually spend the summer.

IRENE: So you and—and that other woman live out there now?

RUBEK: Yes. When my wife and I aren't travelling; as we are this year.

IRENE: Beautiful, beautiful was life on the Taunitzer See.

RUBEK: And yet, Irene—

IRENE: And yet we let all that beauty slip from our grasp.

RUBEK (*softly, urgently*): Is it too late to find it again?

IRENE (*does not answer him, but sits silent for a moment, then points across the plateau*): Look, Arnold. The sun is setting behind the mountains. See how redly it shines on all the heather.

RUBEK (*follows her gaze*): It is a long time since I watched the sun set in the mountains.

IRENE: Or the sun rise?

RUBEK: I don't think I have ever seen a sunrise.

IRENE (*smiles*): I once saw a miraculously beautiful sunrise.

RUBEK: Did you? Where was that?

IRENE: High, high up on a dizzy mountain top. You enticed me up there and promised you would show me all the glory of the world, if—(*stops sharply*).

RUBEK: If—? Well?

IRENE: I did as you told me. Followed you to the mountain top. And there I fell on my knees and—worshipped you. And served you. (*Is silent for a moment, then quietly*) Then I saw the sunrise.

RUBEK (*hesitantly*): Wouldn't you—like to come and live in the villa down there?

IRENE: With you and that other woman?

RUBEK: With me. As in the days when we created together. You can unfasten all the locks that have snapped shut inside me. Will you, Irene?

IRENE (*shakes her head*): I haven't the key any longer, Arnold.

RUBEK: You have the key! You are the only one who has it. (*Beseechingly*) Help me to start living again!

IRENE: Empty dreams. Idle, dead dreams. Our life together cannot be resurrected.

RUBEK (*curtly*): Then let us go on with our game.

IRENE: Our game, yes. Let us go on with our game.

They sit throwing leaves and petals into the stream, and watching them float and sail. Up the hill in the background to the left come SQUIRE ULFHEJM *and* MAJA, *in hunting costume. After them comes the* SERVANT *with the pack of hounds, which he leads out to the right.*

RUBEK (*catching sight of them*): Ah, there goes little Maja with her bear-baiter.

IRENE: Your lady, yes.

RUBEK: Or his.

MAJA (*looks round as she walks, and sees the two figures by the stream. Shouts*): Good night, Professor! Dream about me! I'm going off on an adventure.

RUBEK (*shouts back*): In quest of what?

MAJA (*approaches nearer*): Life. Real life! No substitutes!

RUBEK (*mockingly*): You, too, Maja dear?

MAJA: Yes. I've made up a song about it. It goes like this. (*Sings happily*).

> I am free! I am free! I am free!
> No longer imprisoned! I'm free
> I can fly like a bird! And I'm free!

Yes, I believe I have awoken at last.

RUBEK: It sounds like it.

MAJA (*takes a deep breath*): Oh, how heavenly it feels to be awake!

RUBEK: Good night, Maja, and good luck to your—

ULFHEJM (*shouts warningly*): Don't say it! We don't want any of your goddam blessings! Can't you see we're going hunting?

RUBEK: What will you bring me home from the hunt, Maja?

MAJA: I'll bring back a fine hawk for you to model. I'll wing one for you.

RUBEK (*smiles bitterly*): Yes, winging birds is rather in your line, isn't it?

MAJA (*tosses her head*): Just let me take care of my own life from now on. (*Laughs mischievously*) Goodbye! Have a nice quiet summer night on the mountain!

RUBEK (*jovially*): Thank you! And damn bad luck to you both—and to your hunting!

ULFHEJM (*guffaws*): Now that's the kind of blessing I like to hear!

MAJA (*smiles*): Thank you, thank you, Professor.

They go out through the brushwood to the right.

RUBEK (*after a pause*): Summer night on the mountain! Yes, that would have been life.

IRENE: Would you like to spend a summer night on the mountain? With me?

RUBEK (*spreads his arms wide*): Yes! Yes! Come!

IRENE: My love, my lord and master!

RUBEK: Oh, Irene!

IRENE (*smiling, as she gropes for the knife*) It will only be an episode. (*Whispers quickly*) Ssh! Don't look round, Arnold!

RUBEK (*as quietly*): What is it?

IRENE: There's a face staring at me.

RUBEK (*turns involuntarily*): Where? (*starts*) Ah!

The NUN'S *head is half visible among the bushes on the path down to the right. Her eyes are fixed on* IRENE.

IRENE (*gets up and says softly*): We must part now. No, don't move. Do as I say! You mustn't come with me. (*Leans over him and whispers*) We'll meet tonight. On the mountain.

RUBEK: Will you come, Irene?

IRENE: Yes, I shall come. Wait for me here.

RUBEK (*repeats, as in a dream*): Summer night on the mountain. With you. (*His eyes meet hers*) Oh, Irene, that could have been our life. And we have wasted it—

IRENE: We only find what we have lost when—(*Stops abruptly*).

RUBEK: When—?

IRENE: When we dead awaken.

RUBEK (*shakes his head sadly*): What do we find then?

IRENE: We find that we have never lived.

She goes across and climbs down the hill. The NUN *makes way for her, and follows her.* PROFESSOR RUBEK *remains seated motionless on the bench.*

MAJA (*is heard singing happily higher up the mountain*):

I am free! I am free! I am free!
No longer imprisoned! I'm free!
I can fly like a bird! And I'm free!

ACT THREE

A wild, broken mountain top, with a sheer precipice behind. To the right tower snowy peaks, losing themselves high up in drifting mist. To the left, on a scree, stands an old, tumbledown hut. It is early morning. Dawn is breaking; the sun has not yet risen.

MAJA RUBEK, *out of breath and excited, comes down across the scree.* SQUIRE ULFHEJM *follows her, half angry, half laughing, holding her fast by the sleeve.*

MAJA (*trying to tear herself loose*): Let me go! Let me go, I tell you!

ULFHEJM: Steady, now, or you'll be biting me next! You're as snappish as a vixen.

MAJA (*hits him over the hand*): Let me go, I say! Try to behave yourself!

ULFHEJM: I'm damned if I will.

MAJA: Then I won't go a step further with you. Do you hear? Not a step!

ULFHEJM (*guffaws*): How do you think you'll escape from me up here?

MAJA (*points down into the ravine*): I'll run down there, if need be.

ULFHEJM: And smash yourself into dogs'-meat? A fine, savoury blood-pudding you'd make! (*Lets go of her*) All right, go ahead. Run down the mountainside if you want to. It's as sheer as a wall, there's only one narrow path down, and that's as near as dammit impassable.

MAJA (*dusts her skirt with her hand and glares angrily at him*): You're a fine one to go hunting with!

ULFHEJM: It's all in the sport.

MAJA: Oh, you call this sport, do you?

258

ULFHEJM: Yes, my fine lady, the kind of sport I like best.

MAJA (*tosses her head*): Well, I must say! (*After a moment*) Why did you let the hounds loose up there?

ULFHEJM (*winks and smiles*): To give them the chance to hunt a little on their own, too.

MAJA: That's quite untrue. It wasn't for their sake you let them loose.

ULFHEJM (*still smiling*): Well, why did I, then? Tell me.

MAJA: Because you wanted to be rid of Lars. You told him to run after them and catch them; and meanwhile—

ULFHEJM: And meanwhile—?

MAJA: Never mind.

ULFHEJM: Lars won't find them. You don't need to worry about that. He won't come back before his time.

MAJA (*angrily*): No, I'm sure he won't.

ULFHEJM (*tries to take her arm*): Lars knows my—my hunting habits, you see.

MAJA (*evades his grasp and measures him with her eyes*): Do you know what you're like, Squire Ulfhejm? You're exactly like a faun.

ULFHEJM: A faun? Isn't that some kind of monster? A wood-demon or something?

MAJA: Yes. Just like you. With a beard like a goat and legs like a goat—yes, and horns, too.

ULFHEJM: By Jove, horns too?

MAJA: A pair of beastly horns, just like you.

ULFHEJM: What, can you see my poor little pair?

MAJA: Yes, quite plainly.

ULFHEJM (*takes the dog-leash from his pocket*): Hm. I'd better tie you up, then.

MAJA: Have you gone mad? Tie me up?

ULFHEJM: If I'm a monster, I might as well play the part properly. So that's the way of it? You can see my horns, can you?

MAJA (*soothingly*): Now, now, please try to behave yourself, Squire Ulfhejm. But where's this hunting lodge of yours you were talking so much about? You said it was around here somewhere.

ULFHEJM (*points with a flourish at the hut*): There it is, right in front of your eyes.

MAJA (*stares at him*): That old pigsty?

ULFHEJM (*chuckles*): It's housed more than one princess in its time.

MAJA: Was it there that that horrid man you told me about went in to the princess disguised as a bear?

ULFHEJM: Yes, my fair huntress, this was the very place. (*With an inviting motion of his hand*) If it should please you to step inside—

MAJA: Ugh! Set foot in that place? Ugh!

ULFHEJM: Oh, two people can while away a summer night very comfortably in there. Or a whole summer, for that matter.

MAJA: Thank you, I've no taste for that kind of thing. (*Impatiently*) Well, I'm tired of you and your hunting expedition. I'm going down to the hotel, before people wake up.

ULFHEJM: How do you suppose you're going to do that?

MAJA: That's your business. There must be a way down somewhere.

ULFHEJM (*points upstage*): Bless you, yes, there's a way down. Down there.

MAJA: You see? You can be a gentleman when you want to—

ULFHEJM: Just you try it.

MAJA (*doubtfully*): Don't you think I dare?

ULFHEJM: You wouldn't have a chance. Unless I help you—

MAJA (*uneasily*): Well, come and help me, then. What else are you here for?

ULFHEJM: How would you rather I carried you, on my back—?

MAJA: Don't be ridiculous.

ULFHEJM: Or in my arms?

MAJA: For heaven's sake don't start that nonsense again!

ULFHEJM (*suppressing his anger*): I did that to a young girl once. Picked her up out of the gutter, and carried her away in my arms. Carried her on my hands; I'd have carried her right through life like that, so that she shouldn't hurt

260

her pretty foot against a stone. Her shoes were worn to shreds when I found her—

MAJA: And yet you picked her up and carried her on your hands?

ULFHEJM: Lifted her up out of the mire, and carried her as high and as gently as I knew how. (*Laughs roughly*) Do you know what thanks she gave me?

MAJA: No, what?

ULFHEJM (*looks at her, smiles, and nods*): She gave me horns. The ones you can see so clearly. Isn't that a funny story?

MAJA: Oh, yes, quite funny. But I know one which is even funnier.

ULFHEJM: What's that?

MAJA: Once upon a time there was a silly girl. She had a father and mother, but they were very poor. One day a great and powerful man appeared in their poor little house, and picked the girl up in his arms, just like you, and carried her far, far away.

ULFHEJM: Wanted to live like he did, eh?

MAJA: Yes. She was stupid, you see.

ULFHEJM: And he was tall and handsome, no doubt.

MAJA: No, he wasn't so terribly handsome. But he made her believe he was going to take her up to the top of the highest mountain, where the sun would always shine.

ULFHEJM: He was a mountaineer, was he?

MAJA: Yes. In his way.

ULFHEJM: So he took the wench up with him?

MAJA (*tosses her head*): Took her up with him? Oh, yes! No; he led her into a cold, damp cage, which the sun and the fresh air never reached—or so it seemed to her— though the walls were gilded, and lined with great stone ghosts.

ULFHEJM: Serve her right, damn it!

MAJA: Yes, serve her right. It's a funny story, though, isn't it?

ULFHEJM (*looks at her for a moment*): Look now, listen to me—

MAJA: Well, what is it now?

ULFHEJM: Why don't we two stitch our tattered lives together?

MAJA: Is the Squire turning poor man's tailor?

ULFHEJM: Yes. Couldn't we try to draw the rags together here and there so as to patch some kind of a life out of them?

MAJA: And when those poor rags have quite worn out, what then?

ULFHEJM: Then we shall stand there, free and unashamed. Ourselves, as we really are.

MAJA (*laughs*): You with your goat's legs?

ULFHEJM: And you with your—well, let that pass.

MAJA: Come on, let's go.

ULFHEJM: Where to?

MAJA: Down to the hotel, of course.

ULFHEJM: And then?

MAJA: Then I shall bid you a polite farewell, and say: "Thank you, sir, for the pleasure of your company."

ULFHEJM: I can offer you a castle—

MAJA (*pointing to the hut*): Like that?

ULFHEJM: It hasn't fallen down yet.

MAJA: And all the glory of the world?

ULFHEJM: A castle, I said—

MAJA: Thank you. I've had enough of castles.

ULFHEJM: With splendid hunting grounds for miles around—

MAJA: Is it full of great works of art, this castle of yours?

ULFHEJM: I can't offer you any of those.

MAJA: I'm glad to hear it.

ULFHEJM: Will you come with me, then?

MAJA: There is a tame bird of prey which keeps guard over me.

ULFHEJM: We'll wing him, Maja!

MAJA: Come and carry me down this path, then.

ULFHEJM (*throws an arm round her waist*): Yes, it's time we went. The mist is on us.

MAJA: Is it very dangerous, the way down?

ULFHEJM: Not as dangerous as a mountain mist.

She tears herself loose, goes to the edge and looks down, but starts quickly back.

ULFHEJM (*goes over to her and laughs*): Does it make you giddy?

MAJA: Yes, it does. But look down there! Those two climbing up—

ULFHEJM (*leans over the edge*): It's only your bird of prey. And his strange lady.

MAJA: Can't we get down without their seeing us?

ULFHEJM: Impossible. The path's too narrow. And there's no other way down.

MAJA: Oh, well. Let's face them here, then.

ULFHEJM: Spoken like a true bear-baiter!

PROFESSOR RUBEK *and* IRENE *come into sight above the edge of the ravine. He has his plaid over his shoulders, she has a fur coat thrown loosely over her white dress and a swansdown hood over her head.*

RUBEK: Hallo, Maja! So we meet again?

MAJA: At your service. Come right up.

RUBEK *climbs up and reaches down his hand to* IRENE, *who joins him.*

RUBEK (*coldly, to* MAJA): So you've been on the mountain all night too? Like us.

MAJA: Yes, I've been hunting. With your permission.

ULFHEJM (*points over the edge*): Have you come up that path?

RUBEK: As you see.

ULFHEJM: The strange lady, too?

RUBEK: Yes, of course. (*With a glance at* MAJA) The strange lady and I will not be going separate ways any more.

ULFHEJM: Don't you know that this path you've just climbed is a deathtrap?

RUBEK: We tried it, anyway. It didn't look too difficult at first.

ULFHEJM: Nothing looks difficult at first; but then you come to a tight corner where you can't go on or turn back, and you're stuck there fast, Professor. Fast as a rock.

RUBEK (*smiles*): Are these meant to be words of wisdom, Squire?

ULFHEJM: Words of wisdom be damned! (*Points up towards the mountain top*) Can't you see the storm's about to break? Don't you hear the wind rising?

RUBEK (*listens*): It sounds like the prelude to the Day of Resurrection!

ULFHEJM: It's the wind blowing from the mountain, man! Look how the clouds are heaving and sinking! They'll be all round us soon like a winding sheet.

IRENE: A winding sheet! I know that feeling!

MAJA (*pulls at* ULFHEJM's *arm*): Let's go down, quickly.

ULFHEJM (*to* RUBEK): I can't take more than one. Get into that hut and stay there till the storm's past. Then I'll send men up to fetch you down.

IRENE: To fetch us! No, no!

ULFHEJM (*roughly*): Take you down by force, if need be. This is a matter of life and death. Now you know! (*To* MAJA) Come on, now, don't be afraid, trust me.

MAJA (*clinging to him*): Oh, get me down, get me safely down!

ULFHEJM (*as he begins to climb down, shouts to the others*): You wait in the hut. Till they come with ropes to fetch you.

ULFHEJM, *with* MAJA *in his arms, descends hastily yet cautiously down the mountainside.*

IRENE (*stares frightened at* RUBEK): Did you hear that, Arnold? They are coming up here to fetch me. Men—coming here—!

RUBEK: Be calm, Irene.

IRENE: And she—the one in black—she'll come too! She must have missed me long ago by now. She'll take hold of my arms, Arnold! And put me in the straitjacket! She's got it with her, in her trunk. I've seen it!

RUBEK: No one will be allowed to touch you.

IRENE (*smiles*): Oh, no. I've a way to stop them.

RUBEK: What do you mean?

IRENE (*takes out the knife*): This.

RUBEK (*tries to take it*): A knife?

264

IRENE: Always, always. Day and night. In bed, too.

RUBEK: Give me the knife, Irene.

IRENE: I meant it for you, Arnold.

RUBEK: For me?

IRENE: As we were sitting there last night, down by the Taunitzer See—

RUBEK: The Taunitzer—?

IRENE: Outside the farmhouse. Playing at swans and water-lilies—

RUBEK: Go on.

IRENE: I heard you say, clear as ice, cold as the grave, that I was only an episode in your life—

RUBEK: You said that, Irene, not I.

IRENE (*continues*): I took out my knife. I was going to stick it in your back.

RUBEK: Why didn't you?

IRENE: I suddenly realized you were already dead. You'd been dead for years.

RUBEK: Dead?

IRENE: Dead. Like me. We sat there by the Taunitzer See, two clammy corpses, playing our little game together.

RUBEK: I don't call that death. But you don't understand me.

IRENE: Then where is the burning passion you fought against when I stood naked before you as the woman rising from the dead?

RUBEK: Our love is not dead, Irene.

IRENE: The love which belongs to our life on earth—that beautiful, miraculous life so full of riddles—that love is dead in us both.

RUBEK: I tell you, that love burns as passionately in me now as it ever did!

IRENE: And I? Have you forgotten who I am now?

RUBEK: Whoever you are, whatever you are, to me you are only the woman I see in my dreams of you.

IRENE: I have stood on a stage, naked, and showed my body to hundreds of men since you—

RUBEK: I was blind, I drove you to it. I set that dead figure of clay above life, and happiness, and love.

IRENE: Too late. Too late.

RUBEK: Nothing that has happened since has cheapened you one whit in my eyes.

IRENE (*raising her head*): Nor in mine!

RUBEK: Well, then! We are free! There is still time for us to live, Irene!

IRENE (*looks at him sadly*): The desire to live died in me, Arnold. Now I am risen from the dead, and look for you, and find you. And see that you are dead, and life is dead— as I have been.

RUBEK: No, you are wrong, wrong! Both in us and around us life rages as fiercely and joyously as ever!

IRENE (*smiles and shakes her head*): The woman whom you created, rising from the dead, sees life cold and lying on its bier.

RUBEK (*throws his arms tightly round her*): Then let us two dead people live life to the full for one short hour before we go down again into our graves!

IRENE: Arnold!

RUBEK: But not here in this half-darkness! Not here, with this hideous dank shroud flapping around us!

IRENE: No, no! Up into the light, where glory shines. Up to the promised mountain top.

RUBEK: Up there we shall celebrate our wedding feast, Irene, my beloved.

IRENE (*proudly*): The sun may look on us, Arnold.

RUBEK: All the powers of light may look on us. And all the powers of darkness, too. (*Grips her hand*) Will you come with me now, my bride of grace?

IRENE (*as though transfigured*): Freely and willingly, my lord and master.

RUBEK (*leading her*): First we must pass through the mists, Irene. And then—

IRENE: Yes, through the mists. And then up, up to the top of our tower, where it shines in the sunrise.

The mist closes tightly over the scene. RUBEK and IRENE, hand in hand, climb upwards over the snowfield to the right, and soon disappear into the low clouds. Sharp gusts of wind hunt and whine through the air.

The NUN comes over the scree to the left. She stops, and looks round silently, searchingly.

MAJA (*is heard singing happily from far down in the ravine*):
I am free! I am free! I am free!
No longer imprisoned! I'm free!
I can fly like a bird! And I'm free!

Suddenly a roar like thunder is heard from high up on the snowfield, which rushes down, whirling, at a fearful pace. RUBEK and IRENE are glimpsed momentarily as they are whirled round in the snow and buried beneath it.

THE NUN (*utters a shriek, stretches out her arms towards them as they fall, and cries*): Irene! (*She stands silent for a moment, then makes the sign of the cross in the air before her*) Pax vobiscum!

MAJA'S song continues from further down the mountainside.

NOTE ON THE TRANSLATIONS

The Pillars of Society is, like *A Doll's House* and *An Enemy of the People*, a fairly straightforward play to translate. The chief problems are Hilmar Toennessen and Lona Hessel. Hilmar talks in a fanciful manner, overloaded with adjectives and ridiculous flights of imagination, like Hjalmar Ekdal in *The Wild Duck*. Lona has a breezy, slangy way of speaking which contrasts markedly with the prim speech of the local stay-at-homes, and since she and Johan have spent the past fifteen years in America I have tried to make them talk like Americans.

The Norwegian word *samfund* can mean either society in general, or a specific community. Ibsen uses it in both senses, and I have translated it sometimes as society and sometimes as community, as the context demanded.

The chief characters in *The Pillars of Society* are a good deal younger than they are generally played. The "incident" with Dina's mother took place fifteen years ago. Johan was then nineteen, so he is now thirty-four. Bernick was then four years older than Johan, so he is thirty-eight. Martha is the same age as Johan. Mrs. Bernick is older than her brother Johan, so is presumably in her middle to late thirties; and Lona Hessel is older than Mrs, Bernick and therefore presumably in her late thirties or early forties. She should not be more than a few years older than Bernick, if at all, since he nearly married her.

In contrast to the simple, colloquial style of *The Pillars of Society*, much of the final act of *John Gabriel Borkman*, and most of *When We Dead Awaken*, are written in a heightened prose very near to poetry. When translating the latter play, I continually found myself feeling how much easier my task would have been if Ibsen had written it in verse. There is a certain kind of high-flown writing which in any prose sounds grandiose, even windy (when I translated *Brand* I tried at first to put it into prose, and found exactly this result). I cannot but feel that *When We Dead Awaken* would have been a much greater play if Ibsen had written it in poetry—as he nearly did. He told C. H. Herford, a Welshman who translated

Brand into English, that he would probably write his last play in verse "if only one knew which play would be the last." To have done this with *When We Dead Awaken* would have been tantamount to an acceptance that he would never write any more. Yet the straining is clearly there.

The shortness of the last act is a mystery; not merely its shortness but its (to my mind) inadequacy. It is the only less-than-great final act that Ibsen wrote after *The Pillars of Society* (whatever objections may be raised against the endings of *The Lady from the Sea* and *Little Eyolf*, they both work wonderfully well if—to borrow Henry James's phrase—really *done*). A possible explanation is physical exhaustion; he was within a few weeks of his first stroke, may have sensed that he had not an indefinite time left, and perhaps felt unequal to the immense strain of composing a final act, especially to so self-searching a play. In performance, the way to minimise the briefness of the last act is to have no interval between Acts Two and Three; the scene-change, from one level of the mountain to another, may easily be made during a brief black-out.

I gladly acknowledge my thanks to Mr. Casper Wrede for much invaluable advice and criticism in connection with the translations of *John Gabriel Borkman* and *When We Dead Awaken*.